American Sport in International History

New Approaches to International History covers international history during the modern period and across the globe. The series incorporates new developments in the field, such as the cultural turn and transnationalism, as well as the classical high politics of state-centric policymaking and diplomatic relations. Written with upper-level undergraduate and postgraduate students in mind, texts in the series provide an accessible overview of international diplomatic and transnational issues, events, and actors.

Published:

American Sport in International History

The United States and the World since 1865

Daniel M. DuBois

BLOOMSBURY ACADEMIC
LONDON · NEW YORK · OXFORD · NEW DELHI · SYDNEY

BLOOMSBURY ACADEMIC
Bloomsbury Publishing Plc
50 Bedford Square, London, WC1B 3DP, UK
1385 Broadway, New York, NY 10018, USA
29 Earlsfort Terrace, Dublin 2, Ireland

BLOOMSBURY, BLOOMSBURY ACADEMIC and the Diana logo are
trademarks of Bloomsbury Publishing Plc

First published in Great Britain 2023

Series design by Catherine Wood.

Cover image © United States Air Force Staff Sgt. Casey Carlin relaxes
by shooting hoops April 10, 2002 at the Bagram Air Base in Afghanistan.
Photo by Joe Raedle/Getty Images.

A catalogue record for this book is available from the British Library.

A catalog record for this book is available from the Library of Congress.

ISBN: HB: 978-1-3501-3471-3
         PB: 978-1-3501-3470-6
       ePDF: 978-1-3501-3472-0
      eBook: 978-1-3501-3473-7

Series: New Approaches to International History

Typeset by Integra Software Services Pvt. Ltd.

To find out more about our authors and books visit www.bloomsbury.com
and sign up for our newsletters.

To the memory of my grandfather,
and first editor,
Thomas Driscoll

CONTENTS

FIGURES

ACKNOWLEDGMENTS

This book depended on an immeasurable amount of kindness, support, patience, and guidance from many different people. That begins with the series editor, Thomas Zeiler, the wonderful editorial team with Bloomsbury Press, and the anonymous reviewers whose critiques and suggestions made this project a reality. I also benefited from the help of my colleagues at Saint Leo University, including the wonderful interlibrary loan team at Cannon Memorial Library, as well as Tim Jussaume, Frank Orlando, Heather Parker, Janis Prince, Marco Rimanelli, and Mary Spoto who patiently encouraged and helped support my research and writing. I especially want to thank my retired colleague and dear friend, Jack McTague, who reviewed drafts of every chapter and talked to me for hours about his longtime love of sport and his memories of some of the famous episodes that make up this book. Other friends and colleagues who helped support my work over the last several years include Michael Butler, Rob Morrison, Mike Ortiz, and Doug Snyder. They indulged every obnoxious "did you know?" I could throw at them as I waded through the research, helped me find sources, and commented on various drafts along the way.

Then there are my students. I started teaching my sport history class six years ago in my first semester at Saint Leo, and it was then I began to wish for a book that would work as a class reader and put America's sport history in a global context. In the last two years, my sport history students took on a huge role in the development of this project and, as promised, they deserve mention. Cale Adsett, Jack Bator, Michael Brewer, Christian Buenavides-Diaz, Aliceison Brown, Shannon Byrne, Aurel Ciocanu, Justin-Sahin Colak, Claudio Cuba Campero, Rhiannon Flanagan, Abigail Gangemi-Hague, Amaya Gomez, Erika Haugen, Andres Higuera, Yasmin Jalamdeh, Dalton Lang, Skylar Lewis, Giselle Estrada, Katherine Lynch, Nina Michelangelo, Emma Nieman, Noah Nixon, Ashley Quero, Gabriel Quinn, Quiwanaki Ramsey, Steven Richardson, Joseph Rojas, Brenika Russell, Lindsey Samuel, Rex Soderlund, Arthur Sodermark, Joshua Theis, Marlen Tiscareno, Alex Tomberlin, Haley Totos, Paul Vitaliti, and Ryan Young—thank you all for your hard work in class and enthusiasm for this project. Emma Crafton and John Macht deserve special thanks for taking on research projects that supported portions of this book. Above all, my sincerest thanks to Kylie Culver who has been my research and editorial assistant for the last two years. Kylie helped track down sources, corrected citations, fact-checked, and proofread. She went above and beyond what was expected when I enlisted her help. I cannot thank her enough.

Finally, my family has been a source of endless support, motivation, and love. My father-in-law, Bill Maloney, and mother-in-law, Susan Craven, shared helpful memories and shepherded my kids on family excursions so I could stay home and write. My parents, Mike and Mary DuBois, have been sounding boards, research assistants, and clutch-time babysitters who helped me find the hours and energy to keep writing, even as the world around us went mad. My father's love of sport has been a huge part of my life and, thankfully, he handed it down to me. I treasured the opportunity to talk with him about these subjects and to learn about the great teams, athletes, and moments that made up his lifetime of sport fandom. He also helped with the research for the case study on Jim Thorpe and the section on the American Basketball Association (ABA). Working with him on those parts was very special for me. Lastly, thank you to my amazing, selfless wife Melissa and our incredible two sons Dodge and Liam. The patience and love they showed me while I toiled away in my office can never be repaid—but I will try. This project was possible only because of their support and faith in me.

Introduction

Internationalizing the History
of American Sport

On February 28, 2013, Dennis Rodman, the National Basketball Association (NBA) Hall-of-Fame power forward and legendary provocateur, shocked audiences again. Photographers captured the mercurial Rodman, nicknamed "The Worm," sitting courtside at a North Korean basketball game in box seats next to the young dictator and lifelong NBA fan Kim Jong-Un. Kim reportedly "had a blast at the game" and invited Rodman along with players from the Harlem Globetrotters back to his palace for a post-game celebration. Together "they had a grand old time," and during the festivities Rodman pledged to the ruthless autocrat that "you have a friend for life."[1]

It was the first of two visits Rodman made that year to the hermit kingdom—visits that bookended several major flashpoints in US-North Korean relations. Rodman at first insisted he was not a diplomat (a sentiment US Secretary of State John Kerry publicly shared as well), but later described his sojourns as attempts at "basketball diplomacy," by which he meant using Kim's well-documented love of the Michael Jordan–era Chicago Bulls to improve relations between the United States and the Democratic People's Republic of Korea. Media critics and some traditional foreign policy observers scoffed at Rodman's antics as obtuse and inconsequential. Calling Kim "cool and pretty nice" was certainly tone-deaf, to put it mildly, but his visit was not immaterial. Rather, it showed basketball's enormous global power to puncture even the most cloistered cultures and make fans out of adversaries. It was also part of a larger picture coming into focus that proved how culturally immersive basketball had become all over the world.[2]

About eighteen months before the courtship between Rodman and Kim tipped off, the reigning NBA Most Valuable Player (MVP), Derrick Rose, toured China, where he promoted his Adidas-brand shoes. Rose, the most famous Chicago Bull since Jordan, had just signed one of the largest endorsement deals in professional sport history: a whopping

$250 million "lifetime" contract. When explaining the company's rationale for inking Rose to such a lucrative and long-term deal, Adidas executives stressed above all Rose's appeal in the China market. Citing the unrivalled popularity of the NBA throughout Asia, one executive predicted that an Adidas-clad Rose would someday "be the number one basketball icon and potentially the biggest sports icon in all of China."[3] A big deal, indeed, given that an estimated 300 million Chinese *play* the game of basketball and around 500 million (more than the entire US population) watch NBA games streamed in China. Considering how tense the US relationship is with both North Korea and China, the popularity of such a distinctly American cultural export in these authoritarian states is truly remarkable. But it should not come as a surprise.[4]

Sport has been a tool used to expand US influence abroad since the nineteenth century. And for just as long, major international developments—including mass migrations, world wars, and changes to the global economy—have likewise shaped the evolution and significance of sport in America. Rodman and Rose's respective experiences in Asia were by-products of that history. They also reinforced important truths about how sport affects America's place in the world. In a country where US and other world diplomats had struggled for half a century to make inroads with North Korea's violent and reclusive leaders; and in another, whose famous "China Market" captivated yet eluded most major US businesses for over two centuries: in both cases, the game of basketball achieved what more traditional instruments of American power by comparison could not.

To make sense of these stories and to understand more broadly the way American sport operates in the world today, one must look back to sport's evolution alongside America's rise as a great power since the end of the Civil War. Fortunately, we live in a golden era for sport history. No longer relegated to history's hinterlands, sport history today flourishes as a major subfield in its discipline and a popular course option for students in and out of the history major. National histories of American sport and sport culture in particular are ever-growing, but increasing numbers of historians are trying to understand how sport shaped America's relationship with the rest of the world.[5]

Scholars have shown that sport can function as a seminal example of what Joseph Nye first called "soft power." According to Nye, a "country's soft power rests on its resources of culture, values, and policy," which work "through attraction rather than coercion or payment."[6] Under the right circumstances, soft power can advance national interests and gain global influence akin to more traditional forms of "hard power" like military strength, population size, and economic productivity. Sport, like music, literature, and art, works as a reflection of a national identity on the world stage, fashioned according to whomever controls its spread. Sport not only helped grow US power, but as historians demonstrate, Americans from many walks of life recognized its broad utility and harnessed it as a source for political, economic, and cultural strength. This book stitches together some of this great scholarship to give readers a narrative history of US sport in the world.

Overview

American Sport in International History is both a synthesis of groundbreaking research in the fields of history, sport journalism, and kinesiology and a meditation on the international community's considerable influence over the development of sport in the United States. It strives for as many salient examples as possible but prioritizes Olympic history and the histories of America's "Big Three" sports: baseball, basketball, and American football. Other sports, including boxing, cycling, golf, gymnastics, hockey, soccer, and tennis, play important roles in the narrative. However, US national sport along with the three major professional sports forms its foundation.

The chapters, which begin in the mid-nineteenth century and extend through the 2020 Tokyo Olympics, frame certain topics and themes—in particular, sport's interaction with gender, race, economics, and politics—in the context of America's ascent as a major world power. It is undeniable that sport has played an outsized role in pushing the United States into becoming a more inclusive and dynamic nation. Widening the lens beyond America's shores shows how many of these changes were often the result of powerful global events.

Conceptually, this book is by and for the classroom. The narrative was written in a way that I hope a general audience of sport fans and history enthusiasts finds inviting. But it was born on the lectern and designed with students and teachers in mind. The students to whom I have taught my sport history course over the last several years—including many non-history majors—have been my earliest editors, reviewers, researchers, and, above all, inspiration as I worked through teaching and writing this history in tandem. From questions raised in class and points made during discussion, to the essays written and projects researched, the students gave me a clear sense of what they wanted from a classroom reader and how a narrative history of American sport in the world should sound.

A recurring feature in the story is an emphasis on individuals whose importance spanned both cultural and national borders. The life and times of Babe Ruth, Jesse Owens, Jackie Robinson, Muhammad Ali, Billie Jean King, Michael Jordan, Simone Biles, and many more help mark and measure the ways American sport has changed over the years. Additionally, each chapter includes a case study spotlighting an important athlete whose career deserves special consideration because of the individual's contributions to America's international sport history. These spotlights include the uber-athletes Jim Thorpe and Babe Didrikson Zaharias, Wimbledon champion and professional golfer Althea Gibson, Olympic legend Carl Lewis, and world-champion ice skater-turned-diplomat Michelle Kwan. My hope is that a balanced blend of athlete biographies presents readers with different perspectives on the world over time, as well as a sampling of American superstars who made huge impacts on the world of sport.

Writing the international history of American sport as a narrative has meant strategizing when and where to introduce certain sports in the chronology. Soccer was legitimately popular in America in the early 1900s, but faded when the professionalization of sport began after the First World War. Because the US experience with soccer became broadly noticeable and high-level only much later in the century, I waited until the book's latter sections to introduce its history to readers. The same is true for boxing, cycling, golf, hockey, gymnastics, and tennis. They provide important entries at various points along the way. Admittedly, however, they do not get the full attention they each deserve. My editorial priorities centered on capturing the big picture and doing it in a way students and a more general readership would find accessible. That has meant cutting more than I would have preferred so that the book's length stayed manageable and the narrative as coherent as possible.

Just as certain sports get more attention than others, so too do different levels of athletic competition. This book draws mostly from the Olympics and professional sport to frame the history. The Olympics are an obvious point of contact between American sport and the world. They are a key example of what sport historians refer to as "mega-events": large-scale, international gatherings "used to showcase economic achievements, to signal diplomatic stature or to project ... soft power."[7] The Olympic movement's revival at the turn of the twentieth century helped spark the politicization of sport domestically and globally. The United States was an early adopter of using the Olympics as a forum to prove its national and cultural strengths. Other nations recognized the political implications of the Olympics as well, and its usage as political theater intensified as the twentieth century wore on. Olympic history shows the evolution from "sport-as-diplomacy," where international sporting events can have the auxiliary effect of promoting cross-cultural, economic, and political exchange, to formal "sport diplomacy," where countries deliberately "use sport, including teams, athletes, tours, and events, as a means of public diplomacy."[8]

Professional sport has likewise evolved into a dynamic and consequential point of contact between the United States and the world. Several professional US leagues have substantial foreign audiences and feature scores of international players on their teams. With varying success, these leagues have sold their products in foreign markets and, in the case of the NBA and Major League Baseball (MLB), hugely profit from extensive international operations. By comparison, collegiate athletics, while not entirely absent from this history, are often in the background. True, colleges have been essential to the formation of sport in America, and for more than a century, universities have recruited international students to play on their teams.

This book tries to account for the importance of collegiate sport but spends most of its time analyzing events involving the Olympics and the pros.

I learned quickly that applying an international context to American sport history only enhances the prominence of race and gender. These themes play essential roles in how sport has evolved in the United States and how foreign audiences have interpreted American sporting culture. The global reach of American sport must be understood in the context of capitalism and US foreign policy—and those themes inform the narrative, too. But trying to write about Jesse Owens's heroics in Berlin in 1936, for instance, or Billie Jean King's impact on the world of women's tennis would be impossible without foregrounding the racial and gender barriers they and others overcame to achieve their dreams. Their lives prove that athlete activism is one of the oldest and most durable traditions in US sport, although critics often pretend otherwise. The international fame of American women and athletes of color, coupled with their determined calls for justice, drew global attention to the fault lines in US society and, in some cases, helped make American democracy more reflective of its diverse population.

Sources

It is worth stressing that this is *an* international history of American sport. Any attempt at *the* history of this topic would require many more pages—and a better historian than the one you are saddled with here. Sport history buffs might notice certain athletes, teams, and moments that make up America's international sport history are missing from the text. As contrition for what is left out, the notes section contains references with additional sources that help fill in the gaps. Readers wanting to learn more about a particular topic or looking for something that I left out might consult the notes for some guidance on where to keep digging.

Among the book's sources, certain historians and sport scholars loom large. Like the history itself, the historiography in this book is not exhaustive, but it aims to showcase the incredible research and writing of other scholars as broadly and often as possible. Among the many historians cited herein, the individual and edited works of Heather Dichter, Mark Dyreson, Gerald Gems, S. W. Pope, Toby Rider, Susan Ware, and Kevin Witherspoon help pin everything together, as do several monographs of particular importance by scholars Adrian Burgos Jr., Robert Elias, Frank Josza Jr., Barbara Keys, Alan Klein, Walter LaFeber, Louis Moore Jr., Robert Peterson, Stephen Riess, Randy Roberts, Damion Thomas, and Thomas Zeiler.

When prudent, articles from newspapers like the *New York Times*, the *Pittsburg Courier*, and the *New York Amsterdam News*, among others, enliven the narrative, along with essays from magazines such as *Outing* and *Sports Illustrated*. State Department documents help us decipher how government officials viewed the evolving role of sport within US foreign policy. Biographies, especially their own, and interviews with newspapers, on television, and in documentaries furnish the athlete's perspective. Finally, databases maintained by professional leagues and organizations like the International Olympic Committee (IOC), as well as online repositories such as *Basketball Reference* and *FanGraphs*, provide statistical measurement of athletic performance and records of achievement.

Structure

The book is arranged into five chapters and a conclusion. They move chronologically, beginning around the end of the American Civil War and finishing at the 2020 Tokyo Olympics. The chapters are divided into three sections, and each section into two or more smaller subsections. One section in each chapter is reserved for the history of US national sport—often framed around the Olympics—another covers the professional development of one or more of the Big Three sports, and a third highlights other key themes from the era. At the end of every chapter is a case study spotlighting the singular achievements of a particularly remarkable athlete.

Chapter 1 begins with the emergence of a modern sporting culture in America in the late nineteenth century. Sports like basketball, boxing, and baseball became important vehicles of assimilation for the country's growing and diversifying population. Through sport, immigrants and marginalized groups like Blacks and women found ways to demonstrate resilience, toughness, and—for a few of them—a means to climb the socioeconomic ladder. The elite also attached cultural value to sport—particularly amateur sport—and on university campuses, American football became a fulcrum for ideas about industry, masculinity, and war. A national spirit that privileged amateur athletics defined early US Olympic history, while the country's surging militarism and maturing business culture propelled baseball's evolution into the national pastime.

The story of how MLB built an early advantage as a professional sport leads off Chapter 2. Thanks to the infusion of new media technologies, plus the arrival of the larger-than-life Babe Ruth, baseball became an American obsession and a popular global export. Other sports tried to follow suit, with mixed results. The National Football League (NFL) formed in the 1920s, just a few years after professional hockey organized into the National Hockey League (NHL), with franchises in Canada and the United States. Basketball tried to professionalize around the same time, but the initial returns were less impressive. Prizefighting, meanwhile, which the Progressive Era tried to bury, resurfaced when America joined the Great War and returned to professional form in the decades after, thanks to the dominance of Jack Dempsey and Joe Louis. War shaped Olympic sport as well. With Hitler gaining strength in Europe, Berlin hosted the 1936 Olympics, where Jesse Owens became a symbol of hope in the global fight against white supremacy.

Chapter 3 examines the role of sport during the early Cold War (1945–70). The rabid consumerism that supercharged the US economy after the Second World War had huge benefits for professional sports, especially American football. At the national level, the intensity of Cold War rivalries spilled out into Olympic and other international athletic competitions. Athletes on both sides of the Iron Curtain were expected to prove the superiority of their respective government's economic and political systems by winning gold medals. Cold War pressures meant international sport became more competitive and politically loaded than ever before. Both sides relied on propaganda to impugn the other, and for the United States, its long history of cultural and institutional racism became fodder for its communist adversaries. This chapter explores how Black sport stars like Jackie Robinson, Bill Russell, Wilma Rudolph, and Muhammad Ali became activist athletes by using sport to advance the cause of civil rights, including as official representatives of the US government, throughout the world.

The activist athlete tradition established in the early Cold War evolved in different directions over the rest of the twentieth century. After exploring how sport functioned in the Cold War's final decades, Chapter 4 looks at how political activism broadened into athlete economic empowerment in the 1970s, particularly in the world of men's and women's professional tennis. Led by Arthur Ashe and Billie Jean King, efforts to maximize professional athletes' economic rights soon became evident in other corners of sport, as well. That was especially true for MLB, where the era of free agency intensified the league's interest in finding cheaper foreign talent from baseball's international community. The NBA's transition from a rickety league on the fringe of professional sport to a billion-dollar global operation by the end of the century rounds out the rest of the chapter.

The fifth and final chapter considers the international history of American sport since 2000. It explains how foreign sports that had been peripheral to US sporting culture took on greater prominence in the new millennium, thanks especially to the dominance of American stars like Tiger Woods in golf and Lance Armstrong in cycling. Additionally, those two individuals provide instructive lessons on how athletes can go from celebrities to outcasts in the blink of an eye. This chapter is also where soccer emerges as a major subject of inquiry and explores how, despite very modest growth at the men's level, the US Women's National Team (USWNT) has become the gold standard for women's soccer around the world. The chapter concludes by chronicling the recent history of USA Gymnastics (USAG), host to some of the greatest athletic accomplishments and acts of individual bravery, as well as the most horrifying scandal and dereliction of duty, in the history of US national sport.

The conclusion brings the narrative through the Tokyo 2020 Olympics that were postponed until 2021 due to the Covid-19 pandemic. The Tokyo Games encapsulated many of the very themes, and some of the key athletes, underpinning the chapters in this book. They also presented a bizarre and unique portrait of what global sport looks like in a plague.

Notes

1   Lynne Zinsler, "Rodman Meets with North Korean Leader, Courtside," *New York Times* [hereafter *NYT*], February 28, 2013, URL: https://www.nytimes.com/2013/03/01/sports/basketball/dennis-rodman-meets-north-korean-leader.html [accessed 12.18.21].

2   Ibid.

3   Lawrence Norman quoted in Melissa Isaacson, "No. 1 in Chicago, No. 1 in China?" *ESPN*, July 20, URL: https://www.espn.com/chicago/nba/columns/story?columnist=isaacson_melissa&id=6787878 [accessed 4.27.22].

4   "Factbox: NBA Taking Flak in China," *Reuters*, October 7, 2019, URL: https://www.reuters.com/article/us-china-basketball-market-factbox/factbox-nba-taking-flak-in-china-a-valuable-market-with-500-million-fans-idUSKBN1WM1WI [accessed 12.18.21].

5   There are several excellent comprehensive histories of American sport, some of which include international perspectives, that deserve mention here. This includes Linda Borish, et al., eds., *The Routledge History of American Sport* (New York: Routledge, 2016); Richard Davies, *Sports in American Life: A History*, Third Edition (Malden, MA: Wiley Blackwell, 2017); Elliot Gorn, *A Brief History of American Sports*, Second Edition (Champagne: University of Illinois Press, 2013); S.W. Pope and John Naught, eds., *Routledge Companion to Sports History* (New York: Routledge, 2011); Steven Reiss, ed., *A Companion to American Sport History* (Malden, MA: Wiley Blackwell, 2014).

6   Joseph S. Nye Jr., "Public Diplomacy and Soft Power," *Annals of the American Academy of Political and Social Science* 616 (2008): 94; see also Joseph Nye Jr., *Soft Power: The Means to Success in World Politics* (New York: Public Affairs, 2005).

7   Scarlett Cornelissen, "The Geopolitics of Global Aspiration: Sport Mega-Events and Emerging Powers," *The International Journal of the History of Sport* [hereafter *IJHS*] 27 (2010): 3010.

8   Heather L. Dichter, "The Diplomatic Turn: The New Relationship between Sport and Politics," *IJHS* 38, no. 2–3 (2021): 3. See also Peter Beck, "Conclusion: 'Good Kicking' Is Not Only 'Good Politics' but Also 'Good Diplomacy'," in Heather L. Dichter, ed., *Soccer Diplomacy: International Relations and Football Since 1914* (Lexington: University Press of Kentucky, 2020), 222–7.

1

The Huddled Masses

America, Sport, and the World at the Turn of the Twentieth Century

Introduction

Two global events transformed American sporting culture around the turn of the twentieth century. The first was the swell of immigrants that landed in the United States between 1840 and 1920. As millions of migrants from Europe, Latin America, and Asia settled into US cities and farmlands, they remade the face of recreational and professional sport all over the country. The second was the arrival of US sport and athletes on the world stage. Akin to its growth as an imperial power, America's influence on international sport advanced swiftly and suddenly.

This chapter explores how both forces—immigrants coming to America and the exportation of US sport to global audiences—recast the purpose of American sport beginning after the Civil War. By the outbreak of the First World War, sporting events and athletic competitions helped facilitate the assimilation of America's diversifying population and announce US power to audiences around the world. Gradually more observers wondered about the implications of the "land of immigrants" reshaping the world of sport. Advocates proclaimed with missionary zeal that sport could both vitalize a nation and promote unity among a growing, multiethnic population. Meanwhile, thanks to what historians call the US government's "promotional" relationship with businesses at the turn of the century, American sport became an export that followed US commercial and military advancements around the world.[1]

To understand how these processes unfolded, and how they contributed to America's international sport history, we begin with the role sport played in assimilating new immigrants from all over the world. In her 1909 book *The Spirit of Youth and the City Streets*, Progressive reformer, women's rights activist, and sport enthusiast Jane Addams captured the mood in America quite well. "Many Chicago citizens," she wrote, thinking about her own city's rapidly diversifying population:

> will never forget the long summer day in the large playing field filled during the morning with hundreds of little children romping through the kindergarten games; in the afternoon with the young men and girls contending in athletics sports; and the evening light made gay by the bright colored garments of Italians, Lithuanians, Norwegians, and a dozen other nationalities, reproducing their old dances and festivals for the pleasures of the more stolid Americans. Was this a forecast of what we may yet see accomplished through a dozen agencies promoting public recreation which are springing up in every city of America?[2]

Immigration and the Emergence of Modern Sport in America

The historian Robert Wiebe once argued that amid an unprecedented surge in immigration, emerging out of a cataclysmic Civil War, and in the throes of late-stage industrialization, the United States in the late nineteenth century was a "distended society," a country "without a core" that "lacked those national centers of authority and information which might have given order to such swift change."[3] Americans' "search for order," the title of Wiebe's famous history of this era, reached into every corner of society and, eventually, helped bring about the era of Progressive reform as well as America's budding interest in imperialism.

Of all the forces driving America's distension, immigration was perhaps the most acute. Around thirty-seven million Americans, more than one-third of the US population, were either first- or second-generation immigrants in 1920.[4] Factory work and farming opportunities drew them to America, and ethnic enclaves gave migrant communities a semblance of safety and familiarity. But the workplace and homelife did not always promote the cultural assimilation of these new Americans. As the United States began to look more like the places its immigrants came from, the country needed new ways to break down ethnic barriers and promote a greater sense of community throughout its towns and cities. Schools, novel technologies like the radio, amusement parks, and other cultural attractions helped spur the assimilation of the nation's diversifying population. Sport, however, offered a particularly powerful means of generating shared experiences and common identities. No surprise that amateur athletics and organized sport became important touchstones during this dramatic demographic transformation. Among them, the early histories of basketball, boxing, and football demonstrate the value, and limitations, of sport as a vehicle of assimilation.

Basketball and Urban Space

If there is a genuinely "American" sport, it is basketball—not least because its inventor, James Naismith, was a first-generation immigrant from Canada. Unlike baseball and football, each with deep roots in traditional English sports, basketball was made in America. Akin to other great innovators at the time, Naismith came to the United States and created a global phenomenon seemingly out of thin air. And while other sports played important roles assimilating America's diversifying population, basketball's particular suitability to urban communities accelerated the sport's adoption throughout the country. It took time and a great deal of structural change for the game to reach its true potential, but even in its earliest days, there should have been no dismissing the obviously broad appeal that basketball has to the masses.

Basketball's invention was really a happy accident, the outcrop of young athletes needing something to do indoors during chilly winter months. In 1890, Naismith joined a physical education program run by the Young Men's Christian Association (YMCA) as an instructor. For one of his courses, YMCA administrators charged Naismith with developing a new indoor team sport—something that the YMCA could use to occupy its members when the snow fell. Just before Christmas in 1891, in a small gymnasium in Springfield, Massachusetts, Naismith took the simple step of nailing peach baskets to a balcony ten feet in the air and instructed students to toss balls into them for points. With that, and a few rules he jotted down on a piece of paper, Naismith and his friends invented what would become a global sport sensation.[5]

Evidence of the game's potential for growth showed immediately. Within a year, Americans were playing Naismith's new game all over the country. Naismith's friend Luther Gullick remarked it was "doubtful ... a gymnastic game has ever spread so rapidly over the continent as has 'basket ball.' It is played from New York to San Francisco and from Maine to Texas by hundreds of teams and associations, athletic clubs and schools."[6] Thanks also to the YMCA, basketball was being played as far away as the Philippines by 1910.[7]

Several factors contributed to basketball's proliferation at the turn of the century. One of them was Alonzo Stagg, who knew Naismith through the YMCA and later became the athletic director at the University of Chicago, where he brought the game with him. Basketball's early adoption in US cities like Chicago also foreshadowed the game's potential for rapid growth in America and beyond. Indeed, compared to other sports like baseball and football, which require a lot of space and are, even today, mostly played outdoors, basketball fulfilled the need for an indoor sport that fit inside America's ever-crowded cities. Thanks to its minimal equipment costs, and highly individualized skill requirements, basketball was a sport Americans of every class could practice either alone or in groups. Sport historian Pamela Grundy explains that "[b]asketball has always appealed to a broad cross-section of the nation. Many of the teams and players of the early era ... reflected the class and cultural backgrounds of recent immigrants or of crafts and industries of the time."[8] Grundy adds that basketball was "flexible enough to be played by anyone with enough ingenuity to corral a barrel hoop and roll up a pair of socks, and was new enough that women had the chance to seize on it before it was defined as a 'men's' activity."[9]

Women were, in fact, a key demographic responsible for basketball's adoption in America. Women at Smith College began playing in 1893 and helped implement rule changes to make the women's game run as smoothly as the version initially reserved only for men.[10] In Chicago, Jane Addams's settlement house—known as Hull House—started teaching the game as early 1895 and by the end of that decade Hull House boasted two full women's basketball teams. Addams envisioned Hull House as a terminal for Chicago's diverse immigrant communities, where they could learn American history and the English language, as well as a safe space for the city's ethnic groups to socialize. Sport, particularly basketball, advanced Addams's goal of assimilating her city's residents, as well as her broader mission of promoting women's rights. According to historian Stacy McDermott, "Hull-House celebrated female athletics. Women's basketball games at Hull-House were announced in the Chicago papers, encouraging attendance, and scores were published the next day." Over the bellyaching of all-male sporting associations like the Illinois State High School Athletic Association, who called women's basketball "immodest and not altogether ladylike," by the First World War, Hull House sponsored sixteen basketball teams. McDermott concludes that "[w]omen who had the opportunity to engage in physical activities like basketball in the Hull-House gymnasium took those experiences out into the world with them. Playing the sport gave them confidence in their bodies and ... stretched the boundaries of their own imaginations."[11]

Basketball's professional development had a stuttered start, beginning with the quickly defunct National Basketball League (NBL). The sport's primary league today—the NBA—did not form until 1946, and it was only a decade before that when basketball became an official Olympic sport. In the early twentieth century, the game prospered thanks to local recreational leagues and a bustling playground movement, which included groups like the Playground Association of America and the Outdoor Recreation League that promoted amateur athletics as a means of national unity and strength.[12] Irish immigrants in New York City formed a local team they called the "Celtics" in 1914, a namesake that garnered great fame for the city of Boston later in the century.[13] In some areas, basketball became known as the "Jewish game," thanks to its popularity among younger Jews. Historian Peter Levine states that it was no surprise that basketball, "in urban, ethnic working-class neighborhoods, a game open to improvisation and requiring little space or equipment, proved attractive" to the Jewish community. When Jewish basketball players earned public acclaim for their skills, he adds, "along the way they became culture heroes in their own communities for people both proud of their Jewish connections and eager for American acceptance."[14]

Other urban enclaves, including pockets of African American neighborhoods that were beginning to grow amid the Great Migration, found joy and community in basketball. Harlem's own Alpha Physical Culture Club sponsored an all-Black team beginning in 1907.[15] Prior to its successful professionalization at mid-century, however, basketball remained, like Wiebe's view of America, still a sport for "island communities." Nationwide basketball circuits were slowly emerging, but nonetheless basketball proved hugely popular with audiences wherever it traveled, including in rural areas in the Midwest and West. One remarkable example of basketball's appeal and capacity to draw people together was the Fort Shaw Indian School women's basketball team, which competed and won a tournament championship at the 1904 World's Fair in Saint Louis. In Linda Peavy and Ursula Smith's oral history titled *Full-Court Quest*, they describe "a time when a fledgling game was being embraced by women and girls whose gender had thus far excluded them from participation in team sports." For the young women at Fort Shaw Indian School, basketball highlighted "the abilities of Indian youth and … the importance of providing them with academic, artistic, and athletic opportunities equal to those available to their white counterparts."[16]

Despite marginal professional growth and limited international reach, basketball's potential to capture large audiences and draw in huge public participation was evident in the early twentieth century. It took time to incubate, and rule changes that continued well into mid-century added more creativity and beauty to the game. But basketball's emphasis on spontaneity and tempo, the way it fits into cramped corners, and how it could be played alone or in large groups made it an attractive amateur sport and forecasted real potential for professional growth. Before long, basketball would begin challenging the other major American sports in both popularity and participation.

Jack Johnson and the Global Business of Boxing

Boxing is a prime example of a non-American sport sinking deep roots in US culture by the turn of the twentieth century. Evidence of organized boxing-like competitions dates back to the ancient Egyptians and Greeks, but England often gets credit for the first recorded prizefight in the late seventeenth century. In America, boxing became wildly popular in the nineteenth century as an amateur form of athletics in rural and urban settings, while the professional world of prizefighting cultivated a fervent subculture of followers and impressive fighters. Like basketball and other sports, boxing held out the possibility of assimilation and social mobility for immigrants. Gerald Gems, who has written on Italian immigrants and American sport, argues that for a "young Italian boy capable of reading the story or hearing about the successes of Italian boxers, the message clearly suggested that one's physicality was a means to recognition and wealth."[17] Historian Louis Moore, author of *I Fight for a Living: Boxing and the Battle for Black Manhood, 1880–1915,* writes that "black prizefighters represented a symbol of black mobility as they moved around the country or crossed oceans to find work."[18] And for Jewish immigrants, boxers like Benny Leonard, who reigned as the lightweight champion of the world between 1917 and 1925, "confirmed Jewish toughness and the will to survive, while providing a vivid counterpoint to popular anti-Semitic stereotypes. They also served as touchstones for attempts to reconcile traditional, ethnic values with mainstream American culture."[19]

One way to understand this period of boxing history is to explore the life and professional career of the African American prizefighter Jack Johnson. Johnson's legacy as an American athlete is among the most complicated that exists in US history. He was born and raised in turn-of-the-century Galveston, Texas, where the brutality of white supremacy was ubiquitous. Violence shaped Johnson's early life, and his mother demanded he learn to defend himself. As an adolescent, Johnson became involved in local boxing events that Randy Roberts, a sport historian and one of Johnson's biographers, describes as "Battle Royals," wherein "eight or more black youths were told to get into the ring and fight a free-for-all," sometimes blindfolded, while onlookers "threw pennies and nickels to the victor."[20] Roberts explains that the Battle Royals were designed to "debase black youths before the white enforcers of the Southern racial system" and teach them that "rewards came from defeating your brother, not from joining him."[21]

Johnson emerged from the crucible of his early childhood a powerhouse of a fighter, blending unrivaled strength and size with a defensive style he learned in the Battle Royals as a boy. These years also kindled in him streaks of rage and violence that later became assets in the ring—and dangerous liabilities for others outside it. Johnson horribly abused multiple women in his life. One of them, Etta Duryea, Johnson beat so badly she required hospitalization. While she coalesced, Johnson was with his mistress. He and Duryea stayed together a little longer, and even married briefly, but the abuse and infidelity persisted. In 1912, Etta shot and killed herself in their apartment in Chicago. Johnson moved on, remarried, and continued to engage in other reckless and illicit behavior. Yet amid several major personal crises—including a racially fueled FBI investigation into his personal and financial activities—Johnson could channel his emotions into an eerie calmness in the ring that belied the explosiveness of his fists.[22]

Johnson's career took off within a boxing world struggling to stay alive. Racial barriers would eventually become an issue for him, but initially anti-prizefighting activists put up the biggest hurdle to his career. As we have seen, Progressive-era reformers preached the value of sport to a diverse society, but many also abhorred the brutality that professional boxing celebrated as well as the sport's commercialization. Not only were prizefighters paid for brutalizing one another in the ring, but the sport was awash in one of the oldest and most controversial of all sporting traditions: bawdy gambling. States began outlawing prizefighting in 1900, sending most of America's boxing subculture underground.[23] The broadsides leveled at the commercialization of boxing reflected a much larger phenomenon taking place in American and foreign sporting communities. Roberts writes that "the crusade against boxing had strong class overtones …. Indeed, many upper-class gentlemen noted that boxing inculcated worthy virtues" and supported amateur boxing as a healthy feature of a modern, masculine society.[24] With money mixed in, however, the sport's shine wore off. To well-heeled Americans, prizefighting looked more like a barfight. President Theodore Roosevelt, who often spoke as the vanguard of Progressivism, lamented that when "money comes in at the gate, sport flies out at the window."[25] The president's outlook carried weight in other corners of the sporting world as well, while in boxing it preceded a dramatic reduction in the size of the fighters' purses.

Somehow, under these conditions, Jack Johnson evolved into a global boxing sensation. After dominating the competition in Texas and California, Johnson sought out America's heavyweight champion, Jim Jeffries, who was based on the East Coast. Jeffries, however, refused to fight a Black boxer, stating publicly that he was "determined not to take the chance of losing the championship to a negro."[26] Amid the crackdown on prizefighting in the country, Jeffries retired as heavyweight champion until eventually the title was awarded to the Canadian Tommy Burns, who quickly left for England, where the business of boxing still boomed. Johnson followed him across the Atlantic, but Burns rejected Johnson's request for a showdown and then left for Australia, which in those years was the epicenter of the boxing world. Finally Burns agreed to a fight, and when Johnson dispatched the champion with no trouble—even mocking Burns and toying with him like a cat with a wounded bird—Jim Jeffries came out of retirement to reclaim the title from a man he openly despised because of the color of his skin. In the pages of the *New York Herald*, the legendary journalist Jack London set the tone for white Americans before the fateful showdown: "Jim Jeffries must now emerge … and remove that golden smile from Jack Johnson's face. Jeff, it's up to you. The White Man must be rescued."[27]

In Reno, Nevada on the Fourth of July in 1910, before 20,000 rowdy spectators and for a total purse and movie rights estimated in the hundreds of thousands of dollars, Johnson annihilated Jeffries. When the news broke that Johnson had won, race riots erupted all over America. Historians

FIGURE 1.1 *Jack Johnson stands over a fallen and bloodied Jim Jeffries in Reno, Nevada on July 4, 1910. In the days after Johnson's victory, throughout the United States angry whites killed nineteen Black Americans who were seen celebrating the outcome of the fight. (Bettman/Contributor via Getty Images).*

have shown that the psychological effect of Johnson's victory over Jeffries, the "great white hope" of the boxing world, was profound. When news of the fight's outcome spread, cities began passing laws prohibiting Black boxers from fighting whites. Newspapers like the *Memphis Commercial Appeal* warned that "no fool negro get biggity because of the result of the fight," while other white supremacists wanted blood.[28] From Baltimore to Los Angeles, almost every major US city witnessed rioting and racially motivated violence in the days after Johnson's victory over Jeffries. Angry whites—including police and military personnel—attacked and murdered Blacks seen celebrating Johnson's win.[29]

For Johnson, the victory over Jeffries proved fleeting. His career continued, he fought other challengers, and went on world boxing tours, stopping in Germany, Spain, Cuba, and Mexico to box as a celebrity. But by the 1930s, according to Roberts, Johnson had "become a figure of humiliation in tinsel surroundings."[30] Despite achieving fame and wealth as an American sport star, Johnson was never welcomed into the white society that defined his world. He died as he had lived, violently, in 1946 after losing control of his car and slamming into a light post outside of Raleigh, North Carolina.

Johnson's career anticipated so much of what generations of Black American athletes endured over the twentieth century. His response to the white power structure around him provides instructive comparisons, as well, with how other athletes, like Jackie Robinson, Muhammad Ali, and Arthur Ashe, reacted to their own day's oppression. Johnson attacked white supremacy in the ring, where he took a particular delight in bloodying white opponents. Johnson's persona outside of prizefighting was loud and performative, designed to poke racist whites in the eye. But his behavior differed from the concerted social activism Black athletes pursued later in the century. Johnson had more interest in living large and stayed in the headlines because of his boxing feats and notoriously risky behavior. His ostentatious living also fed into the narrative that professional sport eroded the virtue of athletic competition by putting greed over sportsmanship. The amateur movement briefly managed to sap boxing of its cash flow for a few years, but not permanently. In other corners of sport, however, amateurism had become gospel.

American Football, Collegiate Athletics, and the Amateur Sport Movement

Football is a hybrid US sport, drawing partly from international traditions but stamped with important characteristics from turn-of-the-century America. "Prior to 1880," write sport historians Elliot Gorn and Warren Goldstein, American football "resembled English rugby more than today's football," but soon thereafter the game underwent major alterations.[31] What led the sport to transition from the ceaseless, roving scrum of players like in rugby to a carefully measured, stop-and-go sport that put a fixed defense and offense on the field was primarily the influence of the industrial workplace. The sport's most important early figure, and leading innovator during football's nascent development, was Walter Camp, who started playing the rugby-like version of American football in the 1870s. Camp was a standout on the field before taking a job with the New Haven Clock Company, after which he returned to the world of football to become a coach at Yale and then Stanford. According to Gorn and Goldstein, "Camp frequently noted the connections between the structure of football and the world of business," and eventually put his particular experience in clockmaking, plus his general knowledge of industrial management, toward reshaping and improving his favorite sport.[32]

Under Camp's direction, football transitioned to a more orderly game shaped by deliberate strategizing and a routinization of positional skill sets that made the sport resemble the modern factory floor. Camp envisioned eleven players (down from fifteen) each performing a clear and distinct job on every play, just like a clock: a series of individualized parts working toward the success of a bigger, multifunctioning unit. By following the industrial blueprint he learned in the business world, Camp "constructed a sport that was probably the fullest expression of industrial organization—on the playing field and at the training camp—that the world of play had ever seen."[33]

There are some examples of football bridging ethnic and cultural divides like other sports did early in the century—perhaps most famously in the case of the US Olympian Jim Thorpe, who learned the game at the Carlisle Indian Industrial School.[34] But since its inception, football was a collegiate sport, which meant that mostly college-bound white men from America's upper crust played the game. Its affiliation with collegiate athletics—the first recorded American football game took place in 1869 between Rutgers and Princeton—placed football on the frontlines in the turn-of-the-century battle between amateur and professional sport. East Coast Ivy League schools were the first adopters, and once Camp took over the Yale team as a player and coach, New Haven became the mecca of college football programs. "Far more than academic achievement," argue Gorn and Goldstein, "the experience and culture of football linked different generations of American leaders in a collegiate socialization process that helped provide class cohesion for the children of the American upper classes." Thanks to its intense physicality and frequent comparisons to war, the full effect of tying football to collegiate sport was that it became "a means of defining and testing physical and psychological masculinity, a kind of initiation ritual" for the country's elite white men.[35]

The amateur athletic movement that exerted heavy influence over America's broader sporting culture in the early twentieth century looked at football as testament for its cause. Teddy Roosevelt, who loved football and constantly complained about the commercialization of sport, argued for its permanence on university campuses because it was "a game appropriate for a nation ripe for a clean, violent, virile, yet gentlemanly sport."[36] Roosevelt did have some worries about the direction the sport seemed headed. Despite his legendary jingoism, he once intervened to try to make the game less violent, to no avail. His most serious concern, however, was that football players, or any other athlete, might forget the true value of sport and make it, instead, a professional pursuit. "When a man so far confuses ends and means as to think that fox-hunting, or polo, or foot-ball, or whatever else the sport may be, is to be itself taken as the end, instead of as the mere means of preparation to do work that counts when the times arise," Roosevelt once warned, "when the occasion calls—why, that man had better abandon sport altogether."[37]

Other influential athletic boosters echoed Roosevelt's rebuke of the profit-seeking side of sport. That included Walter Camp who helped found what became the National Collegiate Athletic Association (NCAA) in 1906. The defense of amateur sport, much like football itself, began in Britain where upper-class Englishmen told a story about the purity of amateurism that was, in fact, designed to prevent working-class athletes, who needed to be paid to play, out of the wealthy worlds of English soccer and rugby. Sport historian S. W. Pope argues that the "invention of amateurism, then, must be understood within the larger context of how a national middle class elite was formed in the late nineteenth century."[38] Influential Americans like the sport journalist Caspar Whitney applied English thinking to American sport and wrote that "money, money seems to be the cry, and it will be the curse, if indeed not the downfall of honest university sport."[39] In reality, "amateur" athletes found ways of making money under and above the table, and even the amateur sport movement took on a conspicuously professional patina in order to promote its brittle vision of sporting culture. No matter how hypocritical the amateur movement was, however, the fact is it made a lasting impact on the landscape of American sport. Perhaps nowhere was that more evident in the early 1900s than in the revived Olympic movement.

America and the Modern Olympic Movement

In the first half of the twentieth century, Americans used the Olympic revival to show off their new sporting culture to the world. US Olympians, and their trove of early victories at the Games, became messengers of their country's rising power. This period of Olympic history reflects what sport historians call "track-two diplomacy," where cultural exchange functions to the benefit of nation-states, but not entirely under their control. "People to people exchanges," writes historian Simon Rofe, "organized by private individuals or organizations ... can also contribute to the changing of perceptions."[40] During the first four decades of the Olympic movement's revival, international athletics functioned indirectly as a powerful means of public diplomacy through the efforts of mostly private enterprise.

That would not always be the case. By mid-century, governments took firmer control over the management of sport as an instrument of soft power. But initially, an amateur sport movement, unfettered by overt government direction, conveyed to the world what American competitiveness and sport culture were all about. Some countries grumbled about the arrogance of American athletes during the first few Olympiads, while others wondered if the melting pot had, in fact, produced a special brew that gave the United States an unfair advantage over its competitors.

Pierre de Coubertin and the 1896 Revival of the Olympic Games

Toward the end of the nineteenth century, a bold French baron named Pierre de Coubertin looked back to history for a means of rejuvenating flagging French nationalism. The historian Mark Dyreson describes how Coubertin "fervently believed that if France would adopt Anglo-American sporting culture, it would regain its status as the leading nation of modern civilization."[41] The baron insisted that the original Olympic tradition, dating back to 776 BCE, had bolstered Greek culture and society—and he wanted the same for modern France. In 1896, the United States was one of fourteen countries to answer Coubertin's call and sent athletes to Athens for the Olympic movement's rebirth. Whether the baron's original goal of reinvigorating French nationalism through athletic competition was a success is debatable. There is, however, no questioning the impact his efforts to restart the Olympic Games had on the twentieth-century world of sport.[42]

Early in the revival, the Olympics primarily consisted of track and field events, which many considered the purest measure of amateur athletic performance. Women were not allowed to participate in the 1896 Olympics, so the United States sent a handful of college-age men from Ivy League schools to compete before a crowd of 40,000 fans packed into the recently refurbished Panathenaic Stadium, the cradle of the original Olympic Games. Olympians competed for ten days, and the Americans did not disappoint, winning the majority of the track and field events. Victory in 1896 introduced the world to another enduring feature of US Olympic culture: swagger. "I think it was on the third or fourth day of the Games," hammed the US hurdler Thomas Curtis, "that the Americanization of Europe began."[43]

Coubertin set in motion a new Olympic tradition that still grows and thrives today. Given how the Games matured, and the international sport community with them, perhaps the most salient outcome for US Olympic athletes in 1896 was that their performances had captured the attention of the most serious-minded amateur athletic boosters in the United States. Heading into the 1900 Olympics, which Coubertin engineered to occur in Paris, the Amateur Athletic Union (AAU) and other apostles of amateurism took up the Olympic cause and made victory at the Games a top priority within the US sporting community. Sport barons like James E. Sullivan, A.G. Spalding, and Caspar Whitney believed the United States could dominate Olympic competitions and elevate American sport to new heights.

The 1900 Olympic Games in Paris

Constituted in 1894, but uninvolved with the 1896 Games, the American Olympic Committee (AOC) took over US Olympic operations in 1900. Key members of the AAU staffed the AOC's top posts, but no one loomed larger than AAU secretary, and later president, James E. Sullivan. "Under the command of Sullivan," Dyreson writes, "the AAU and the AOC pushed their beloved track and field athletics to center stage at the Olympic Games," and in the process turned the American Olympic movement "into an instrument of athletic nationalism."[44] The AOC's fixation on curating an even stronger collection of Olympians than the 1896 team brought a wider group of athletes into the mix, now including women. By the time the US Olympic team headed to Paris for the 1900 Games, the AOC and the broader US public expected a decisive victory. According to Pope, the revitalized Olympic movement "provided an arena in which certain Americans could invent and popularize symbols of their political and sporting culture by linking athletic prowess to national mythology. As such, the Olympics became a self-perpetuating forum for discussion of athletic superiority as a national characteristic."[45]

Led by Alvin Kraenzlein, who finished first in four contests, the US Olympic team once again dominated the vaulted track and field events, winning seventeen of twenty-two competitions in 1900. That year the United States also competed in non-track-and-field games, after avoiding them in Athens, and won several, including men's golf and rowing. One final victory—which for years was omitted from official Olympic records—was in women's golf when Margaret Abbot became the first American woman to win an Olympic competition. An international cohort of twenty-two women competed in the 1900 Games, although Olympic officials restricted them to just four events. Olympians placing first, second, or third in Paris received "objects of art," and the US women tallied four of the decorative awards.[46] A *New York Times* article reported that the "feature of the [Olympics] was not only the number of events the Americans won, but the ease with which they outstripped their competitors, often finishing first and second, laughing side by side, and in a canter."[47]

The *Times* was fair to highlight the manifest arrogance of US athletes. Foreign audiences certainly paid attention to the Americans' behavior in victory and defeat. Historians note that the US Olympic team's penchant for raucous cheering annoyed French onlookers, who wished their foreign guests would accept victory with a quiet grace. But that was never the American way. The US team whooped and hollered during the events, while the AOC leveled blunt criticisms about the way French officials handled the Paris Games, as there were several logistical mishaps along the way. Behind their impressive performances in 1896 and 1900, Americans convinced the International Olympic Committee (IOC) to grant the 1904 Games to the United States. As Dyreson writes, the Olympic Games "were coming to the 'new Athens', and the Americans planned an ode to the strength of their conception of sport."[48]

The 1904 Games and the St. Louis World's Fair

The popularity of international expositions, also called world's fairs, was at an all-time high in the early twentieth century. World's fairs date back to the mid-1800s and were intended to introduce global audiences to new technologies and other major national achievements, all according to the tastes of the sponsoring country. Like sport, world's fairs could have powerful effects on a society and the international community at large. David Nasaw, who writes on public amusements and assimilation, describes world's fairs as "paeans to progress, concrete demonstrations of how order and organization, high culture and art, science and technology, commerce and industry, all brought together under the wise administration of business and government, would lead inevitably to a brighter, more prosperous future."[49] To some sport boosters in America, linking the 1904 Olympic Games to the coinciding St. Louis World's Fair (also called the Louisiana Purchase Exposition) made good sense. Indeed, the 1900 Paris Games had occurred simultaneously with a French exposition, although there was evidence to suggest the exposition sapped Parisians' interests in the Olympic festivities.[50] Prominent US businesses and politicians lobbied for the games to be in Chicago or Philadelphia, but in the end, the Missourians landed the 1904 Games.[51]

Turn-of-the-century St. Louis was a growing, ambitious city, and it hosted an impressive world's fair. The 1904 Louisiana Purchase Exposition—celebrating the centennial (plus one) anniversary of Thomas Jefferson's famous territorial purchase from Napoleon that effectively doubled the size of the United States—unveiled modern technologies including airplanes, automobiles, X-ray machines, and wireless telegraph. Almost twenty million people from around the world attended the event and took in marvelous architecture designed specifically for the exposition. In their book *Anthropology Goes to the Fair*, Nancy Parezo and Don Fowler write that the "federal government, states, and historical societies sent precious iconic heirlooms and reproductions to document American history, patriotism, and nationalism."[52] The St. Louis exposition made a strident attempt to promote US nationalism indeed, and one increasingly predictable method for doing so involved the denigration of non-Anglo-Saxon cultures and people. The exposition brought in thousands of "Native peoples" from around the world and hosted a culturally skewed anthropological exhibit designed, according to Parezo and Fowler, "to celebrate the assumed racial and cultural superiority of Northern European and American nations and to justify their imperial and colonial ambitions."[53]

It was with this unseemly feature of the 1904 exposition that the AOC decided to involve itself and organized what it called "Anthropology Days." Sullivan helped orchestrate the event and recruited men from various ethnic and national backgrounds, including Pygmies, Aborigines, Filipinos, Syrians, as well as several Native Americans tribes, to compete against one another in athletic events before the fair's more "civilized" onlookers.[54] Sullivan billed the contest as a case study that would help determine the *true* athlete in the world: the "primitive" man or the "modern" Olympian. A few days before the Olympic Games began, the men Sullivan selected faced off in track and field events, as well as others that the *St. Louis Star* described as "suited to the nature of the contestants." Native Americans won the most points during the competition, but what Sullivan boasted about was what he called proof that "adult 'savages' had abilities that were the equivalent of civilized children." He insisted there was no hope "for their evolutionary advancement or assimilation" and concluded "that Native peoples were destined to disappear or remain wards of the state."[55]

As for the official 1904 Games, once again the United States dominated, albeit this time without Britain or France to worry about since neither country sent full Olympic delegations. Remembered as an "all-American affair," the lack of foreign competition did nothing to dampen the nationalistic fervor that American audiences felt for their Olympians. Facing just eleven other countries, the United States easily walked away with the most Olympic medals—which became a modern Olympic tradition after they were handed out in St. Louis—including seventy-eight golds. Watered down or not, the US public and Olympic team read the results as irrefutable proof that America was the world leader in sport. The "confirmation of national athletic supremacy," writes Dyreson, "complemented what Sullivan insisted was the central purpose of the St. Louis Olympics—educating the world in the doctrines of American athletics."[56]

Olympic Fatigue, European Rivalry, and the 1908 London Games

How telling that the United States, when given its first chance to host an Olympics, chose foremost to mock and degrade non-white, indigenous communities, and then held a party mostly for itself where it won all the awards. The combination of human cruelty and self-idolatry on display at the 1904 St. Louis Games spoke volumes about the condition of American society in the early 1900s. During those same years, in the name of white Christian civilization the US military was on the march around the world, killing and displacing native peoples, taking their lands and resources by force and extortion, all the while securing US businesses lucrative trade and investment opportunities. American success in Olympic sport put a fine point on the ascendance of the United States as a new world power— at least for American sport fans. Their sense of national importance was becoming more pronounced, and sport—particularly the Olympics—offered a powerful new way to show themselves off to the world.

Conversely, after 1904 international interest in the Olympic revival movement tapered off.[57] But thanks to Greece's offer two years later to host another international sport competition—what became the 1906 Intercalated Games—the movement caught a gust of wind and regained its momentum. The 1906 games no longer count in the IOC official records, but contemporaries viewed them as another Olympic installment. Judging by participation and attendance, the games were more popular and representative of the state of international sport than the 1904 St. Louis Olympics. Twenty-four countries sent 901 athletes to compete in front of an estimated 80,000 fans—double the crowd that had watched the inaugural 1896 Games. Sullivan was so impressed by Greek enthusiasm that he considered supporting a permanent resettlement of the Games in Athens.[58]

The 1906 results mirrored prior Olympic competitions, with the United States winning the most medals. The US minister plenipotentiary to Greece John B. Jackson boasted back to Washington that the Americans won a plurality of the "real Olympic contests" (meaning track and field), and also claimed they "won much popularity by their sportsmanlike qualities and their discipline," giving their country "every reason to be proud of them."[59] Although many foreign audiences disagreed about the sportsmanship of US athletes, the team's success certainly helped to support a burgeoning vision of American exceptionalism back home. More significant than the medal count, however, was the effect the Intercalated Games had on international support for the Olympic movement. Heading into England for the 1908 Olympics, expectations soared over what the British could pull off on their home turf.

Historians often highlight the intense transatlantic rivalry that simmered between the United States and Great Britain by the time the 1908 Games kicked off. There were, in fact, several testy moments, but they were little more than nationalistic bravado brought on by competition between two close international allies. The 1908 Games only hinted at the politicization of the Olympics, and the attending rise of hyper-nationalism, that occurred toward midcentury. Still, national rivalries were a noteworthy aspect of the London Games. According to historian George Matthews, Britons and Americans saw that year's Olympics "as a means of demonstrating [their] overall cultural superiority and promoting nationalism."[60]

Once again, the rowdiness of the US contingent stood out, keeping "everything and everyone alive with their shouts of encouragements and applause," according to the London *Times*.[61] American journalists further inflated the US team's swelling vanity by promising the Americans would "knock the spots off the Britishers," and invoking memories of the American Revolution.[62] One of the most symbolically rich moments occurred during the opening ceremonies, when the US delegation failed to dip its flag before the British royal family during an introductory procession—a custom the other countries had all observed. Allegedly, the Irish-American shot-putter Ralph Rose, who carried the American flag for the US team, uttered "this flag dips for no earthly king" as he marched along. Apocryphal or not, the story became a small sensation among the American press and helped stoke the inherent imperial rivalry between Britain and its rising former colony.[63]

Pre-game rivalries grew into full-fledged controversies once the trials started, beginning with the 400-meter race. In that event, US sprinter J. C. Carpenter finished first, only to have British Olympic officials disqualify him for impeding another runner, the British braggart Wyndham Halswelle, who before the race had guaranteed victory over the Americans. Recalcitrant American journalists questioned the disqualification and named Carpenter the real winner of the event.[64] In another case, during the marathon competition, an Italian runner named Dorando Pietri collapsed

FIGURE 1.2 *British officials help carry the Italian runner Dorando Pietri across the finish line to keep the American John Hayes from winning the 1908 Olympic marathon. IOC judges ultimately awarded Hayes the gold medal after the United States protested the initial result. (Photo by © Hulton-Deutsch Collection/CORBIS/ Corbis via Getty Images).*

not far from the finish line. Rather than let an advancing American runner win, the judges helped the Italian to victory.

The US team protested and the IOC quickly reversed the decision and awarded the US runner, John Hayes, a gold medal. English observers, however, found it distasteful that the Americans demanded the gold medal. The British journal *Academy* claimed that if Hayes had only let Pietri win, he "would have done much to wipe out the feeling of disgust which had been generated by the conduct of the American athletes and their rowdy supporters."[65] By 1908 foreign audiences often accused American athletes of bending the rules and taking the competitive spirit of the Olympics too far. The American sportswriter Caspar Whitney dismissed the accusations as "violent prejudice" and countered plainly that his country's cutthroat approach to athletics reflected the same national spirit "that has made us what we are."[66]

Yet at these particular Games, American bravado did not translate to Olympic supremacy. Great Britain enlisted over 500 athletes on their home turf and walked away with the most medals by far, more than doubling the United States in golds. Rather than temper its approach to Olympic preparation, however, British success motivated the AOC to intensify its planning for the 1912 Games set for Sweden. According to Dyreson, after the 1908 Games, "Americans dreamed of more glory. The AOC had grand plans. They wanted more money, bigger and better tryouts, and a training ship to carry their champions to Sweden."[67]

Melting Pot Athletes and the 1912 Stockholm Games

The AOC had no trouble securing its desired funding ahead of the 1912 Games. American business tycoons like John Rockefeller, Andrew Carnegie, J. P. Morgan, T. C. DuPont, and Cyrus McCormick joined the AOC as vice-presidents and helped turn the US Olympic recruiting process into an expansive operation. The *New York Times* characterized the 1912 squad the "most representative team ever sent abroad." Dipping from the well of American jingoism, the paper boasted that "[n]ever before in the forces of any of our invading teams has the make-up of the athletic army been so truly National."[68] Bad war metaphors aside, the 1912 US team was even more representative than in previous years. White American women participated in the 1900 Olympics, and African Americans began competing in the Olympics in 1904 (despite the fact Black Americans were not permitted to attend the Games or the St. Louis exposition) when George Poage medaled in the 200-meter and 400-meter hurdles. Four years later, John Taylor, the son of former slaves, won the gold as part of the US 400-meter relay team. In 1912, the US team brought on Native Americans, including the legendary multisport star Jim Thorpe. That year's Olympians also featured the African American sprinter Howard P. Drew, considered by many "the world's fastest human," who was poised to challenge for a gold medal in the 100-meter sprint before pulling a muscle and withdrawing from the final round of competitions.[69] One historian writes that "bellboys, clerks, and mechanics; the doctors, lawyers, and policemen; the Anglo-Saxons, Irish, African Americans, Slavs, Scandinavians, Native Americans, and Hawaiians; the Jews, Catholics, Protestants, and Christian Scientists of the American squad—together they faced the assembled might of the athletic world."[70]

Based on how Americans remembered the Games, one might have missed that Sweden walked away with the most total medals, edging out the United States by two.[71] But the United States had once again performed very well in track and field and left Stockholm with the most total gold medals (twenty-seven), giving them ample reason to celebrate. And celebrate they did in their famous American style which had been on display throughout the 1912 Games. The British press once again complained about the "exultant Americans" who sought victory "not to delight in their strength and prowess, but to show that these United States can whip the universe."[72] Back home, a New York City ticker-tape parade awaited the returning Olympians. The *New York Times* adumbrated how "the returning conquering athletes" would soon be "riding in a string of touring cars through the streets lined with school children, who will cheer themselves hoarse with the American Olympic team's yell just as it was given in Stockholm."[73]

With the Olympic wind at its back, US sport continued to grow. Robust domestic athletic programs—both amateur and professional—enjoyed broad interest and participation from the American public. Olympic success enhanced Americans' awareness of their aptitude in the world's greatest arenas, just as business growth and military gains fueled the country's aspirations for more imperial power. While not every American played or cared about sports, around them grew a pervasive sporting culture that, like everything American, seemed primed for export. The credibility of America's early Olympic success paved the way for a global sport marketing campaign that professional sporting leagues, the sporting goods industry, and the US government pursued for decades after.

Yet at the forefront of America's global sport ascendance stood a paradox. Was US sport, like the nation it covered in glory, the product of a modern, pluralistic, democratic society, or the extension of an aggressively militaristic state determined to enhance white Americans' power at home and abroad? The Olympics suggested the former might be true. Other sports like baseball, however, offered plenty of evidence to conclude that on many levels, sport served primarily as veneer for an oppressive US empire. When baseball arrived at the Great War, it rode a wave of US military expansion and economic imperialism that reached from the Caribbean to East Asia.

Baseball and American Empire

In the early twentieth century, baseball embodied the spirit of American sport from all angles. The game's short-lived reign as the most popular US sport at home and overseas reflected a billowing sport culture that served the state in many ways. Domestically, broad public participation and interest in baseball, like other sports including basketball, functioned as an assimilative force in a country rapidly diversifying both culturally and ethnically. Unlike the other major sports, baseball successfully professionalized over these years, and used its leverage as a business to join the march of American commercial growth in foreign markets. The business of baseball behaved the same as other industries run by rampant capitalists. Professional baseball's history of labor strife, market consolidation, and cutthroat business tactics reflected the evolutionary status of capitalism in the late industrial period. Like others of their era, baseball's early tycoons worshipped the almighty dollar and, in their greed, set a precedent for a tendentious business culture that persists in the sport to this day.[74]

Baseball also went to war. It was the sport US soldiers carried into the Caribbean and Latin America, across the Pacific to East Asia, and eventually deployed in Western Europe. To quote Mark Twain, everywhere "the eagle put its talons on any other land," baseball seemed to sprout. The game's popularity among foreign audiences was uneven (and remains so today) but nonetheless exceeded the other major US sports in global relevance through the mid-twentieth century.[75]

There were several formative developments between 1865 and 1920 that set the course for America's global sport history. The US dominance from the onset of the modern Olympic Games standardized the kind of performance Americans would expect from their Olympians while preparing other countries for what US power looked like. Sports like basketball made themselves indispensable by helping assimilate a nation of new and old immigrants. And football's expression of the amateur spirit became an enduring, if often insincere, fixture within the country's sporting tradition. Still nothing captured the prominence and frenetic growth of American sport at the turn of the century quite like the game of baseball.

Foreigners to Fans

Of the three major US sports, baseball is arguably the least "American" of them all. The game's design, its early fans, and its rapid introduction to foreign audiences combined to give baseball the most international heritage of any US sport. Early American adopters borrowed baseball's conceptual framework and skill requirements from British sports, including cricket, rounders, and even a version the English were already calling "base ball" as early as 1744.[76] Evidence of organized play resembling the modern game of baseball in America reaches back to the colonial period. George Washington played catch in camp with Continental soldiers during the Revolutionary War, while Thomas Jefferson, channeling a slaveowners' aversion to physical exertion, complained that "base ball was too violent for the body and stamped no character on the mind."[77]

Baseball's popularity grew with the country, often surfacing in the wake of America's conquests that wrangled more territories and people into a burgeoning US empire. The Indian Wars that still raged in the nineteenth century opened the interior of the country and brought US soldiers and settlers into the plains and Rocky Mountains, and some carried bats and gloves with them. The Mexican–American War (1846–8) accomplished the goal of continental dominion. Like the railroads, baseball advanced into blood-soaked western terrain and developed a new regional audience. Political cartoonists used baseball as metaphor for Lincoln's 1860 election, and during the Civil War both Union and Confederate soldiers recorded playing baseball in their camps. After defeating the Confederacy and helping end slavery, Union troops began outfitting semiprofessional baseball clubs as far west as Colorado, where they called themselves the "Rocky Mountain Boys."[78] Historian Robert Elias writes that during the period of westward expansion, the "US military helped spread baseball wherever it went, a practice it would soon extend well beyond America's borders."[79] Despite continued regional polarizations in the era of Reconstruction, by the 1870s baseball flourished in every corner of the country.

Baseball's growth helped the sport become an important vehicle of assimilation. As Nasaw argues in *Going Out*, not only did playing sports facilitate assimilation by fostering teamwork, communication, and shared goals, but attendance at major sporting events, especially professional baseball games, helped accelerate the integration of diverse ethnic neighborhoods into unified sporting communities. Tiered ticket prices created a "de facto segregation" of poor and wealthier white Americans within the stadiums, while for African Americans segregation in public areas was often absolute in the early twentieth century.[80] Still, mingling and bonding across ethnic and class lines occurred in the parks. Polish and Czech immigrants might arrive for a game at Weeghman Park (renamed Wrigley Field in 1926) members of separate communities, with distinctive identities reinforced by their ethnic enclaves. But once inside the friendly confines they transformed into a unified bloc of Chicago Cubs fans. Mix in some alcohol, and the exhilaration of seeing a home run or a nifty backhand in the hole, and the metamorphosis was complete: for a least a few hours, ethnic differences melted away, replaced by the collective experience of Cubs fans together taking in a ballgame.[81] Noting the municipal and civic value that Madison Square Garden served to New York's diverse community, in 1900 the *New York Times* confessed to one worry: "whether there is public spirit enough among the rich men of New York to retain for public uses the place which has so admirably served those uses ever since it was built."[82] The paper was not wrong to wonder about the future of public sporting events. Rising ticket prices at major venues increasingly impeded the access of lower- and even middle-class Americans throughout the twentieth century, thus blunting the assimilative power stadiums once served to their communities.

Nasaw's work also highlights the stress fractures that formed between first- and second-generation immigrants over how best, and how deeply, to assimilate into their new surroundings. In the early twentieth century, baseball became a point of friction in these intergenerational culture wars. Surrendering old-world cultural traditions to new ways of life can be a painful burden for first-generation immigrants. And baseball, which flaunted a foreign language of its own built on intricate rules and an elaborate scoring system, presented a unique threat to more cloistered communities. Watching their children fall in love with the game, Jewish parents in New York editorialized that the sport wasted their kids' time and energy. The *Jewish Daily Forward*, however, stood up for the youngsters and asked the parents not to "raise the children that they should grow up foreigners in their own birthplace."[83] In other cases, like in Italian and Polish quarters, the non-English newspapers often refused to carry box scores or cover local baseball teams.[84]

Baseball's allure, however, overwhelmed the efforts by first-generation immigrants to keep their children from wasting time on the game. Even as other sports like football and basketball were becoming more popular, none enjoyed the enthusiasm Americans felt for baseball. Little leagues, saloon leagues, municipal leagues, up to semiprofessional leagues—in the early twentieth century organized baseball seemed everywhere and for everyone. Peter Levine, who has written on Jewish immigrants and American sport, explains that for Jewish youth baseball "symbolically permitted an immediate sense of belonging to a larger American community" that helped define "the game's special contribution as middle ground in the process of becoming American."[85] The sport itself reflected the American public's broad reciprocating interest. A Chicago resident in the early 1900s, for example, could attend games of the First Ward League and watch the all-Jewish team (the Matzas) take on the all-Italian team (the Kennas), or an all-Chinese team (the Hip Lungs) play the All Nations team "comprised of Jews, Swedes, Italians, Irish, Chinese, Spaniards, Japanese, African-Americans, and French players."[86]

Of course, at the highest professional level baseball was anything but democratic. The rise of MLB—comprising the National League (NL), formed in 1876, and the later-joining American League (AL), established in 1901—is a story of broad popularity and narrow accessibility. When Moses Fleetwood Walker left the league in the 1880s, for a half century thereafter MLB instituted a de facto "color line" and refused to sign Black ballplayers. Barred from the major leagues until after the Second World War, African Americans created their own baseball organizations, and eventually a professional circuit for Black baseball players known as the Negro Leagues, which became widespread in the 1920s.[87]

The slightest of paths to the majors was available to Latino communities in America, where baseball was also growing in popularity. The first was Cuban immigrant Esteban Bellán, nicknamed "The Cuban Sylph," who starred for the short-lived National Association's Troy Haymakers from 1871 to 1873, followed soon thereafter by Vincent Nava from Mexico, who played in the NL following the National Association's collapse in 1875. According to historian Adrian Burgos, "[t]hirteen of the sixteen major league teams that existed prior to 1947 had at least one Latino player perform in uniform before Jackie Robinson's 1947 debut." He adds that because "these players, most of whom were racialized as nonwhite Others or of 'Spanish' ancestry, secured access [to the majors] illuminates how team and league officials manipulated their league's racial policy to sign players who occupied locations along the color line other than that of blacks."[88]

Small numbers of Native Americans played professional baseball, but their place was likewise contingent and complicated. Louis Sockalexis from the Penobscot tribe broke into the NL in 1897, only to be greeted by white fans donning feathers and "Indian garb."[89] Nonetheless, the presence of even a few non-white ballplayers began a subtle movement to integrate the game more fully. In 1901, for instance, N.Y. Giants manager John McGraw unsuccessfully tried to sneak a Black ballplayer on his team by claiming the player was Native American.[90] Efforts to integrate MLB persisted for decades and eventually brought down the color line, but not without fierce resistance from baseball's old guard.

Even for certain white ethnic communities, structural obstacles put the professional game out of reach. Southern and Eastern European communities were heavily underrepresented in MLB into the 1920s. Some of this stemmed from intergenerational culture wars, as we have seen, but historians have shown that the urban/rural divide was a major determinant of who was good enough to play the game professionally. By 1920, roughly 40 percent of all professional ballplayers were from rural parts of the country, which suggests the majority hailed from cities. But as scholars such as Stephen Riess have shown, that percentage is misleading without the proper context. The ethnic communities living in the densest areas of the cities—often Italians, Jews, Eastern Europeans, and African Americans—typically lacked access to the space needed to master the game.[91]

Indeed, a baseball field is a cavernous design. The requisite space for a proper *infield* would have been hard to find in most inner cities in America. Thus, the popular variation of baseball known as "stickball"—a game that fit in alleyways or abandoned lots—became an acceptable substitute for city youths. Among the professional ballplayers who grew up in cities, most were born to upper-middle-class families, or above, who could afford to join private clubs where their children learned the game. By comparison, less than 4 percent of MLB players by 1920 were born to factory workers or other "unskilled" laboring classes.[92] Wealthy children and those who grew up in semirural or rural settings had a huge advantage over poorer, inner-city youth in skill development. In conjunction with MLB's color line, well into the 1920s league rosters consisted mainly of English, German, and Irish Americans, who grew up either well-off or in farming communities where land and space were plentiful.[93]

Cannons in the Outfield

Baseball enjoyed unrivaled popularity among a diverse cast of Americans in the early twentieth century, but it found less receptive audiences abroad. As in the game itself, how baseball was pitched mattered a good deal. For some, baseball was an appendage of a US military occupation. The Civil War paused Americans' drive for new territory, but once the war ended, they were back in the mood for more. By the early 1900s, the United States had unleashed a sweeping approach to empire building, deploying at various times the country's economic, military, and diplomatic power centers to take lands and open markets.[94] When the remnants of Spain's empire became engulfed in revolutionary independence movements, the United

States pounced on former Spanish colonies, while adding a few other new possessions for good measure. Along the way, US soldiers carried baseballs in their packs and helped plant the seeds for the global baseball community that exists today.

Americans stretched their military and economic influence from Puerto Rico to the Philippines, but two examples from this era—US interventions in Hawaii and Cuba—illuminate what became of baseball, and empire, in lands beyond US shores. With its lucrative sugar and pineapple cultivation, and its proximity to East Asia, by the 1890s the "Hawaiian pear," according to one US statesman, "is now fully ripe and this is the golden hour for the United States to pluck it."[95] Americans had been devising ways of acquiring a foothold in the Pacific since the Revolutionary era, and some of the country's most important developments—including the transcontinental railroad—originated with China's markets particularly in mind.[96] American businessmen helped foment a coup against the Hawaiian monarchy in the 1880s, and in 1893, after Queen Lili'uokalani tried to reassert sovereign rule over the islands, US marines surrounded the royal palace until the queen abdicated her claims to power. An ostensible national government operated at the bequest of US business interests until the US Senate formally voted to annex the islands in 1898. "One hundred years later," writes the historian George Herring, "without acknowledging United States responsibility, Congress would pass a bill formally apologizing to the people of Hawaii for the overthrow of its government."[97]

Amid the US takeover of Hawaii, some Americans became baseball boosters and launched the Oahu Plantation League and the Maui Athletic Association.[98] The leagues helped popularize the sport to diverse new audiences, including growing numbers of Chinese and Japanese immigrants in Hawaii. By the early 1900s, Chinese migrants in Hawaii organized what the historian Xiaowei Yu calls "the Great Chinese-Hawaiian Baseball Tours." The tours featured an all-Chinese team that trained in Hawaii, traveled to the United States several times between 1905 and 1916, and played against various levels of amateur and professional talent. In 1910 alone, this traveling Chinese baseball team played 114 games, winning sixty-six of them, good enough for a .580 winning percentage. Yu notes that Chinese ballplayers—touring America in the age of Chinese Exclusion—grew accustomed to xenophobic and racist attacks from white audiences, who mocked them for their hairstyles and clothing, among other things. Most teams they faced, however, showed more respect for the visiting ballplayers, often commending them for their quality of play and sportsmanship.[99]

Hawaii was far from America's only colonial target at the turn of the century. The 1898 Spanish–American War, which punctuated the end of the Cuban War of Independence against Spain (1895–8), transferred Spain's Caribbean colonies into America's imperial orbit. Initially, the United States insisted its only goals in Cuba were to support the island's independence and revitalize America's martial spirit—which some American jingoes, like Teddy

FIGURE 1.3 *The 1898* USS Maine *baseball team, led by the team's only Black player, and ace pitcher, William Lambert (back right). Ten of the players died when an explosion sunk the* USS Maine *in Havana, Cuba in February 1898, an event that helped spark the Spanish-American War. (Photo by Buyenlarge/Getty Images).*

Roosevelt, believed was needed to make the United States a more formidable world power. After the United States dispatched the Spanish from Cuba—what one US official called afterward a "splendid little war"—America withdrew its pledge not to take control of the island and instead began intermittently occupying Cuba and dictating its economic policies through the 1950s.[100] In addition to the natural resources US businesses sought, Cuba became an important outpost for a rapidly growing United States Navy.

Apart from the revolutionary reckoning the US occupation of Cuba ensured, America's newfound dominance over the island accelerated baseball's growth in the Caribbean. Burgos explains that the "end of Spanish colonial rule in 1898 turned Cuba into a regular winter stop for teams and players from the elite minor leagues, the major leagues, and the Negro leagues."[101] He writes that between 1900 and 1920:

a transnational baseball circuit emerged that linked New York, San Francisco, and Chicago with Havana, San Juan, and Santo Domingo. This period saw teams from organized and black baseball make regular tours of Cuba and other parts of Latin America. Big-league teams started annual barnstorming tours in 1900. Two years later, African American teams began to tour Cuba, and by 1907 African American players were formal participants in the Cuban league.[102]

Baseball attended other colonial acquisitions at the turn of the twentieth century, in places like Puerto Rico (which the United States took from Spain and annexed as a territory in 1917) and the Philippines (also seized from Spain and controlled by the United States from 1898 to 1946). Anchored on either side of America's coasts, baseball continued to grow throughout the western hemisphere and Pacific Rim, evolving into a dynamic international game that flourished throughout the twentieth century. The military was not the only catalyst behind baseball's globalization, however. The other face of US imperialism—the American businessman—left its own mark on baseball's early global history.

Baseball's World Tours

Compared to the more provincial expectations that basketball and football's progenitors had for their sports, the vision and ambition of baseball's first patrons help explain its enormous popularity in the early twentieth century. Nowhere was that more evident than in the world baseball tours that took the game to far-flung audiences beginning in the 1870s. With mixed results, these world baseball tours elevated the game's participatory and commercial appeal while, simultaneously, stressing its connection with American nationalism. As Albert Goodwill (A.G.) Spalding, one of baseball's most important early architects and personal sponsor of the 1888–9 world tour, liked to put it: "Everything is possible to him who dares."[103]

Daring is a fair way to describe Spalding's world baseball tour—and so is racist. His dream of exporting the game to various global hubs—which in the end included the Philippines, Australia, Ceylon (Sri Lanka), Egypt, Italy, and England—was nothing if not bold. Spalding called for "wherever a ship floating the stars and stripes finds anchorage today, somewhere on a nearby shore the American national game is in progress."[104] What he was most after, however, was to grow his own Spalding sporting goods company by attaching it to America's most popular game. Like so many other US global businessmen at the time, Spalding's sprawling worldview made no attempt to hide its racist disdain for people of color. The team's mascot was an African American with dwarfism who performed "plantation dancing" in front of bewildered foreign audiences.[105] Captained by Chicago's star first baseman and outspoken white supremacist, Cap Anson, the team Spalding assembled struggled mightily to appear inviting. The tour's visit to Egypt, according to historian Thomas Zeiler, was "notable for offensive behavior indicative of the tourists' profound racism." Beneath the Great Pyramids, the team posed for pictures and, over the reproach of their Egyptian audience, hurled baseballs at the Sphynx.[106]

Zeiler argues in his book *Ambassadors in Pinstripes* that the Spalding World Tour embodied a key dilemma of the new American empire. Driven at its core by profit-seeking, decorated in nationalism and performative wonder, Spalding's tour revealed the kind of arrogance and ethnocentrism "that typified norms of late nineteenth-century imperialism." He writes that the players adopted "ideas of identity and power relationships critical to the projection of America's brand of empire. The tourists travelled in the context of race, a context that shaped their views of and experiences with the nonwhite domestic and foreign cultures to which they were exposed."[107] Spalding and his business continued to influence American sporting culture well into the twentieth century. All throughout his life, Spalding remained devoted to the idea that one day "Base Ball will become the established and recognized Field Sport of the world."[108]

By the time of baseball's next world tour, the United States had ascended as a true imperial power. In 1913, two baseball giants, John McGraw and Charles Comiskey, promised "the tour to end all tours," and enlisted an imposing squad of major league stars, including recent Olympic hero Jim Thorpe. The MLB tour ran for five months, and expanded the Spalding tour's itinerary to include Mexico, Japan, and China. The 1913–14 tourists behaved with more cultural sensitivity than Spalding's group, save for the tour organizer, Ted Sullivan, whom the historian James Elfers calls "as repulsive a racist as one could find in America at the time," which is really saying something. But Sullivan was a formidable white supremacist, notorious for bringing watermelons to games against all-Black teams, just to explode them with a hammer in front of African American fans while he spewed racist invective.[109] Sullivan's bigotry was on display in Cairo too, where he frequently disparaged his Egyptian hosts.[110]

The 1913–14 MLB tour added more hubs to a global baseball circuit that both the US military and baseball's business class together forged at the turn of the century. Audience attendance was mixed, as was the game's reception throughout the world, but, by 1914, clearly a global baseball ecosystem had formed.[111] The MLB tourists sometimes complained that foreigners misunderstood or ignored the game's fundamental rules, bending baseball to their own cultural sport tastes, but none could ignore that by the outbreak of the First World War, baseball had become a known commodity throughout much of the world. When General Pershing and the American Expeditionary Force (AEF) arrived in Europe in 1917 to fight the Triple Alliance, they discovered Australians and Canadians were already playing the game with British and French soldiers, or at least some of them. America's doughboys, who played baseball wherever they went in Europe, noted that "Baseball will never be popular in France." Christy Mathewson, the Hall of Fame pitcher and AEF enlistee, quipped that the French were "more afraid of a hard-hit grounder or liner than a German shell."[112]

With baseball's global visibility rising in the early 1900s, its bosses decided their game needed a more marketable genesis story. Bothered by its English roots and nebulous point of origin in the United States, men like A.G. Spalding worried that the "national pastime" was insufficiently American. To give the game a proper heritage, baseball's executives decided to lie about its early history and falsify a new beginning, rinsed clean of foreign influence and painted over in red, white, and blue. Although the effort was a scam, by denying the sport's authentic history and projecting what its business leaders wanted to pretend was true, MLB was following in a familiar American tradition of whitewashing the past to accommodate a fawning, mythologized history that comforted the powerful.

Conjuring the National Pastime

The modern game of baseball owes a great deal to the international environment into which it was born. A global mix of players and fans shaped and reshaped the game to give it meaning and vitality beyond the terrific drama and athletic feats that sparkled on its diamonds. Yet baseball's most powerful early patrons worked feverishly to bury the game's global roots. Men like A.G. Spalding and AAU president James E. Sullivan fabricated for baseball a distinctly *anti-foreign* origin story that says much about the importance Americans attached to sport as an expression of national identity in the early twentieth century. As the *Outlook* crowed in 1913, "baseball is something more than the great American game—it is an American *institution* having a significant place in the life of the people."[113]

Absent any identifiable progenitor, birthplace, or birthday, in the early 1900s a small group of wealthy white men invented baseball's backstory to sell to the American public and the world. With the help of Sullivan and another baseball nativist, former president of the NL, Abraham Gilbert Mills, Spalding commissioned a formal investigation into the game's origins, where he conjured up the Doubleday Myth. The Mills Commission (as it was called) first had to untie the strings connecting baseball to English sporting traditions, particularly rounders, which resembles baseball greatly. The British-born, American-based journalist Henry Chadwick, who grew up playing rounders, was an outspoken proponent of its clear lineage with baseball.[114] But Spalding and the commission rejected its international heritage, declaring in 1907 that "Base Ball is of American origin and has no traceable connection whatever with 'Rounders' or any other foreign game." Rather, they claimed it was the invention of one man, Abner Doubleday, who, according to their fiction, organized the first discernable baseball game in 1839 in Cooperstown, New York—home to what is today Major League Baseball's Hall of Fame.

In fact, Doubleday did not invent baseball in 1839, and quite possibly never played the game.[115] But baseball canonized the commission's story and cast the game as an American conception. Like the broader US sporting community, baseball in the early twentieth century was struggling to balance two countervailing pressures that warred within a distended country. So much of its success was attributable to immigrants and other countries, yet baseball's gatekeepers and profiteers kept its highest realms—the major leagues—a game of white privilege through racist policymaking and nativist storytelling. The tension between these forces intensified within baseball and American sport over the coming decades.

Notes

1　See Emily Rosenberg, *Spreading the American Dream: American Economic and Cultural Expansion, 1890–1945* (New York: Hill and Wang, 1982).

2　Jane Addams, *The Spirit of Youth and the City Streets* (New York: Macmillan Press, 1909), 102.

3　Robert Wiebe, *The Search for Order, 1877–1920* (New York: Hill and Wang, 1967), 12.

4　Charles Hirschmann and Elizabeth Mogford, "Immigration and the American Industrial Revolution from 1880 to 1920," *Social Science Research* 38, no. 4 (December 2009): 1.

5　Robert Peterson, *From Cages to Jump Shots: Pro Basketball's Early Years* (New York: Oxford University Press, 1990), 15–16.

6　Douglas Andrew Stark, *Wartime Basketball: The Emergence of a National Sport during World War II* (Lincoln: University of Nebraska Press, 2016), 15.

7　Gerald Gems, *Sport and the American Occupation of the Philippines: Bats, Balls, and Bayonets* (Lanham: Lexington Books, 2016), 95.

8　Pamela Grundy, et al., "The Emergence of Basketball as an American National Pastime: From a Popular Participant Sport to a Spectacle of Nationhood," *International Journal of the History of Sport* 31, no. 1–2 (2014): 138.

9　Ibid., 135.

10　Linda Peavy and Ursula Smith, *Full Court-Quest: The Girls from Fort Shaw Indian School, Basketball Champions of the World* (Norman: University of Oklahoma Press, 2008), 60.

11　Stacy Pratt McDermott, "Women's Hoops at Hull House," Jane Addams Papers Project, URL: https://janeaddams.ramapo.edu/2019/12/womens-hoops-at-hull-house/ [accessed 7.8.20].

12　Stephon Wessen, "How the Playground Movement Made a Case for Play," Teaching with the Library of Congress, URL: https://blogs.loc.gov/teachers/2018/05/how-the-playground-movement-made-a-case-for-play/ [accessed 7.6.20].

13　Steven Riess, *City Games: The Evolution of American Urban Society and the Rise of Sports* (Urbana: University of Illinois Press, 1991), 107.

14　Peter Levine, *Ellis Island to Ebbets Field: Sport and the American Jewish Experience* (New York: Oxford University Press, 1993), 27–8; 53.

15 Peterson, *Cages to Jump Shots,* 11–13; Grundy, et al., "The Emergence of Basketball as an American National Pastime," 146.

16 Peavy and Smith, *Full-Court Quest,* 344.

17 Gerald R. Germs, *Sport and the Shaping of Italian American Identity* (New York: Syracuse University Press, 2013), 23.

18 Louis Moore, *I Fight for a Living: Boxing and the Battle for Black Manhood, 1880–1915* (Urbana: University of Illinois Press, 2017), 5.

19 Levine, *Ellis Island to Ebbets Field,* 147.

20 Randy Roberts, *Papa Jack: Jack Johnson and the Era of White Hopes* (New York: The Free Press, 1985), 6–7.

21 Ibid.

22 Ibid., 68–84; 108–23.

23 Ibid., 38–43.

24 Ibid., 41.

25 Theodore Roosevelt quoted in ibid., 42.

26 Jim Jeffries, quoted in ibid., 31.

27 Jack London quoted in ibid., 68.

28 "That Fight," *Memphis Commercial Appeal,* July 5, 1910, quoted in Moore, *I Fight for a Living: Boxing and the Battle for Black Manhood, 1880–1915,* 156.

29 Ibid. See also Moore's interactive digital history project about the riots, titled "July 4, 1910: America, Racism, Violence and the Jack Johnson-Jim Jeffries Fight," URL: https://uploads.knightlab.com/storymapjs/3107230e5eafea9f5e74496d4a1a0f40/jack-johnson-riots/index.html [accessed 6.24.2020]; see also Roberts, *Papa Jack,* 109–12.

30 Roberts, *Papa Jack,* 220.

31 Elliot Gorn and Warren Goldstein, *A Brief History of American Sports* (Urbana: University of Illinois Press, 2004), 154.

32 Ibid., 158.

33 Ibid., 159.

34 For examples of Jewish immigrants playing football, see Levine, *Ellis Island to Ebbets Field,* 208–15.

35 Ibid., 164; 163.

36 Roosevelt quoted in Robert Elias, *The Empire Strikes Out: How Baseball Sold US Foreign Policy and Promoted the American Way Abroad* (New York: New Press, 2010), 50.

37 Theodore Roosevelt, "The American Boy," reprinted in the *Project Gutenberg E-Book of The Works of Theodore Roosevelt, Volume 12* (2019), 152.

38 S.W. Pope, *Patriotic Games: Sporting Traditions in the American Imagination, 1876–1926* (New York: Oxford University Press, 1997), 28.

39 Caspar Whitney quoted in ibid., 30.

40 Simon Rofe, ed., *Sport and Diplomacy: Games within Games* (Manchester: Manchester University Press, 2018), 4.

41 Mark Dyreson, *Making the American Team: Sport, Culture, and the Olympic Experience* (Urbana: University of Illinois Press, 1998), 34.

42 Ibid., 35–7.

43 Thomas Curtis quoted in Dyreson, *Making the American Team*, 46.

44 Ibid., 60–1; see also Pope, *Patriotic Games*, 44.

45 Pope, *Patriotic Games*, 40–1.

46 See Sheila Mitchell, "Women's Participation in the Olympic Games, 1900–1926," *Journal of Sport History* 4, no. 2 (Summer 1977): 208–28; Paula Welch and D. Margaret Costa, "A Century of Olympic Competition," in D. Margaret Costa and Sharon Guthrie, eds., *Women and Sport: Interdisciplinary Perspectives* (Champagne, IL: Human Kineticks, 1994); Jennifer Hargreaves, "Olympic Women: A Struggle for Recognition," in Jean O'Reilly and Susan K. Kahn, eds., *Women and Sports in the United States: A Documentary Reader* (Boston, MA: Northeastern University Press, 2007).

47 "American Athletes Win," *NYT*, July 15, 1900.

48 Dyreson, *Making the American Team*, 72.

49 David Nasaw, *Going Out: The Rise and Fall of Public Amusements* (Cambridge: Harvard University Press, 1999), 66.

50 Ibid., 56–8.

51 George R. Matthews, *America's First Olympics: The Saint Louis Games of 1904* (Columbia: University of Missouri Press, 2005), 5–39.

52 Parezo and Fowler, *Anthropology Goes to the Fair: The 1904 Louisiana Purchase Exposition*, 1.

53 Ibid., 3.

54 Dyreson, *Making the American Team*, 81–2.

55 Parazo and Fowler, *Anthropology Goes to the Fair*, 352.

56 Dyreson, *Making the American Team*, 92.

57 Ibid., 127.

58 Ibid., 131.

59 Letter from Foreign Minister John B. Jackson to Secretary of State Elihu Root, March 5, 1906, in United States Department of State *Foreign Relations of United States* [hereafter FRUS], 1906, Greece, 814.

60 George Matthews, "The Controversial Olympic Games of 1908 as Viewed by the *New York Times* and the *Times of London*," *Journal of Sport History* 7, no. 2 (Summer 1980): 40.

61 Quoted in ibid., 45.

62 *NYT* quoted in Pope, *Patriotic Games*, 46.

63 Dyerson, *Making the American Team*, 136–7.

64 Pope, *Patriotic Games*, 47.

65 October 1908 *Academy* article quoted in Caspar Whitney, "The View-Point," *The Outing Magazine* 53, no. 2 (November 1908): 248.

66 Ibid; see Pope, *Patriotic Games*, 47.

67   Dyreson, *Making the American Team*, 153.

68   "American Olympic Team Is Selected," *NYT*, June 11, 1912, 10.

69   See howarddrew.com [last accessed 7.4.2020].

70   Dyreson, *Making the American Team*, 158.

71   Ibid., 162.

72   "The Folly of International Sport," quoted in Dyreson, *Making the American Team*, 238.

73   "Olympic Victors to Parade," *NYT*, August 24, 1912, 18.

74   See Harold Seymour, *Baseball: The Early Years* (New York: Oxford University Press, 1989).

75   Mark Twain, *New York Herald*, October 15, 1900, https://www.loc.gov/rr/hispanic/1898/twain.html [accessed 9.7.2021].

76   David Block, *Pastime Lost: The Humble, Original, and Now Completely Forgotten Game of English Baseball* (Lincoln: University of Nebraska Press, 2019).

77   Thomas Jefferson quoted in Elias, *The Empire Strikes Out*, 6.

78   George Kirsch, *Baseball in the Blue and Gray: The National Pastime during the Civil War* (Princeton: Princeton University Press, 2013), 53; John P. Rossi, *Baseball and American Culture: A History* (Lanham: Rowman and Littlefield, 2018), 23.

79   Elias, *The Empire Strikes Out*, 16; 6–15.

80   Nasaw, *Going Out,* 100.

81   See Gorn and Goldstein, *A Brief History of American Sport*, Chapter Five.

82   "Madison Square Garden," *NYT*, February 28, 1900, 6.

83   Gorn and Goldstein, *Brief History of American Sport*, 188. For similar anecdotes, see Levine, *From Ellis Island to Ebbets Field*, 92.

84   Riess, *City Games*, 104–6.

85   Levine, *From Ellis Island to Ebbets Field*, 89.

86   Xiaowei Yu, "'Let's Cut Queues and Play the Game': The Origins and Evolution of Chinese Involvement in American Baseball, 1870–1935," *International Journal for the History of Sport* 34, no. 12 (March 2018): 1–16.

87   Robert Peterson, *Only the Ball Was White: A History of Legendary Black Players and All-Black Professional Teams* (New York: Oxford University Press, 1970), 82; see also Elias, *The Empire Strikes Out*, 58.

88   Adrian Burgos and Adrian Jr Burgos, *Playing America's Game: Baseball, Latinos, and the Color Line* (Berkeley: University of California Press, 2007), 36; 77; 4.

89   Ibid., 77.

90   Elias, *The Empire Strikes Out*, 59.

91   Riess, *City Games*, 87; Levine, *From Ellis Island to Ebbets Field*, 89.

92   Riess, *City Games*, 87.

93   Ibid. Levine, *Ellis Island to Ebbets Field*, 100–3.

94   For more on the emergence of the American empire at the turn of the twentieth century, see Daniel Immerwahr, *How to Hide an Empire: A Short History of the Greater United States* (New York: Farrar, Straus and Giroux, 2019).

95 Letter from Foreign Minister John L. Stephens to Secretary of State John W. Foster, February 1, 1893, in United States Department of State *FRUS*, 1894, Affairs in Hawaii, 402.

96 Gordon Chang, *Fateful Ties: A History of America's Preoccupation with China* (Cambridge: Harvard University Press, 2015), 45.

97 George C. Herring, *From Colony to Superpower: US Foreign Relations since 1776* (New York: Oxford University Press, 2008), 297.

98 Elias, *Empire Strikes Out*, 42.

99 Yu, "Let's Cut Queues and Play the Game," 1–16.

100 The historiography on the Spanish–American War is extensive, but some helpful primers include: Kirstin Hogenson's *Fighting for American Manhood* (New Haven, CT: Yale University Press, 1998) and Louis A. Perez Jr., *The War of 1898: The United States and Cuba in History and Historiography* (Chapel Hill: University of North Carolina Press, 1998).

101 Burgos, et al., *Playing America's Game*, 8.

102 Ibid., 88.

103 Spalding quoted in Thomas W. Zeiler, *Ambassadors in Pinstripes: The Spalding World Baseball Tour and the Birth of the American Empire* (Boulder, CO: Rowman & Littlefield Publishers, 2007), 13. The first world baseball tour occurred in 1874, under the direction of Harry Wright, but was much less grand than Spalding's.

104 Spalding quoted in Elias, *Uncle Sam Strikes Out*, 21.

105 Zeiler, *Ambassadors in Pinstripes*, 25.

106 Ibid., 105.

107 Ibid., 75–6.

108 Spalding quoted in Ibid., 188.

109 James Elfers, *The Tour to End All Tours: The Story of Major League Baseball's 1913–1914 World Tour* (Lincoln: University of Nebraska, 2003), 194.

110 Elias, *The Empire Strikes Out*, 71.

111 Ibid., 40–52.

112 Christy Mathewson quoted in Elias, *The Empire Strikes Out*, 91.

113 H. Addington Bruce, "Baseball and the National Life," quoted in Reiss, *Major Problems in American Sport*, 219 [emphasis added].

114 "Henry Chadwick," Society for American Baseball Research *Biography* Project, URL: https://sabr.org/bioproj/person/henry-chadwick/ [accessed 7.5.2020]; James A. Vlasich, *A Legend for the Legendary: The Origin of the Baseball Hall of Fame* (Bowling Green: Bowling Green State University Popular Press, 1990), 19.

115 Elias, *The Empire Strikes Out*, 47–8.

Athlete Spotlight #1:
Jim Thorpe

FIGURE 1.4 *The uber-athlete Jim Thorpe poses for a photograph in his Carlisle Indian Industrial School football uniform. One of the most prodigious American football players of the twentieth century, Thorpe also played professional baseball and won two Olympic gold medals at the 1912 Stockholm Games. (Photo by Hulton Archive/Getty Images).*

Jim Thorpe was born May 22, 1887, near Konawa, Oklahoma. His father, Hiram, was part Sac and Fox and part Irish; his mother, Charlotte, was French and Potawatomi. Young Jim attended the Sac and Fox Mission School, a vocational boarding school for Indian youth focused on "civilizing" Native Americans like Thorpe by inculcating aspects of Anglo-Saxon culture. To his parents and teachers, Thorpe was an "incorrigible youngster."[1] His athleticism, however, was what others noticed. When he was sixteen, Thorpe accepted an offer to attend the Carlisle Indian School in Pennsylvania, which became renowned in the 1890s for pummeling many of the best college football programs in America.[2]

Carlisle's coach, Pop Warner, was one of the most influential football boosters in the country. Warner came to Carlisle from Cornell University in 1899 at the recommendation of Walter Camp, five years before Thorpe arrived. Thorpe's sheer talent amazed Warner, but the coach also called Jim a "lazy Indian" and accused him of squandering his talents. In 1908, he was Carlisle's starting half-back and named third-team All-American at season's end. Thorpe was equally dominant in track and field and starred in other sports as well. In the summer of 1909, Thorpe went to North Carolina to play semiprofessional baseball—a routine practice for collegiate athletes—and earned about $20 a week. As Thorpe later said, it was a decision he "paid for ... for the rest of my life."[3]

He returned to school in 1911 and won first-team All-American honors in football, leading Carlisle over Georgetown, Harvard, and Brown on the way to an 11–1 season. No one "ever carried a pigskin down the field with the dazzling speed of Thorpe," Warner remarked later. "He knew everything a football player could be taught and then he could execute the play better than the coach ever dreamed."[4] The next year, Warner introduced Thorpe to James Sullivan, who oversaw US Olympic recruitment, and helped Jim qualify for the 1912 Stockholm Games. In Sweden, he won gold medals in the Decathlon and Pentathlon—two intensely strenuous events—against twenty-eight competitors. Thorpe "so dominated the Fifth Olympiad," writes one biographer, "that it became known as the 'Jim Thorpe Olympics.'" During the medal ceremony, Sweden's King Gustav V crowned Thorpe with a laurel wreath and declared him "the greatest athlete in the world."[5]

Warner and Sullivan both knew Thorpe had played semiprofessional baseball prior to the Olympics, but when investigations into Jim's amateur status became public after the 1912 Games, the two men turned on Thorpe to save themselves. Driven by the mania of amateurism and tinged with racial animus, critics hounded the Native American star. In January 1913, Warner and Sullivan announced they were stripping Jim of his gold medals and permanently banning him from amateur sport.[6] Scandalized but unbroken, Thorpe began playing professional baseball the same year for the New York Giants and joined the team for the 1913–14 World Baseball Tour. He stayed in the league until 1919, but it was a modest career next to his football and Olympic glory.[7]

Thorpe's athletic career ended where it began—on the gridiron. He played professionally for the Canton Bulldogs, New York Football Giants, and Chicago Cardinals, and in 1920 was named the first commissioner of what became the NFL. After retiring in 1928, Thorpe starred in movies, inked endorsement deals, and earned money as a public speaker. Personally and professionally, however, he struggled in later life. Thorpe passed away in 1953, and only then garnered the recognition he fully deserved. Outlets like the Associated Press began referring to him as the greatest athlete of the twentieth century. In 2022, the IOC finally reinstated his gold medals. As for his proper legacy, Thorpe's biographer Kate Buford argues that, in the end, he was "the central figure at the dawn of American and international popular sports."[8]

Notes

1   Bill Crawford, *All American: The Rise and Fall of Jim Thorpe* (Hoboken, NJ: Wiley & Sons, Inc., 2004), 20.

2   Ibid., 8–51.

3   Jim Thorpe quoted in Kate Buford, *Native American Son: The Life and Sporting Legend of Jim Thorpe* (Lincoln: University of Nebraska Press, 2010), 83.

4   Pop Warner quoted in Crawford, *All American*, 144.

5   Crawford, *All American*, 175; 176.

6   Ibid., 204.

7   Buford, *Native American Son*, 193–221.

8   Ibid., x.

2

In Service of the State

The Business and Politics of Sport between the World Wars

Introduction

American society changed markedly as the country wound down from its first world war. New laws and cultural attitudes combined with the Republican Party's economic platform of deregulation, tax cuts, and conspicuous consumption together challenged social norms once strictly governed by Victorian-era values. For many Americans, their traditional society, often cast in the light of Christian fundamentalism, was under attack, and the signs of aggression were everywhere. The only heirloom of the nineteenth century that Progressivism and the Great War had spared, it seemed, was white supremacy. But apart from Jim Crow, the United States entered the 1920s visibly transformed. Technologies like radios and automobiles that had been for the few were becoming more affordable and prominent in society. Prohibition was law but bootlegging thrived, and with it flourished organized crime. Immigrants helped the country urbanize along with increasing numbers of Black Americans fleeing the South's violence and persecution. Sexual mores, like birth control and casual sex, once taboo suddenly threatened Americans' decency in magazines, movies, and music. America was becoming modern, and at each step of this transformation there came reactionary pushback by fundamentalists, law enforcement agencies, xenophobes, and sexists. The nation's new "modern temper," as Lynn Dumenil writes, was "distinguished by Americans' growing consciousness of change, a perception that a yawning gulf separated them from the world of only a decade before."[1]

The country's experience in the First World War was a primary contributor to the cultural upheaval and sense of change that overwhelmed America in the 1920s. Unsurprisingly, the war also transformed how Americans viewed their role in the world. Along with the culture, US foreign policy was likewise in a state of flux, careening from the international overtones that Wilsonianism had popularized to an America-first type of isolationism that, nevertheless, made every effort to expand America's global economic influence. Beginning with President Warren G. Harding's administration, the Republican Party held the White House for twelve years (1921–32), during which they pursued US foreign relations with the principal goal of further positioning the business community as the primary point of contact with the rest of the world. US foreign policy swerved again in 1933 amid a worsening Great Depression and the inauguration of Franklin Roosevelt as the thirty-second president of the United States. Roosevelt took office needing not only to save capitalism from demise but also to reorient US foreign relations within an international community once again engulfed in the fires of militant nationalism.

Driving much of this era's excesses and despair was a capitalist system that for about a decade ran red hot until it collapsed and derailed a fragile global economy. But before the fall, as corporate power grew and entrenched itself further in the business of government, America's flowering sport landscape took on a bigger role in the US economy. Unlike the prior decades, the commercial gains that awaited a professionalized, market-oriented sporting league came into better focus. Other major sports in America followed baseball's path to chase after the considerable possibilities that lay in professionalizing a game for mass consumption. Between the world wars, boxing, football, hockey, and basketball all started commercializing by forming professional leagues and selling their products to American consumers. Not all these efforts panned out: attempts at a professional basketball league, for instance, fell short until after the Second World War. Nonetheless, the surge in professionalized organizations during the 1920s and 1930s was a watershed moment in the history of American sport and positioned those sports for even bigger gains later in the century, at home and abroad.

Business and sport mixed happily when the economy boomed, and war was a memory. But when the Depression set in, and a tide of extremism brought the world back to war, sport took on different meaning throughout world. The authoritarian regimes that rose in the 1930s each blended into their toxic ideologies a lethal dose of nationalism, promising their people a great struggle to achieve the power and glory their countries, and ethnic identities, deserved. No surprise that sport and athletes would become tangled up in the competition over national greatness in the years prior to the Second World War. This chapter concludes by exploring how sport matured as a form of public diplomacy and cultural currency amid an international community ablaze in nationalism and war.

The Growing Business of Baseball

The 1920s were the salad days of baseball's run as America's favorite sport. The game sailed into the heyday of Babe Ruth with a new, voracious sport media industry to broadcast all about it. Americans as never before began to follow the exploits of their favorite baseball heroes—and no one stood out like Ruth. The structure of the major leagues changed during this era as well. The creation of a league president, management's tightening grip on player rights, and baseball's legal exclusion from anti-trust laws strengthened its institutional framework and kept it well ahead of other major US sports that were only beginning to professionalize.

Baseball's professional growth made it more lucrative and cutthroat, yet even the competitive advantage of adding talented Black players could not disabuse MLB of its deep, abiding racism. So, Black ballplayers made their own major leagues. The history of the Negro Leagues, which took decades for MLB to appreciate and only very recently to recognize in its record books, demonstrates the profound affection so many Americans had for baseball in the early twentieth century. This era also highlights the deepening connections baseball was forming with the rest of the world. Players of any color could make respectable sums of money playing in foreign leagues, particularly in the Caribbean, and many Black Americans chose to do so. The sport's expansion throughout the western hemisphere, and Pacific Rim, was an enduring feature of these years and shaped MLB's growth throughout the rest of the century.

Babe Ruth and the New Sport Media

Americans' relationship with the news and media industry was one of many social arrangements changing in the 1920s. A sign of the times was when major newspapers started printing daily columns covering stock exchange prices, as a wider share of Americans began investing in risky, speculative ventures amid one of the great bull markets. Similarly, the profiles of famous American athletes, or the outcomes of important sporting events, appearing in the pages of major US newspapers and over radio broadcasts were, in fact, another seminal development of this era. The historian Frank Jozsa Jr. has shown that by the 1930s, publishers regularly began printing statistics and accounts of player performances in newspapers across the United States, reaching more and more Americans every year. In addition to "[g]ame scores and a team's errors, hits, home runs and win-loss percentages," Jozsa writes, newspapers printed "batting averages of hitters and earned run averages of pitchers in baseball, the point-per-game and rebounds-per-game of players and teams in basketball, the number of touchdowns scored and total yards gained from passing and running of players and teams in football, and the assists, goals, points earned and shutouts in ice hockey games."[2] As a broader, more ravenous and diverse sport consumer market emerged, the commercial benefits of professionalizing major sports, or re-professionalizing them in the case of boxing, became irresistible. At the bleeding edge of the new sport media, baseball showed how leagues could turn athletes into celebrities and carry their brands to new heights.

Baseball's adoption of emerging information technologies, particularly radio and television, helped create a new sport media industry—and, with it, more cash for league operatives, owners, and teams. Some in MLB worried that radio and television would discourage in-game attendance, but before long, the value was too great to ignore. The first World Series broadcast on the radio was in 1921 and involved a journalist phoning in the play-by-play to a New Jersey-based announcer who "called" the game to a very local audience. Within a couple of years, baseball broadcasts resembled the medium as it exists today. One commenter described the 1924 World Series radio broadcast as "one of the greatest heartbumping events of American sport. It made the game bigger," exhilarating baseball fans with "almost as much of a thrill as though they were at the Polo Grounds."[3]

Once radios became fixtures in more American households—by 1929, about one-third of the population owned a personal radio—the fan experience with the game changed dramatically. Initial concern among the owners that radio broadcasts were going to sap stadium attendance proved unfounded. In fact, in cities where games ran on the radio, average attendance climbed during the 1920s. Historian Jules Tygiel writes that the radio "democratized major league baseball, transmitting a more intimate sense of being at the game to millions who could never attend."[4] Radio's ability to further nationalize the game also generated enticing returns for baseball executives. By 1933, MLB was bringing in $18,000 a year in radio broadcasts rights. The season after that, Ford Motor Company paid $100,000 to be the official sponsor of the World Series. And when television entered the game, profits soared higher: in 1939, MLB soaked up nearly $900,000 in broadcast revenue.[5]

Of course, honeymooning in the era of Babe Ruth helped ensure a happy marriage between baseball and America's new sport media. Few US sport stars have ever enjoyed the level of fame and adoration—nationally and internationally—like George Herman Ruth, Jr., known affectionately by his nicknames "The Babe," "The Great Bambino," and "The Sultan of Swat." Ruth was a larger-than-life figure, on and off the diamond, and profoundly transformed the major leagues. Arguably his most lasting legacy was in the particular skillset he showcased and with which he pummeled his opponents and reset baseball's record books. In 1919, Ruth slugged twenty-nine home runs, the most all-time and making him one of only six major league players at that time to record more than twenty home runs in a season. The next year, Ruth erupted for fifty-four longballs—more homeruns than fourteen NL and AL *teams* hit that season. That year, the total number of homeruns hit in the majors was 630 (and Ruth accounted for nearly 10 percent of those). Just two years later, in 1922, that number had climbed to 1,055, and by the 1930 season, more than 1,500 baseballs left the park.[6] By cranking more balls over the fence, Ruth reoriented how players, teams, and owners judged offensive talent, and revolutionized the way the sport was played down to the present day. The homerun, once an oddity, is now understood as the most valuable outcome a player can produce in a baseball game. And that it was Ruth, who lived as large as he played, to take hold of the nation's favorite sport and give it new juice only further enhanced MLB's fortunes.[7]

The Babe's fame was due to his play but also, over time, a persona built around public appearances, product endorsements, motion pictures, and the vaudeville circuit. Tygiel argues that "Ruth became the first true celebrity of the modern era," symbolizing "not only the exuberance and excess of the 1920s, but the emergent triumph of personality and image in modern America."[8] Baseball's Sultan believed firmly in player enrichment and empowerment, even if doing so violated what baseball's rules permitted beyond the ballpark. When Ruth and a teammate went on barnstorming tours of the United States—playing against local teams and collecting payment for their appearances—baseball's favorite gladiator clashed with its new emperor, Kennesaw Mountain Landis, the first commissioner of MLB.

Prior to becoming commissioner in 1920, Landis had been a federal judge and was involved with one of the antitrust lawsuits that the major leagues faced from the rival Federal League. That case ultimately reached the US Supreme Court in 1922, when the high court ruled that the sport of baseball was exempt from antitrust law.[9] Landis served as MLB commissioner for twenty-four years and made several infamous rulings over his tenure, including instituting life bans to eight players on the 1919 Chicago White Sox for participating in a plan to throw the World Series in return for cash.[10] When Landis learned of Ruth's barnstorming indiscretions, despite the Babe's unrivaled popularity in the game, the commissioner suspended Ruth for six weeks and fined him $3,500. In Landis's words, Ruth's antics represented "a mutinous defiance intended by the players to present the question: who is bigger: base-ball or the individual Ruth."[11] For decisions like the one he leveled against Ruth, the league's owners, managers, and even some in the new sport media praised Landis for maintaining a firm grip on the game and driving its popularity to new heights.

The Negro Leagues and Baseball's Continued Growth Abroad

Another aspect of Landis's legacy to come under more recent scrutiny is his protection of baseball's color line that had been in place since the late nineteenth century. In his book *Conspiracy of Silence*, historian Chris Lamb explores Landis's many shifting statements on the possibility of integrating baseball with Black players. Landis often denied that African Americans were barred from the game and pointed out that no formal rule existed that would stop a team from signing a Black player. The commissioner's stance, however, was disingenuous: all along it had been a "gentlemen's agreement" among racists in professional baseball to keep Black ballplayers off major league diamonds. In fact, Landis's tendency to dismiss the issue out of hand or defer to the judgment of owners and managers had the clear effect of upholding baseball's segregation throughout his tenure as commissioner. Lamb argues that "Landis ruled baseball with absolute control. If he wanted blacks in baseball, there would have been blacks in baseball. For twenty years Landis, whom the black press derisively called 'the Great White Father,' enforced baseball's color line with the complete authority of his office."[12]

Barred from the major leagues, Black ballplayers found ways to compete and make the sport their own. In 1920, the inroads carved by Black local leagues, barnstorming tours, and exhibition circuits that stretched around the country led to the formation of the Negro National League (NNL). The talent pool the NNL showcased was incredible—no doubt many of its players would have flourished in MLB had it been integrated at the time— and its stars produced some of the most impressive careers in all of baseball history. Financial difficulties, plus competition from other all-Black leagues like the American Negro League (ANL), hampered the NNL's early growth, and, like most other professional leagues, it required restructuring over the 1920s and early 1930s. But by the Second World War, as the historian Robert Peterson shows, the league "grew to the stature of a two-million-dollar-a-year business, probably the single biggest black-dominated enterprise" in the United States.[13] On teams like the Kansas City Monarchs, the St. Louis Stars, and the Washington Homestead Grays, heroic figures such as the legendary pitcher Satchel Paige, the speedy outfielder "Cool Papa" Bell, and the power-hitting catcher Josh Gibson helped elevate the Negro League's profile around the country and built a case for democratizing the major leagues.

Gibson, who played the majority of his career as the Homestead Gray's ferocious backstop, was one of the most prolific hitters of his era. Fans often called him the "Black Babe Ruth," a comparison that was well deserved. By the end of his career, Gibson had hit an estimated 800 home runs—a total that included NNL games and independent league performances. According to the historian Leslie Heaphy, "Gibson hit some of the longest homeruns and hit them more frequently than almost any other player. Today, when discussions revolve around the greatest home run hitters in the game the conversation cannot be complete without including Gibson's name."[14] Indeed, in 1972 MLB's Hall of Fame committee corrected at least one wrong in baseball's sordid racial history when it made Gibson the second Negro

League star to be elected to Cooperstown—one year after the great pitcher Satchel Paige became the first Negro League player to gain that honor. When asked what it was like to pitch to Gibson, Paige once quipped, "You look for his weakness and while your [*sic*] lookin' for it, he's liable to hit forty-five home runs."[15]

Gibson, Paige, and several other Negro League stars also blazed impressive international careers playing for teams in Central America and the Caribbean. In the early twentieth century, playing abroad, in countries like Mexico, Cuba, Puerto Rico, and the Dominican Republic—places where baseball accompanied US merchants and marines at the turn of the century—afforded Black ballplayers greater freedom and compensation for their talents. "Playing in Cuba," writes Heaphy, "earned the best Negro League players hundreds of dollars a month plus free room and board during the winter months."[16] In 1929, Cuba's championship team, the Cienfuegos, had seven Negro League players on its roster. Gibson was especially fond of playing in Latin America, earning monthly salaries around $700 while punishing the competition, racking up Most Valuable Player awards, and even managing a team in Puerto Rico.

While in the United States he was the "Black Babe Ruth," in Latin America Gibson was called "Trucutu," the name of a popular cartoon character best known for carrying around a big club.[17] In 1937, the US-backed Dominican dictator Rafael Trujillo constructed a team made up of the Negro League's most elite players, including Gibson, Bell, and Paige (whom Trujillo paid $1,000 a month to play in the Dominican league), and won the league's title after a championship round the historian Alan Klein calls "among the best series ever played anywhere."[18] The truth was, for some Negro League stars, the Latin American baseball circuit offered treatment and rewards more commensurate with their talent and basic humanity than what they could get in their own country.

Sensing the rising popularity of baseball beyond its borders, US government officials and businessmen continued to pump the game throughout the western hemisphere and Pacific Rim. According to Elias, when governments throughout the Caribbean and Latin America invested in baseball, they helped line the pockets of US sporting goods companies along the way. "The Yucatan government," Elias highlights as one example, purchased "$18,000 worth of baseball gear from the United States for the public schools, where youngsters used it for free."[19] Baseball tours, like Spalding's from the late nineteenth century, also continued apace. Most famously during this era was the East Asian baseball tour of 1934, which brought Babe Ruth face to face with adoring foreign audiences. "Already a legend in Japan, Ruth did not disappoint his hosts, hitting fourteen home runs as his team won all seventeen games played," writes Elias. "Millions lined the streets and more than 65,000 fans crammed Tokyo's Jingu Stadium to see him play."[20]

FIGURE 2.1 *George Herman "Babe" Ruth flashes the homerun power that made him famous and changed the game of baseball forever, while playing an exhibition game at Miji Shrine Stadium in Tokyo, Japan in 1934. (Photo by New York Times Co./Getty Images).*

Japan's budding baseball fandom in the 1930s offers a compelling glimpse at how sport and athletes can bridge cultural divides and, at other times, obscure them. In her excellent book *Transpacific Field of Dreams*, historian Sayuri Guthrie-Shimizu chronicles the relationship between Japan and the United States by following the roads that baseball paved between both societies earlier in the century. She writes that prior to the Second World War, the United States and Japan often "espoused comparable visions and formed individual and collective bonds neither totally amenable to state control nor summarily replaceable with local or national allegiances." Baseball's role in that relationship, she adds, "highlights this enduring undertow of affinity and comparative historical parallels in multiple realms of US-Japanese relations."[21] The state of the game in both countries changed markedly once the war tore through the cultural bonds forged in prior decades. But before that, and through the help of baseball tours like the one in 1934, the cultural and business exchange efforts that MLB and players like Ruth made in Japan "led to the organization of Japan's first commercially viable professional baseball enterprise later in the decade." When the guns were silent and the US occupation of Japan began in 1945, "the dawning of a new era in transpacific baseball" appeared.

Professionalization in Other Corners of US Sport

MLB was clearly the gold standard in professional sport prior to the Second World War, but competition was on the way. Boxing, football, hockey, and basketball all sought to capitalize on the era of big business and commodify their games for a growing sport consumer market. Each one had varying levels of success toward this goal. If the 1920s seemed ripe for growth and investment, bankruptcy and foreclosure was the story of the 1930s. Like it did for many US industries and households, the Great Depression upended most professional sports. Absent the same sturdy commercial foundation on which MLB had built its empire, many leagues were wiped out while others tried to consolidate their market share and protect their solvency by any means necessary.

Nevertheless, sports like boxing, football, and hockey saw significant professional gains between the world wars. Military drafts carried away some of the best athletes in America, but for boxing and football, the martial atmosphere of these years ultimately enhanced their appeal to American audiences. Even basketball, which struggled the most to professionalize in this era, took important steps to commercialize its product. How these major sports and their best athletes weathered the Second World War to become instruments of US power during the Cold War is a story tied to their maturation between 1920 and 1945.

Professional Football, Hockey, and Basketball in Interwar America

The commercial enticements of the 1920s were so potent that even American football, one of the great bulwarks for the amateur sport movement, decided to sell out. In 1920, George Halas inaugurated the American Professional Football Association (APFA) in Canton, Ohio—now home to the American football Hall of Fame. League representatives unanimously voted for Jim Thorpe, the US Olympian, professional baseball player, and football prodigy, to be the APFA's first president. Thorpe also played in the league throughout most of the decade. After his election, the *New York Times* lauded the "first professional football association in the country," and commended its members for agreeing "to refrain from luring players out of college for the professional game."[22] The APFA lasted only two years, however, before major reshuffling occurred, including renaming the organization the National Football League (NFL) in 1922.[23]

Financial trouble, franchise failures and relocations, and marginal fan interest—at least by baseball and boxing's standards—dented the NFL's early history between 1920 and 1945. Rule changes, divisional structure, and championship format all varied in the first dozen years of its existence. But by 1933, when the league settled on a formal playoff system to determine the league champion, the NFL became more functional. Rival leagues began to compete with the NFL for franchises and talent, yet the NFL withstood these pressures, and those of the Great Depression, to retain its position as the premier professional football league through the Second World War. The NFL certainly tried to make itself more relevant to Americans by harnessing the same media, like radio and newspaper coverage, that baseball and boxing were riding to new heights. In 1930 and 1931, the league solicited the Green Bay *Post Gazette* to select the NFL's All-Pro team. In 1932, the NFL began officially publicizing player and team statistics. And in 1939, the NFL sold broadcast television rights for its championship game and then held the first Pro Bowl game, where its best players showcased their talent at the end of the season. The NFL paused its operations when the United States entered the Second World War and many of its players enlisted. After the defeat of the Axis powers, the NFL found the country even more receptive to its warlike aesthetics and gritty professional stars.[24]

Another sport to grow professionally between the world wars was hockey. Hockey's evolution resembled baseball's, spawning from a mix of other athletic games and lacking a precise birthplace or birthday. However, historians credit Montreal with developing the first modern version of hockey in the 1870s and 1880s. Ice skating's rising popularity in Canada, Europe, and the United States in the late nineteenth century, marked by a growth in public skating rinks in those countries, helped sustain hockey during its formative years. One of hockey's very first international tournaments happened in 1886 in Burlington, Vermont, and by 1893, the US sporting magazine *Outing* was predicting that hockey "if climatic conditions allowed ... would speedily become the leading winter pastime in New York."[25] Historians Stephen Hardy and Andrew Holman explain in their book *Hockey: A Global History* that in the early twentieth century US hockey enthusiasts began scheming "to catch the Canadians and match them at their own game" by "developing an American brand" of play.[26]

Before its professionalization, amateur hockey developed into a popular winter sport in Canada and the United States. Leagues formed in Baltimore, Pittsburgh, New York, Boston, Minneapolis, and Portland, Oregon, at the turn of the century.[27] The sport's appeal early on was quite broad and extended to women and communities of color. But hockey's dominant class of wealthy white men aggressively denigrated all-Black and all-women hockey leagues, causing the sport to wither in those communities. Its popularity among white men in Canada and the United States, however, was all the privilege it needed to begin professionalizing in 1917. That year, the National Hockey League (NHL) was formed and quickly replaced the fledgling National Hockey Association that had stumbled as a professional league since 1909. The NHL had four original teams—all Canadian—but its franchise affiliates often changed and expanded through the 1920s.[28] In 1924, the Boston Bruins became the first US-based NHL team, followed shortly thereafter by the New York Americans, the Chicago Black Hawks, the New York Rangers, the Detroit Cougars, and the Pittsburg Pirates.[29] Between 1920 and 1945, "boom times and hard times led to growth and instability across North American hockey," Hardy and Holman write. "Individual teams … and leagues sprouted and died with regularity, artifacts of free-market capitalism both embraced and challenged during these years."[30]

The NHL used the Great Depression to consolidate its power across hockey's landscape and pushed other leagues into folding or joining its ranks. "The NHL *captured* hockey and reordered it," Hardy and Holman argue, "placing a crown of professional control atop the pyramid of once-thriving amateur organizations."[31] The inclusion of US-based teams certainly helped the league's financial stability as the Depression wore on, while signaling the possibilities attending a truly international professional sport league. "Canada was an ocean of devotion that crossed the continent," they write, and by the onset of the Second World War, "the NHL enjoyed a position of dominance in the broad hockey market."[32] Its postwar fortunes would never match baseball's or football's, but hockey became a popular third major sport in the United States for almost fifty years until the late-blooming professional version of basketball found its footing later in the century.

Indeed, basketball's ascent as the dominant winter sport in the United States was not exactly predictable in the 1920s and 1930s. Quite the opposite, actually. Americans from around the country and all walks of life enjoyed playing the game, but a commercialized professional basketball league was a hard sell to American consumers. Early professional leagues—professional only because players earned small sums per game to play but lacked the bureaucratization and capitalization of baseball—popped up in the early 1900s along the East Coast and the Midwest but struggled to stay alive. Leagues like the Eastern League and the Philadelphia Basketball League, along with several others, vied for respectability, yet none of them developed a sustainable business model or competitive structure.[33]

Lacking the speed and explosiveness of the modern game, which rewards players who can handle the ball, shoot from deep, and generate pressure on a defense by attacking the basket, basketball in the early twentieth century was more stolid, distance shooting was less regarded, and, above all, tall players ruled. Dribbling was not originally a rule—Naismith envisioned players would pass the ball to move it forward—and for a while it was not allowed.[34] Games became lopsided affairs because talent distribution was often uneven. The Buffalo Germans, a team made up of paid players with German heritage, embodied the uncompetitive nature of early professionalized basketball, racking up a ridiculous 111-game winning streak between 1908 and 1911. The Buffalo Germans made a name for themselves by winning a tournament at the 1904 St. Louis Olympic Games, although at that point basketball was not considered an Olympic sport, and the games were presented merely as "demonstrations." Historian Annette Hofmann shows that the Buffalo Germans after the 1904 Olympics "became professionals and in the three decades of their existence they won 762 games with 85 losses," making them known by some as the "Original Dream Team." In 1961, the Buffalo Germans were inducted into the Basketball Hall of Fame.[35]

Another semipro team of great renown from this era was the New York Renaissance, an all-Black team that dominated the fledgling national basketball circuit on the East Coast. The Rens, as they were known, were one of the most exciting, rock-ribbed basketball dynasties in US history, featuring many of the best Black basketball players in the country during the 1930s. According to author Bob Kuska, their style was unique because, ironically, "black basketballers had more freedom than their white counterparts to free-lance and, like jazz musicians, invent or hone popular innovations ... like the precursor to the jump shot."[36] From the mid-1920s through the 1930s, the Rens barnstormed around the country, ripping off incredible winning streaks during their 100+ game seasons. Many of their games came against all-white teams in front of all-white audiences, but the Rens never flinched. In 1939, they won the first-ever World Professional Basketball Tournament (WPBT) held in Chicago, Illinois, that featured the best teams in America, including the Harlem Globetrotters and the Oshkosh All-Stars.[37] When professional leagues recruited Renaissance players, like standout big man Pop Gates, they often came up empty. Gates explained that "we thought we were the premier team in the country. The Renaissance players didn't give a damn about [other leagues] at the time because we thought we were their equal or better." He and his teammates "loved being with the Renaissance because we thought we were the best, and we were happy and proud to represent the Negro people and give them something they could be proud of and adhere to."[38]

The closest basketball came to a sturdy professional league between 1920 and 1945 was with the formation of the American Basketball League (ABL) and the National Basketball League (NBL). The ABL featured teams in the northeast, and from its founding in 1925 until the Second World War it generated moderate interest from fans and developed some memorable teams, including the Original Celtics based in New York City. The NBL, by contrast, focused its efforts on the Midwest, in states like Indiana and Ohio. Neither league thrived in the postwar world, and the NBL would eventually join ranks with another league, the Basketball Association of America (BAA), to form the now-dominant NBA in 1949. Nonetheless, the 1930s were crucial years for American basketball. As the historian Douglas Stark explains, heading into the Second World War:

the game was healthy as it embarked on its next fifty years. The American Basketball League and the National Basketball League both vied for the game's best collegiate talent. Basketball was played in the 1936 Olympics, and the United States was victorious. In the span of two years (1938–39), the National Invitation Tournament (NIT), the National Collegiate Athletic Association (NCAA) tournament, and the World Professional Basketball Tournament in Chicago were all founded.[39]

Once the sport fully professionalized after the Second World War, basketball began its ascent as one of the most beloved sports in America and the world.

Re-Professionalizing Boxing in the Nativist 1920s and 1930s

Jack Johnson's reign as boxing's heavyweight champion prior to the First World War turned many whites away from the sport. Already criticized by Progressive reformers who worried about boxing's brutality, Johnson's dominance over white fighters helped drive prizefighting further underground. In 1915, when Johnson finally lost his title to Jess Willard, boxing officials and supportive lawmakers moved to ban Black boxers from competing against white fighters. "In the context of prizefighting, progressivism, and prejudices, lawmakers wanted to protect white superiority," writes historian Louis Moore. "Each black victory in the ring against white opponents … stripped away at the notion of white male social and political authority, a confidence that partly hinged on whites' racial belief in physical superiority."[40]

When the United States mobilized for the First World War, boxing resurfaced as a useful and iconic feature of US military training. Its prominence in the service indeed helped resuscitate the sport in American society. Americans adopted new attitudes toward pugilism once the war was over and accelerated the re-professionalization of prizefighting at home. The US military itself helped campaign against anti-prizefighting laws. Historian S. W. Pope explains that in 1919, state legislatures "began to reverse their prohibitive statutes, and even conservative newspapers like the *New York Times* weighed in on the side of boxing by characterizing the sport's opponents 'as half a century behind the times.'"[41] Their efforts paid off. The state of New York passed the Walker Law in 1920, making prizefighting once again legal under the regulatory power of the New York Athletic Commission. "Madison Square Garden soon emerged as the mecca of boxing," writes Gerald Gems, "and the income generated by boxing spectacles led other states to follow suit."[42] Swept up by the new sport media that had helped amplify baseball's appeal, by the mid-1920s boxing's popularity soared.

Boxing's rebirth also depended on the emergence of a new generation of boxing heroes. The legendary fighter Jack Dempsey, in particular, who dominated the heavyweight division for a decade, came as close as anyone to challenging Babe Ruth in fame and fortune. The celebrity of its fighters combined with the diversity of its ranks made prizefighting a spectacle that broad swaths of Americans cared about. Ethnic identity had been an integral part of boxing's history in America, even during its down days of the early twentieth century. But in the 1920s, ethnic divisions in the United States were intensifying, much as they were around the world. White Americans, particularly those of Western and Northern European descent, promoted "100 percent Americanism" and pushed for restrictive immigration laws, like the Johnson-Reed Act of 1924. Southern and Eastern Europeans came under attack from paranoid law enforcement agencies hell-bent on rooting out foreign radicalism, as well as a resurgent Ku Klux Klan that had broadened its iniquitous platform to become more xenophobic.

So as professional boxing grew, those who competed for its titles took on outsized importance for the ethnic communities they represented. The careers of the Jewish American boxer Benny Leonard and the African American boxer Joe Louis provide instructive examples of how sport mingled with both ethnic and national identities prior to the Second World War. With racialized extremism on the rise throughout America and the world, the dominance of Jewish and Black prizefighters became a testament to their resilience, pride, and the power of sport to challenge prejudice.

The success of Jewish boxers happened across all eight weight divisions— ranging from flyweight to heavyweight—and included several champions with extended title runs. Greatest among them was Benny Leonard, who reigned as lightweight champion of the world from 1917 to 1925. Leonard's parents were Russian immigrants who worked in a tailor's sweatshop for very little money and raised eight children in New York City. Only when their son began to bring home prize money that exceeded his father's weekly wages did Leonard's parents begin to approve of his boxing career. He made a good fortune in his eight-year run as lightweight champion and rode off at the top of his game. Leonard told the press he was retiring because his mother "has begged me not to fight again."[43]

When the stock market crashed in 1929, Leonard came out of retirement to recover from financial ruin, although he never returned to his championship form.[44] Leonard's dominance punctuated the broader success of several Jewish-American boxers, who between 1920 and 1929 won eight world boxing titles and between 1930 and 1939 won ten more. This included "Slapsy Maxie" Rosenbloom, Barney Lebrowitz, who went by "Battling Levinsky," and Barney Ross. But Leonard's career was special. The historian Leonard Greenspoon writes that "Leonard inspired a generation of young Jewish boys from the ghetto to take up the sport." He was "the most famous Jew in America," according to the Jewish press, "beloved by thin-faced little Jewish boys, who, in their poverty, dreamed of themselves as champions of the world."[45]

Like Leonard, the impact Joe Louis had on boxing and his ethnic community was profound. Dubbed the "Brown Bomber," Louis was an incredible prizefighter, winning twenty-two fights in 1935 alone, eighteen of which came by knockout. His uninterrupted nearly twelve-year run as heavyweight champion is still boxing's all-time record. According to Gems, Louis was known "as the anti-Jack Johnson, never gloating over a beaten foe, never being seen with a white woman, and portraying himself in a humble, religious manner."[46] Louis stayed undefeated through 1936 and raked in huge purses for his victories, even as the country continued to struggle through the Great Depression. When Louis defeated the former heavyweight champion Max Baer, he did so in front of 88,000 fans who paid more than $1 million to attend the fight. He certainly comported himself differently than Jack Johnson, but Louis's success in the ring against mostly white opponents evoked similar feelings of pride and celebration in Black communities. After Louis trounced Baer in just four rounds, one Chicago journalist reported that Black Americans "poured out of beer taverns, pool rooms, barber shops, rooming houses and dingy flats and flooded the streets. They chanted 'Louis! Louis! Louis!' … It was like a revival. Really, there was a religious feeling in the air."[47]

In an era where lynchings were public affairs and the Klan rode again, African American celebrities faced impossible scrutiny and ruthless attacks in the media. For Louis to succeed the way he did, to dominate and overpower his white opponents, and to do so at a time boxing had gained huge cultural, political, and economic relevance in America—it all came together to make his career deeply meaningful for many Black Americans. In her famous autobiography *I Know Why the Caged Bird Sings*, the African American poet laureate Maya Angelou wrote about Louis and her memories of his victories when she was a child in a section of the book she titled "Champion of the World."

> The men in the Store stood away from the walls and at attention. Women greedily clutched the babes on their laps while on the porch the shufflings and smiles, flirtings and pinchings of a few minutes before were gone. This might be the end of the world. If Joe lost we were back in slavery and beyond help. It would all be true; the accusations that we were lower types of human beings. Only a little higher than apes. True that we were stupid and ugly and lazy and dirty and unlucky and worst of all, that God himself hated us and ordained us to be hewers of wood and drawers of water, forever and ever, world without end. We didn't breathe. We didn't hope. We waited ….

> Then the voice, husky and familiar, came to wash over us—"The winnah, and still heavyweight champeen of the world … Joe Louis." Champion of the world. A black boy. Some black mother's son. He was the strongest man in the world ….

> It would take an hour or more before the people would leave the Store and head for home. Those who lived too far had made arrangements to stay in town. It wouldn't be fit for a black man and his family to be caught on a lonely country road on a night when Joe Louis had proved that we were the strongest people in the world.[48]

Thumping white supremacy in the ring became an enduring theme of Louis's career and extended beyond the United States. He defeated the Italian champion Primo Carnera the same year Italy invaded Ethiopia, which carried added political and ethnic significance in Italy and in Italian-American communities in the United States. Twice Louis fought the German champion Max Schmeling, who, although not a member of the Nazi party and even hid two Jewish children in his Berlin apartment during *Kristallnacht* in 1938, became a symbol of the fascist state and much-celebrated favorite of Adolf Hitler.[49] The Nazis had particular contempt for Black athletes like Louis, who challenged the tenets of their racialized world view. The 1935 Nuremberg Laws, to give just one example of the Nazi order, outlawed white ethnic Germans from marrying or having sex with certain "racially suspect" groups and that included people of African descent. As they would during the 1936 Olympics, German Nazis touted their national athletic heroes as proof of their genetic superiority and dared others to prove them wrong.[50]

Louis and Schmeling first fought in 1936, a few weeks before the Berlin Games opened, and much to the delight of the Führer and his Nazis, Schmeling won the fight. Louis admitted later he had underestimated his opponent and failed to train as seriously as he should. Gems writes that "Schmeling returned to Germany to a hero's welcome. The Nazis credited German discipline, intelligence, and courage for his triumph."[51] Louis's defeat stung for several reasons, but it did not last long. He bounced back and beat Jim Braddock for the heavyweight title in 1937, setting up a rematch with Schmeling the next year. Before a paying audience of 66,000 in New York's Yankee Stadium, and with an estimated 60 million Americans listening on their radios, Louis got his revenge. When the fight began, Louis took control of the center of the ring, driving Schmeling along the ropes and into the corners. About sixty seconds in, Louis connected with a devastating right cross that made Schmeling look like a human bobble head and sent him tumbling to the ground. The German champion tried to steady himself, but Louis knocked him down twice more. The fight lasted only one round and Schmeling connected for only two punches before his trainers threw in the towel to stop the match. According to Gems, not long after it had begun, the "German broadcast of the fight to the homeland soon terminated abruptly."[52]

Louis's victory, like the broader greatness of his career, was deeply symbolic. He challenged racism in a way that many white Americans found comfortable. Louis was reserved and respectful, fought proudly for his country in the ring and later as a serviceman during the war. He was not an activist, at least not in the way that Jackie Robinson or Muhammad Ali became activists. Yet there is no questioning his importance to African Americans and a nascent Civil Rights Movement. "The Brown Bomber held the heavyweight title for twelve years, the longest reign in history," writes David Zirin. "In a society so violently racist, boxing became an outlet for

FIGURE 2.2 *Germany's Max Schmeling (right) and the African American boxer Joe Louis (left) fought twice. The first Schmeling won in 1936, to the delight of the Nazis. In 1938, Louis prevailed. Despite the international pressures surrounding their bouts, the two men became close friends later in life. (Photo by Keystone-France/Gamma-Keystone via Getty Images).*

people's anger—a morality play about the thwarted ability, the unrecognized talents, and the relentless fighting spirit that shaped the black experience in the United States."[53]

The history of Louis's career also highlights sport's continuous transformation into political theater for hyper-nationalist governments. Between Louis's role as a prominent Black athlete and the growing importance that states like Germany were putting on national athletic achievement, the 1930s foreshadowed the intense politicization of sport that occurred in the postwar world. With the prospects of another world war rising, sport was becoming a key vector for national and ideological competition.

The Olympics and War

Before the 1930s, foreign audiences often criticized the United States for taking sport too seriously and placing too much importance on winning. Americans generally agreed they could be more zealous than others toward sport, but they saw that as a virtue—evidence of their destiny as a great power. In the decade prior to the Second World War, however, more countries began to think of sport as a means of proving national greatness. Leaders like Benito Mussolini and Hitler doubled down on using international sporting events like the Olympics for diplomatic posturing and to pageant political ideologies.

The Second World War also reshaped the US public's relationship with certain sports and facilitated the spread of US sporting traditions around the world. Sport served as martial training, escapist pastime, and a cultural language the United States would use to help win the Second World War and turn itself into the most powerful—and interventionist—nation in the world afterward. Much as the country still has the Second World War to thank for its enormous privilege and power in the world today, the war helped foster the international growth of American sport.

Olympic Growth in the 1920s and 1930s

As the accelerants of another world war formed in the 1920s and early 1930s, the Olympic movement seemed blissfully unaware of the darkening horizon. The first Olympics after the Great War were held in Antwerp in 1920, and once again Pierre de Coubertin played a leading role organizing the event. US athletes trounced in the medal count, winning ninety-six total medals (twenty-eight more than second-place Sweden), including forty-one gold, also by far the most of any country. "By all systems of athletic scoring used in 1920," writes the historian John Lucas, "the United States emerged as the dominant nation at these Olympic Games." Oddly, however, the press and even members of the Olympic team seemed to believe that "the country had not done as well as the great 1912 US team, and poor management by the AAU and the AOC was the reason."[54] Before long, the United States would have another chance to showcase its athletic prowess on its home soil.

In 1924, the Olympics took the historic step of adding a separate Winter Games to its international sporting agenda, which for the next seventy years occurred in tandem with the Summer Olympics during the same year. Only in 1994 did the Winter Olympics begin running in alternating even-numbered years. The 1924 Winter Olympics were set in the picturesque mountain-town of Chamonix, France. The Games featured nine events, including bobsleigh, curling, ski jumping, and ice hockey. Women were only allowed to participate in figure skating, as individuals and in mixed pairs with men. The American Beatrix Suzetta Loughran took the silver medal in the women's individual event and went on to win medals in the 1928 and 1932 Olympic Games—making her the only American to medal in figure skating in three consecutive Olympics.[55] Loughran's performance was one of the few standout US showings at the first Winter Olympics. Another bright spot was the US hockey team, which lost to the

Canadian national team in the championship by a score of 6–1.[56] "The Canadians, victors though they were," wrote a soothing *New York Times* article, "fully realized they had been through a real hockey match, but the indomitable courage, brilliant individual play and uncanny stick handling of the Americans could not prevail against the smooth clocklike" style of Canada's team.[57] Even in defeat, the American press found ways of rescuing the valor of its athletes.

Amsterdam and Switzerland hosted the 1928 Summer and Winter Olympics, respectively, and in 1932, the United States got its second chance to play host when both Los Angeles and Lake Placid became the sites for that year's Summer and Winter Olympics. Historian Barbara Keys writes in *Globalizing Sport* that staging the Summer Games in the Hollywood Hills "symbolized in geographic terms the leap these Games represented in other terms, toward a more global, more competitive, more commercialized, and more Americanized version of international sport." The Los Angeles Games were a "milestone in the international history of modern sport," she argues, because they "displayed in microcosm the broader tensions that beset the globalizing sport world before World War II."[58] When the foreign teams arrived and took in the sights and sounds of sunny California—"far removed from the soup kitchens and unemployment lines of the Depression," Keys notes—the mixture of athletic competition and the city's glittering material culture ensured the Los Angeles Games would leave a lasting impression on Olympic history.

The media scrum that encircled the 1932 Games personified the changing times in international sport. Despite inadequate radio broadcasts—caused by disputes with various other media entities—the new sport media sent stories on the 1932 Games around the world and film clips of its events to the silver screen.[59] According to Keys, "[s]etting the Games in the capital of the American entertainment industry was a crucial element in their success," because "studios, directors, and actors provided critical funds and celebrity backing." Projected to US and world audiences, the LA Games "added glamour to the events and reinforced the idea that athletes, like movie stars, were fundamentally entertainers."[60] The American Olympians answered the bell and delivered another dominant performance, winning more gold medals (forty-four) than the total medals won by Italy (thirty-seven), who finished second in the medal tally. The United States walked away with 110 total medals, but just as notable was the Games' commercial success, which netted over $1 million in profit. "It is a record of some kind," noted one US journalist, "and the shock is expected to have a shattering effect upon treasury officials."[61]

Gate receipts were not the only coin made in Los Angeles. The 1932 Olympics put on display US material culture and highlighted the growing commercialization of sport in the country and around the world. "Foreign businessmen used their Olympic sojourns to investigate US methods in aviation, textile manufacturing" and a host of other industries, Keys writes.

"Local businesses catering to the tourist trade experienced a welcome boom during the Games," while larger companies sunk their teeth into the marketing potential of the Games:

> US companies devised ingenious ways to "market" the Olympics, in the process pushing Olympic marketing toward a focus on products aimed at the masses rather than at the upper classes. Companies such as Kellogg's Pep Bran Flakes, Weiss Binoculars, Safeway, and Piggly Wiggly inaugurated major Olympic-themed advertising campaigns .... Auto supply stores, railroad lines, hotels, tire manufacturers, and gasoline companies gave out Olympic tie-ins ranging from stickers to paper-holders .... "Olympic" seat cushions, hot dogs, soft drinks, sunshades, caps, and ribbons were hawked everywhere in Los Angeles .... Like the Hollywood studios, US companies wooed Olympic stars, offering hefty contracts to winners willing to give up their amateur status. Springboard diver Jane Fauntz, for example, turned down a shot at a movie career but went on to endorse Wheaties cereal and Camel cigarettes.[62]

The 1932 Los Angeles Games injected new forms of commercialization and cultural popularity into the Olympics and tucked the international sporting community neatly into bed with big business. Yet compared to later Olympics, beginning with Berlin in 1936, the Los Angeles Games seemed far removed from looming global crises, including the worsening worldwide depression and the rise of militarism in Europe and Asia. National rivalry was, of course, a driving force behind the renewed Olympic movement, dating back to 1896 and Coubertin's desire to use international athletics to stir up nationalism in his native France. The US-UK rivalry pockmarked a few testy moments early on and suggested at the fuel Olympic competition could add to international relations. But as Keys shows, in 1932 the leaders of most participating countries appeared "oblivious of the political opportunities the Olympics represented."[63]

With one important exception, that is. Before Italy's Olympians boarded their team ship headed to California, Benito Mussolini, the Italian fascist dictator, surprised the Italian national team with a last-minute visit and beseeched the athletes, whom he called "ambassadors extraordinary of Italy to the United States," to "fight hard for the triumph of Italian sport."[64] Four years later, when the Games moved to Berlin, other heads of state joined Il Duce in publicly attaching nationalist expectations to the performance of their country's Olympians. By then, the feeble guardrails put in place after the First World War had blown away amid economic devastation; militarism was on the rise; and competing claims about national strength had made demonstrations of physical strength, like those in the Olympics, more important and politicized globally. Fascists like Mussolini and the Nazis in Germany had built political movements explicitly around the superiority of certain ethnic stock. The 1936 Berlin Games became a testing ground of fascist ideology and thrust the international sporting community squarely in the crosshairs of festering geopolitical strife. With Hitler watching on, America's complicated relationship with its own national identity came further into focus.

Hitler, Jesse Owens, and the 1936 Berlin Olympics

In the months leading up to the 1936 Berlin Olympics, the US ambassador to Germany, William E. Dodd, began reporting that the German government planned to tamp down public displays of anti-Jewish propaganda and other external pressure on Jewish communities, hoping to hide the extent to which their power rested on a program of ethnic cleansing. Dodd, who earlier noted that party members "appear to be doing what they can to throttle the Jews' means of existence," informed Secretary of State Cordell Hull that the "Nazis are putting great store by the Olympic Games to rehabilitate and enhance the reputation of the 'New Germany.'" Dodd said he expected that foreign Olympic athletes and tourists would only be allowed to speak with German citizens "inclined to reject as libel press reports ... [of] Jewish persecution" and "skillful also in parrying embarrassing questions and insinuating praise on National Socialism in their small talk."[65]

Scrubbing evidence of state-sponsored anti-Semitism in Germany was not the only means by which the Nazis hoped to rebrand their national image and paper over the growing list of atrocities Hitler's regime was committing. Previous Olympic Games had, of course, been opportunities for host countries to display evidence of national achievement—the United States clearly sought to do so in 1904 and 1932—but never before had the Olympics been deliberately used to camouflage the rise of a genocidal, authoritarian regime. In October 1935, the German government announced it was adding a national exposition, aimed at foreign audiences and presenting "ideas of the greatness of German history and the peaceful intentions of the new Germany," to accompany the Berlin Games in the summer of 1936. The "manner in which Germany is pointing the way in the present world crisis will be made evident," the German state asserted in the press, and promised that "the phenomenon of Germany is to be shown in all its characteristics."[66] The US Chargé in Germany, Ferdinand Lathrop Mayer, messaged to Washington that "for the Nazis, this year's Olympiad assumes all the importance of a foreign political drive to obtain the favor and approval of the outside world."[67]

The efforts to cover what Hitler was up to were extensive because his regime's persecution of Jews and plans for war were intensifying. The German government passed the Nuremberg Race Laws in 1935, followed by other laws and decrees designed to drive out non-Aryans from the country by choking off civil rights and economic opportunity. That same year, Hitler announced to the world that Germany was remilitarizing, flouting the terms of the Treaty of Versailles, and then preceded to reclaim territory lost after the First World War. Just a few months before the Olympics kicked off, German troops marched into the Rhineland. The government's concentration camp system was also expanding, and under Hitler's orders police forces like the SA and SS began imprisoning political opponents and members of other targeted groups, sending them to the camps for forced labor or death. By 1938, Germany had taken Austria and a year later, Europe was back at war.[68]

An important element in the Nazi worldview was a belief in "scientific racism"—an ideology which many early boosters of the Olympic movement also embraced. In the early twentieth century "many in the scientific community subscribed to a racial theory that asserted that peoples of European descent were the most advanced products of natural selection—athletically as well as intellectually," Dyreson explains. "In these theories," which became core to Nazi ideology, "Europeans, especially northern Europeans, led the world in every imaginable human category—physical as well as mental."[69] Hallmarks of scientific racism were evident at the 1904 St. Louis Games during James Sullivan's Anthropology Games and continued to gain traction in various corners of white power structures in the United States and Europe. The AOC president in 1936, Avery Brundage, "infamous for his racism, sexism, and anti-Semitism," writes Zirin, openly expressed his admiration for the Nazi's authoritarianism and fixation on national identity in politics.[70] Hitler made sweeping claims about the threat racially inferior groups posed to northern European ethnicities in his 1925 book *Mein Kampf* and even borrowed ideas from Jim Crow governments in the United States for ways to marginalize non-Aryan groups in German society.[71] For well over a century, scientific racism had helped justify slavery, colonialism, and war all over the world. Like some other extremist regimes during the buildup to the Second World War, the Nazis took the ideology to its logical, genocidal conclusion. As the great German writer Thomas Mann later put it, by the 1930s the German people had poisoned themselves on "the phantasm of race."[72]

The potency of pseudoscientific race laws in Nazi policy, culminating in the Holocaust and the Second World War in Europe, forced everyday white supremacists to draw lines in what they believed personally and what they might be willing to support publicly. Despite their country's own bloody history of race-based violence and persecution, many Americans became increasingly critical of Hitler's regime as it rose to power. Calls to boycott the Olympics arose from various foreign governments and in America covered the pages of the *New York Times* and other major newspapers. The Harlem-based *The New York Amsterdam News* asked Black Olympians not to participate in the Games to help delegitimize Hitler's authority and influence. "Under Hitlerism," the paper pointed out, "you would have been denied even the limited opportunities which have been yours in America … Humanity demands that Hitlerism be crushed, and yours is the opportunity to strike a blow which may hasten the inevitable end."[73] In late 1935, the pressure to boycott the Games reached critical mass in the United States. But Brundage, who called the boycott a "Jewish-Communist conspiracy" aimed at keeping the United States from competing, refused to withdraw.[74] Sympathetic to the Nazi cause, Brundage even removed two Jewish sprinters, Marty Glickman and Sam Stoller, from the 1936 team, which many believed was to avoid embarrassing Hitler in the likelihood the two men won their events.[75]

Dependent as it was on an ideology of racial superiority, Hitler's vision of German greatness was indeed vulnerable to public displays of non-Aryan physical dominance. The Nazis had elected to measure athletic success as evidence of their nation's ethnic and cultural primacy, concluding as early as 1933 that "much of a Nation's honor and glory is dependent on its success in the field of sport."[76] Hitler's public support for Max Schmeling, the German boxer who defeated Joe Louis just two months before the Berlin Olympics opened, underscored the Führer's interest in international sport and German athletic performance. For some US athletes, the opportunity to run down Nazi ideology and expose its flaws became a compelling reason to challenge Hitler at the very seat of his growing power.

Enter Jesse Owens. Born to sharecroppers in Alabama and then taken north by his parents to Ohio during the early days of the Great Migration, Owens grew into a phenomenal high school track athlete and in 1933 the Ohio State University successfully recruited Owens to join their track team. In 1935, during the Big Ten conference championships, Owens set new world records in the long jump, 220-yard dash, and 220-yard hurdles.[77] As he became a national figure, Owens evoked a strained sense of pride among many white American fans. Color lines were everywhere in the US sporting community, and the legacy of Black athletes like Jack Johnson reinforced how seriously most whites involved with sport supported racial hierarchies, even if that meant diluting the competition in the arena. Owens walked a fine line simply by being a dominant Black athlete, but, unlike Johnson, maintained a public persona that white Americans decided was acceptable to their worldview. The scholar Charles Fountain writes that even "those Americans who suffered from a less-virulent strain of [Hitler's] poisonous notion of Aryan superiority found themselves in the unlikely position of cheering for a black man."[78] Black journalists were more honest about what Owens and the other Black Olympians meant to the US team. The *New York Amsterdam News* wrote that the ship carrying America's Olympians "bore the strongest track and field teams to have ever left American shores. Ten Negro boys were on that boat as track and field Olympic entries, and these ten boys, so the critics said, were the strongest part of the American forces in that division."[79]

The brilliance of America's Black Olympians, particularly those who shone in the hallowed track and field events, meant they bore a particularly heavy burden in Berlin. They represented not only America's best hopes to outpace the world's greatest athletes but also living proof of the bankruptcy that was the Nazi worldview. Owens would later write, in a biography titled *I Have Changed,* that "my whole life was wrapped up, summed up—and stopped up—by a single incident: my confrontation with the German dictator, Adolf Hitler, in the 1936 Olympics." Owens described his childhood as one spent "watching my father and mother and older brothers and sisters trying to escape their own kind of Hitler," alluding to America's systemic racism and his experience with Jim Crow. "If I could just win those gold medals," hoped Owens, "the Hitlers of the world would have no more meaning for me. For *anyone*, maybe."[80]

FIGURE 2.3 *Jesse Owens in mid-flight, on his way to setting a new world record in the long jump and securing one of his four gold medals at the 1936 Berlin Olympics. Owens was the leading figure in a group of African American Olympians who dazzled audiences and won several gold medals in front of Hitler and the Nazis. (Photo by ullstein bild via Getty Images).*

Historians continue to debate the extent to which Hitler's policies motivated US athletes, particularly Owens, at the Berlin Games.[81] But there is no question that many Americans and other audiences framed Owens's performance as a refutation of Hitler's core racial beliefs. While the Germans crushed the United States in the medal count—finishing with 103 total medals to America's fifty-seven—Owens delivered a show-stopping performance by winning gold in the long jump, 100-meter, 200-meter, and as the first leg of the 4X100 meter relay. While Owens reset Olympic records, other world-class Black Olympians, like the US high-jumper Cornelius Johnson, joined in winning gold medals in front of the Nazis. Ignored by Hitler, hailed by the press, and embraced by many fans who attended the Games, Owens became a global sport celebrity in 1936. His legacy and the legacy of the other Black Olympians who competed in Berlin live on as exemplars of sport's power to challenge intolerance and expose the fault lines in racist ideologies. In 2016, US president Barack Obama honored the 1936 Olympic team during a ceremony at the White House, stating that it "wasn't just Jesse. It was other African-American athletes in the middle of Nazi Germany under the gaze of Adolf Hitler that put a lie to notions of racial superiority—whooped 'em and taught them a thing or two about democracy … [and] the American character."[82]

Obama's remarks were about more than just honoring the Black athletes for what they meant to America, and the world, in 1936. He was also righting the wrong of one of his predecessors, Franklin Roosevelt, who had refused to invite Owens and the other Black athletes to the White House after they returned from the Berlin Games. Owens remarked later that "Hitler didn't snub me; it was our president who snubbed me. The president didn't even send a telegram."[83] Only in 1955, when Dwight Eisenhower named him US "Ambassador of Sports," was Owens allowed in the White House. The international success of athletes like Jesse Owens and Joe Louis pushed a begging question about America closer to the surface: How could white Americans and the US government cheer the achievements of Black athletes while in most other ways deny African Americans' rights as equal citizens and human beings? In 1941, all attention turned to the outbreak of the Second World War and Americans devoted themselves to defeating the Axis Powers. But before long that question reemerged as a glaring vulnerability in postwar US society and foreign relations.

US Sport in the Second World War

The Berlin Olympics forced Americans to grapple with their nation's own cultural and ethnic divisions in ways some found hard to reconcile. America's struggle with itself persisted after the Second World War and became an enduring feature of US foreign relations during the Cold War. Beyond the racial reckoning it begot, the era of the Second World War triggered

structural changes within US sport as well. The war disrupted many of the
new professional leagues that had risen in the 1920s and 1930s. Those that
tried to play on, like the NFL and NHL, did so with a depleted talent base.
The NFL saw almost 1,000 league employees, mostly players, drafted or
volunteer into service. Military service likewise thinned out a sizable portion
of the NHL's rosters, leading the Canadian sport journalist Dink Carrol
to comment in 1942 that after "three years of war, the ranks of the NHL
teams have been depleted to the point where the vacancies must be filled by
lads only a year or two out of their knickerbockers." A year later, Hap Day,
coach of the reigning champion Maple Leafs, summed up his team's roster
by telling the press it "appears that we have reached 'The Children's Hour'
in the NHL.'"[84] Nevertheless, important change and growth occurred for
several sports. Both basketball and baseball used the war to further grow
their popularity. While their approaches and outcomes differed, each one
made strides toward bringing in new participants and audiences.

Basketball's international growth took an important step at the 1936
Berlin Olympics where, for the first time, the sport counted as a medal event.
Basketball teams like the Fort Shaw Indian all-women's team and the Buffalo
Germans had played in Olympic tournaments prior to 1936, but always
as exhibitions or demonstrations. The 1936 Games marked a new era in
basketball's history and signaled its growing popularity around the world.
In his book *American Hoops*, historian Carson Cunningham shows that,
thanks to organizations like the YMCA, basketball's growth had started to
reach "South America, and parts of Asia—especially China, where crowds at
basketball games routinely numbered over 10,000 (China's 1936 National
Basketball Tournament in Beijing drew an average of 23,000 spectators per
game)."[85] The 1936 Olympics affirmed basketball's legitimacy as a global
sport, although the quality of play was an issue. In the championship game,
which the United States won over Canada by a score of nineteen to eight,
the court turned into a literal slog. Cunningham writes that the "game was
played outdoors in a downpour and on a dirt and clay court described by the
New York Times as a 'sea of mud.'" The *Washington Post* joked afterward
that the contest should have "been played under water polo rules."[86]

The onset of the Second World War coincided with a sad moment in
basketball's history. In November of 1939, James Naismith, the inventor
of basketball, passed away. He was still working at the University Kansas
when he died, where he had coached the sport he designed despite admitting
to actually playing his own game a couple of times. Prior to his death,
Naismith remained circumspect about the future growth of basketball and
deflected personal comparisons to other great sport innovators, including the
mythologized story of Abner Doubleday inventing baseball.[87] Had he lived
a few years more, Naismith would have witnessed an evolution in the sport
that might have changed his mind. Professional basketball leagues in the
United States remained fragmented and regionalized, and with the Second
World War their operations became further hamstrung. But in conjunction

with the sport's global rise as seen through the 1936 Olympics, basketball entered the Second World War years beginning to grow into the modern version of itself.

An important stimulant for basketball's evolution was the World Professional Basketball Tournament (WPBT) that tipped off every year from 1939 to 1948. Nationwide basketball tournaments had become more popular at the college level prior to 1939, but only the WPBT brought together the country's best professional talent. "From 1939 to 1948," writes Douglas Stark, the WPBT "played a significant role in promoting the game, establishing the professional game on a national level, drawing teams from across the country, and providing a forum for quality professional basketball during World War II."[88] Not only did the WPBT bring in the country's best professional teams, but as discussed earlier, invitees included all-Black and integrated teams, such as the New York Renaissance and the Harlem Globetrotters—who each won WPBT tournaments in its earliest years. Stark argues that the "fact that the tournament served as the first venue for all-black and integrated teams to play for a professional championship was the World Professional Basketball Tournament's most important and lasting legacy."[89] Although the regional professional circuits remained segregated even after the war, the WPBT gave Black basketball players the platform to showcase their talents and forecasted the sport's luminous future.

MLB endured some of the same challenges that football and hockey did during the Second World War, with as many as 1,700 major leaguers, and nearly 4,000 minor leaguers, leaving for military service. Baseball kept its competitively diminished product on the field and did so with a heavy dose of patriotism on display. MLB committed itself to the war cause by hosting fundraising efforts to support mobilization; war bond donations based on player performances like hitting a home run and pitching a shutout; special uniforms designed to support the military; and pregame salutations to the American flag behind renditions of "The Star Spangled Banner" and "God Bless America," a sporting tradition inaugurated during the First World War.[90]

Baseball's mandated public displays of nationalism further endeared the sport to many Americans, at home and abroad, but behind the scenes and between the lines the game was struggling. Not only were rosters depleted, but those who did play earned smaller salaries, the rationing of war-valuable material required players to downgrade their equipment, and travel restrictions complicated spring training and regular season schedules. Still, baseball marched on and, despite the inferior product that trotted out day after day, attendance remained strong throughout most of the war, even topping prewar annual numbers in 1945. "Thanks in part to its dedicated support for the war effort," writes Elias, "baseball's patronage would further skyrocket in the next few years."[91]

Baseball changed in other important ways during the war, and one example was the formation of the All-American Girls Professional Baseball

League (AAGPBL). The AAGPBL was founded in 1943 and traveled all over the country, including military camps and professional stadiums, to play before thousands of Americans. More than 600 women played in the AAGPBL. The league became popular due to the high quality of play as well as how the league was marketed. Players became spokeswomen for the war effort and supported the Red Cross and veteran's groups—yet still were forced to accede to gender expectations at the time. The AAGPBL uniform code required skirts, and team practice included charm school lessons. The league ran until 1954 and was capped off by the Fort Wayne Daisies winning their third consecutive league title. More recent efforts to commemorate the AAGPBL have helped elevate its importance in baseball history. In 1992, the Hollywood film *A League of Their Own* canonized the AAGPBL into baseball lore and popular sport memory. The league also maintains an active players association to this day.[92]

The AAGPBL was one of several non-major league baseball organizations to use the game to support the war. Military bases throughout the United States and its territories were home to competitive and cathartic service leagues. Camp games were packed with major league-level talent and in places like Hawaii the military hosted tournaments featuring Joe DiMaggio, Ted Williams, and Stan Musial, among other professional ballplayers-turned-servicemen. Like in all its other wars, the United States brought baseball along as its military advanced around the world. In Europe, US troops played with other Allied forces, and by 1943 they had established the London International Baseball League and that same year hosted a European Theatre of Operations World Series. Baseball's cultural power was on display when soldiers began using baseball trivia to root out Nazi infiltrators from their ranks by asking would-be spies questions about the latest batting title winner or World Series champion. Baseball also made its mark in North Africa, culminating in the 1944 North Africa World Series which the Allies broadcast to troops over radio and included over 150 teams. "When American troops began making headway against the Nazis, baseball accompanied each new advance," Elias writes. "Ball fields were built everywhere US soldiers were posted."[93]

Baseball in the Pacific War carried even heavier weight than in Europe, given the popularity baseball had long enjoyed in Japan. The 1934 world tour that brought the Babe to East Asia obscured the extent to which the US-Japanese relationship was changing. Before the war, throngs of Japanese fans had greeted Ruth and other ballplayers with wild adoration when the tour reached Tokyo. But as it did in America, the war altered the Japanese experience with the sport. Japan's professional teams, which featured some of the world's best international talent, lost many players to the military, as was the case in the United States. But as Guthrie-Shimizu points out, Japanese players faced more extensive military service, "another telltale sign of the pathetically narrow human and material margins upon which the Japanese war machine operated during the Asia-Pacific War."[94] Japan's professional teams tried to hang on, but in 1944 its league, the National Baseball Association, folded.

The breakdown in Japanese baseball did not last long, however. After the war, during the US occupation of Japan, professional baseball restarted and the two countries once again began to rely on the sport as a friendly point of contact. "After World War II," argues Guthrie-Shimizu, "the shared love of baseball assisted postwar reconciliation and formed a cultural underpinning of the [US-Japanese] alliance, helping it weather the wear and tear of clashing national interests and mutual frustrations in the realm of high politics."[95] As the United States emerged from the Second World War one of the strongest and most assertive countries on the planet, sport would continue to serve as a valuable cultural medium through which US national interests could be pursued around the world.

Notes

1   Lynn Dumenil, *The Modern Temper: American Culture and Society in the 1920s* (New York: Hill and Wang, 1995), 9.

2   Frank Josza Jr., *American Sports Empire* (Westport: Praeger Publishers, 2003), 120.

3   Raymond Frances Yates, quoted in Jules Tygiel, *Past Time: Baseball as History* (New York: Oxford University Press, 2000), 71.

4   Ibid., 73.

5   Josza Jr., *American Sports Empire,* 121.

6   "Home Runs Hit in Each League," *Baseball Almanac,* URL: https://www.baseball-almanac.com/hitting/hihr6.shtml [accessed 9.19.21].

7   Tygiel, *Past Time,* 77.

8   Ibid., 85.

9   See Nathaniel Grow, *Baseball on Trial: The Origin of Baseball's Anti-Trust Exemption* (Champaign: University of Illinois Press, 2014). For an excellent primer on that decision, see Grow's article for FanGraphs, "Judge Landis, the Federal League and Baseball's Antitrust Trial," February 2, 2015, URL: https://tht.fangraphs.com/judge-landis-the-federal-league-and-baseballs-first-antitrust-trial/ [accessed 1.9.21]. For details on the 1922 Supreme Court decision, see *The Federal Baseball Club v. The National League* (1922), JUSTIA, URL: https://supreme.justia.com/cases/federal/us/259/200/ [accessed 1.9.21].

10 See Charles Fountain, *The Betrayal: The 1919 World Series and the Birth of Modern Baseball* (New York: Oxford University Press, 2015).

11 Kenesaw Mountain Landis, quoted in Edmund Wehrle, *Breaking Babe Ruth: Baseball's Campaign against Its Star* (Columbia: University of Missouri Press, 2018), 77.

12 Chris Lamb, *Conspiracy of Silence: Sportswriters and the Long Campaign to Desegregate Baseball* (Lincoln: University of Nebraska Press, 2012), 13; 190–8.

13   Robert Peterson, *Only the Ball Was White: A History of Legendary Black Players and All-Black Professional Teams* (New York: Oxford University Press, 1970), 93.

14   Leslie Heaphy, *The Negro Leagues, 1869–1960* (Jefferson, NC: McFarland & Company, 2003), 103.

15   Satchel Paige quoted on "Josh Gibson Hall of Fame Profile," National Baseball Hall of Fame and Museum, URL: https://baseballhall.org/hall-of-famers/gibson-josh [accessed 1.11.21].

16   Heaphy, *The Negro Leagues*, 173.

17   Ibid., 175.

18   Alan Klein, *Globalizing the Game: The Globalization of Major League Baseball* (New Haven: Yale University Press, 2006), 94.

19   Elias, *The Empire Strikes Out*, 112.

20   Ibid., 117.

21   Sayuri Guthrie-Shimizu, *Transpacific Field of Dreams: How Baseball Linked the United States and Japan in Peace and War* (Chapel Hill: University of North Carolina Press, 2012), 14.

22   "Thorpe Made President: Famous Indian Elected Head of Pro Football Association," *NYT*, September 19, 1920.

23   Josza Jr., *American Sports Empire*, 19.

24   "NFL's All-Decade Team of the 1930s," Pro Football Hall of Fame, URL: https://www.profootballhof.com/news/nfl-s-all-decade-team-of-the-1930s/ [accessed 1.15.21].

25   Beverly Bogert, "Ice Hockey," *Outing* 21 (January 1893): 252–6, quoted in Stephen Hardy and Andrew Holman, *Hockey: A Global History* (Champaign: University of Illinois Press, 2018), 100.

26   Hardy and Holman, *Hockey*, 164–5.

27   Ibid., 106–15.

28   Ibid.

29   "NHL Hockey Came to the US on Dec. 1, 1924," *NHL.com*, URL: https://www.nhl.com/news/nhl-hockey-came-to-the-u-s-on-dec-1-1924/c-395417 [accessed 1.17.21].

30   Hardy and Holman, *Hockey*, 208.

31   Ibid., 218 [emphasis in original].

32   Ibid., 228.

33   Stark, *Wartime Basketball*, 21–2.

34   "Where Basketball Was Invented: The History of Basketball," *Springfield.edu*, URL: https://springfield.edu/where-basketball-was-invented-the-birthplace-of-basketball [accessed 9.3.2021].

35   Annette Hofmann, "Between Ethnic Separation and Assimilation: German Immigrants and Their Athletic Endeavors in Their New American Home Country," *International Journal of the History of Sport* 25, no. 8 (2008): 1004.

36   Bob Kuska, *Hot Potato: How Washington and New York Gave Birth to Black Basketball and Changed America's Game Forever* (Charlottesville: University of Virginia Press, 2004), 166.

37 Peterson, *From Cages to Jump Shots*, 96–9.

38 Gates quoted in ibid., 101.

39 Stark, *Wartime Basketball*, 46.

40 Moore, *I Fight for a Living*, 140–1. Chapter six of Moore's book on boxing fully examines the ban on black boxers after 1915.

41 Pope, *Patriotic Games*, 116.

42 Gerald Gems, *Boxing: A Concise History of the Sweet Science* (New York: Rowman & Littlefield, 2014), 64.

43 Benny Leonard quoted in Mike Silver, *Stars in the Ring: Jewish Champions in the Golden Age of Boxing* (Lanham, MD: Rowman & Littlefield, 2016), 60.

44 Levine, *Ellis Island to Ebbets Field*, 152.

45 Leonard Greenspoon, *Jews in the Gym: Judaism, Sports, and Athletics* (Lafayette, IN: Purdue University Press, 2012), 241.

46 Gems, *Boxing*, 106.

47 Richard Wright quoted in ibid., 107.

48 Maya Angelou, *I Know Why the Caged Bird Sings* (New York: Random House, 1969).

49 Earl Gutskey, "The Night Schmeling Risked All," *Los Angeles Times*, December 23, 1989, URL: https://www.latimes.com/archives/la-xpm-1989-12-23-sp-588-story. html [accessed 1.15.21].

50 Barbara Keys, *Globalizing Sport: National Rivalry and International Community in the 1930s* (Cambridge, MA: Harvard University Press, 2006), 138–9.

51 Gems, *Boxing*, 110.

52 Ibid., 112.

53 Dave Zirin, *A People's History of Sport: 250 Years of Politics, Protest, People, and Play* (New York: The New Press, 2009), 84–5.

54 John Lucas, "American Preparations for the First Post World War Olympic Games, 1919–1920," *Journal of Sport History* 10, no. 2 (1983): 41.

55 Olympic Results, Chaminox 1924, *Olympic.org*, URL: https://www.olympic.org/ olympic-results?g=Chamonix%201924 [accessed 1.18.21].

56 Jørn Hansen, "Olympic Winter Games of 1924 (Chaminox)," in John Nauright and Charles Parrish eds., *Sports Around the World: History, Culture, and Practice,* Volume 2 (Denver, CO: ABC-CLIO, 2012), 397–8.

57 "Canada Beats US in Hockey Final, 6–1," *NYT*, February 4, 1924, 24.

58 Keys, *Globalizing Sport*, 91.

59 Ibid., 98–9.

60 Ibid., 100.

61 "$1,000,000 Above Expenses Cleared at Olympic Games," *NYT*, August 21, 1932, 54. "Los Angeles 1932 Medal Table," *Olympics.com,* URL: https://olympics.com/en/ olympic-games/los-angeles-1932/medals [accessed 9.21.21].

62 Keys, *Globalizing Sport*, 104.

63 Ibid., 106.

64 "Mussolini Greets Italian Athletes," *NYT*, July 2, 1932, 12.

65 Ambassador William Dodd to Secretary of State Cordell Hull, January 30, 1936, *FRUS* 1936: Europe, Volume II, 197–9, URL: https://search.library.wisc.edu/digital/AVBWPY35NJ2SV78I/pages/AKDWWAMPXQEQ2Q8F [accessed 1.24.2020].

66 "Olympic Visitors to See Nazi Show," *NYT*, October 14, 1935, 13.

67 The Chargé in Germany (Mayer) to Secretary of State Cordell Hull, July 14, 1936, *FRUS* 1936: Europe, vol. II, 143, URL: https://search.library.wisc.edu/digital/AVBWPY35NJ2SV78I/pages/AWFC6HWSHSTYGB8Y.

68 Nora Levin, *The Holocaust: The Destruction of European Jewry 1933–1945* (New York: Schocken Books, 1968), 35.

69 Mark Dyreson, *Crafting Patriotism for Global Dominance: America at the Olympics* (Oxfordshire: Routledge, 2008), 91.

70 David Zirin and Jules Boykoff, "Racist IOC President Avery Brundage Loses His Place of Honor," *The Nation*, June 25, 2020, URL: https://www.thenation.com/article/society/avery-brundage/ [accessed 9.21.21].

71 See James Whitman, *Hitler's American Model: The United States and the Making of Nazi Race Law* (Cambridge, MA: Harvard University Press, 2017).

72 Thomas Mann, *Germany and the Germans* (Washington, DC: Library of Congress, 1945), 14.

73 "Negro Olympic Ban Urged," *NYT*, August 23, 1935, 9.

74 "In Favor of Participation," *United States Holocaust Memorial Museum*, URL: https://www.ushmm.org/exhibition/olympics/?content=favor_participation&lang=en [accessed 9.21.21].

75 "Jewish Athletes—Mary Glickman & Sam Stoller," ibid., URL: https://www.ushmm.org/exhibition/olympics/?content=jewish_athletes_more [accessed 9.21.21]; Keys, *Globalizing Sport*, 85–8.

76 American Consul, Raymond H. Geist, quoted in Keys, *Globalizing Sport*, 128.

77 Pamela Laucella, "Jesse Owens, a Black Pearl amidst an Ocean of Fury: A Case Study of Press Coverage of the 1936 Olympic Games," in Chris Lamb, ed., *From Jack Johnson to Lebron James: Sports, Media, and the Color Line* (Lincoln: University of Nebraska Press, 2016), 54.

78 Charles Fountain, *Sportswriter: The Life and Times of Grantland Rice* (New York: Oxford University Press, 1993), 250.

79 William Charles Chase quoted in Laucella, "Jesse Owens, a Black Pearl amidst an Ocean of Fury," 68.

80 Jesse Owens Memorial Park, URL: http://jesseowensmemorialpark.com/wordpress1/resources [accessed 9.7.2021].

81 For a competing perspective on the role of anti-fascism among US Olympians, see Keith Rathbone, "Antifascist Athletes? A Reappraisal of the 1936 Berlin Olympics," in *Fascism: A Journal of Comparative Fascist Studies*, 9 (2020): 195–220.

82 Stephen Whyno, "Obama Welcomes Relatives of 1936 African-American Olympians," *Associated Press*, September 29, 2016, URL: https://apnews.com/article/630eebc7bb5441e6b6c06eacec93d1ef [accessed 1.27.2021].

83 Jesse Owens quoted in "The Champion a President Snubbed," *The Newnan Times Herald*, September 1,.2017, URL: https://times-herald.com/news/2017/09/the-champion-a-president-snubbed [accessed 2.1.2021].

84 Dink Carroll and Hap Day quoted in Stan Fischler, "NHL Came Close to Shutting Down during World War II," *NHL.com*, URL: https://www.nhl.com/news/nhl-came-close-to-shutting-down-during-world-war-ii/c-291024550 [accessed 1.31.21].

85 Carson Cunningham, *American Hoops: US Men's Olympic Basketball from Berlin to Beijing* (Lincoln: University of Nebraska Press, 2010), 4.

86 Ibid., 1.

87 Stark, *Wartime Basketball*, 25.

88 Ibid., 60–1.

89 Ibid., 62.

90 Elias, *The Empire Strikes Out*, 136.

91 Ibid., 145.

92 Information gathered from the "League History," "League Season Timeline," and "Players Association" sections on the *All-Girls Professional Baseball League* website, URL: https://www.aagpbl.org/ [accessed 2.1.21].

93 Elias, *The Empire Strikes Out*, 148–52; 149–50.

94 Gurthrie-Shimizu, *Transpacific Field of Dreams*, 150.

95 Ibid., 203.

Athlete Spotlight #2:
Babe Didrikson Zaharias

FIGURE 2.4 *Mildred "Babe" Didrikson Zaharias, arguably the most gifted overall athlete of the twentieth century, showcases her picturesque golf swing at a tournament in 1937. In addition to golf, Didrikson was an Olympic gold-medalist, semi-professional basketball player, and one of the most colorful media personalities of her generation. (Bettmann/Contributor via Getty Images).*

Babe Didrikson Zaharias—born Mildred Ella Didrikson to Norwegian immigrants in Port Arthur, Texas in 1911—burnished a legacy like few others. Babe occupied her own stratosphere throughout most of her career, which stretched from the 1930s until her premature death in 1956. She claimed to have earned the nickname "Babe" because of her propensity to out-slug all the boys she played baseball against growing up. In many ways, though, her career turned out even more exceptional than Ruth's, given her dexterity as an athlete and accomplishments in other parts of her life.[1]

Didrikson became a sensation playing women's basketball in 1931 for the Golden Cyclones, a semiprofessional team out of Dallas, averaging thirty points a game—an astonishing number for that era of women's hoops. Her accomplishments on the hardwood drew the attention of AAU scouts who recruited Didrikson to compete in the 1932 national amateur track and field championships. Again, her athleticism seemed unmatched: she broke two world records; won five events, including javelin, long-jump, and 80-meter hurdles; and qualified for the 1932 Los Angeles Olympics. As her biographer Susan Cayleff writes, Babe was on her way to proving she "was unarguably the most multi-talented athlete of the twentieth century, male or female."[2]

The breadth of her athletic accomplishments was only part of Babe's mystique. She was endlessly quotable to the press, a bully and braggart to her competition, and, in the context of mid-twentieth-century gender norms, an enigma to the public. After a singular performance at the 1932 Games, where she won three medals (including two golds) and set three world records, a reporter asked if there was anything she did not like to play. "Yeah," she said, "dolls."[3] Indeed, her "tom-boy" looks and behaviors became sensationalized topics among sport journalists and audiences. Babe reveled being an iconoclast. However, the questions about her femininity and sexuality privately bothered her and shaped several key personal decisions, including her marriage to the famous professional wrestler George Zaharias in 1938.[4]

Didrikson's signature sport was golf. Like most everything else she tried, Babe uncannily adapted to golf's intense physical and mental requirements. Famous sportswriter Grantland Rice, who helped lionize athletes like Ruth and Dempsey in print and on radio, encouraged Didrikson to pursue golf. Rice became a key media ally Didrikson could count on to ply her exploits to the public. In the 1940s, writes Cayleff, "[w]omen's golf was in need of a superstar player and personality," and with the help of a captivated press, Babe supplied just that. She "devoted herself to perfecting her golf game with the same ferocity that she brought to the Olympic high hurdles and javelin toss," and soon became a sensation on the links.[5]

Women golfers had no professional tour when Didrikson started playing, so she competed in amateur tournaments until the mid-1940s. In fact, her first professional tournaments were against men on the Professional Golfers' Association (PGA) tour. In 1950, the same year the Associated Press named her the Woman Athlete of the Half-Century, Babe co-founded the Ladies' Professional Golf Association (LPGA) and proceeded to put the final touches on her legendary career. She won over thirty tournaments and ten major championships during her career and finished tour-leader in prizemoney three times.

Doctors diagnosed Didrikson with colon cancer in 1953. She promised she would beat back the disease like she did her competition, and for a brief period it seemed she had. But in 1955, after winning an LPGA tournament in South Carolina, Babe was taken to a hospital and told the cancer had spread. Attended to by her companion Betty Dodd—with whom Babe shared the last six years of her life—Didrikson died in 1956 at the age of forty-five. Despite her "lack of self-conscious effort to do so," writes Cayleff, Didrikson "served as a path-breaking role model by virtue of her accomplishments."[6] Her career illuminated both the potential of women's sport in America and the structural obstacles blocking its growth. Babe showed what was possible and set the stage for other American female athletes to flourish later in the century.

Notes

1   Susan Cayleff, *Babe: The Life and Legend of Babe Didrikson Zaharias* (Champagne: University of Illinois Press, 1996).

2   Susan Cayleff, "The 'Texas Tomboy': The Life and Legend of Babe Didrikson Zaharias," *OAH Magazine of History* 7, no. 1 (Summer 1992): 28.

3   Quoted in ibid.

4   Ibid., 29.

5   Ibid., 29–30.

6   Ibid., 31.

3

The Dawn of the Activist Athlete

Consumerism, Civil Rights, and Sport in the Early Cold War

Introduction

"I was naïve about the elaborate lengths to which racists in the Armed Forces would go to put a vocal black man in his place," admitted Jackie Robinson in his autobiography *I Never Had It Made*.[1] In 1941, Robinson was playing professional football for the Honolulu Bears, in one of the only integrated football leagues on US soil, while living near Pearl Harbor until the league season ended in late November. On December 5, two days before Japan attacked, Robinson hopped a passenger ship headed back to California, where he had grown up and attended college as a four-sport varsity athlete, and All-American football player, for the University of California, Los Angeles (UCLA)—the first "four-letter man" in Bruins history. He was at sea the day Japan launched its surprise assault, and later recounted that "like all men in those days I was willing to do my part" and fight for his country. By the summer of 1942, Robinson was in base camp at Fort Riley, Kansas, and in 1943 became second lieutenant and morale officer of his battalion.

From early in life, it was Robinson's nature to challenge stereotypes and prejudice. So, when he learned that Fort Riley had segregated white and Black-only sections in their mess halls and rec centers, true to form Robinson pushed back. He telephoned the provost marshal at the fort and tried to "appeal to the major by saying we were all in this war together and it seemed to me that everyone should have the same basic rights." Major Hafner, the senior officer whom Robinson had rung up, was unaware that the young lieutenant speaking to him was Black. When Robinson finished making his request to amend fort policy and integrate the base, Hafner replied: "Lieutenant, let me put it to you this way. How would you like to have your wife sitting next to a n*****?"[2]

Robinson's encounters with racism in the military were only just beginning. A few months after his call with Major Hafner, Robinson was transferred to Fort Hood, Texas, where once more he found himself "up against one of those white supremacy characters," this time in the form of a military bus driver who demanded Robinson sit in the back of the bus.[3] Robinson protested and again challenged the racist structures surrounding him, only this time his efforts resulted in a court-martial trial. He was acquitted of all charges but by then Robinson was "pretty much fed up with the service," believing he had cultivated a reputation "as a potential troublemaker who would be better off in civilian life."[4] The military granted Robinson's request for an honorable discharge, and he returned to his athletic pursuits where, eventually, he would lead the fight to integrate America's national pastime. After Robinson's retirement from baseball in 1957, Martin Luther King Jr., in an article for the *New York Amsterdam News*, wrote that "back in the days when integration wasn't fashionable, [Robinson] underwent the trauma and the humiliation and the loneliness which comes with being a pilgrim walking the lonesome byways toward the high road of Freedom. He was a sit-inner before the sit-ins, a freedom rider before the Freedom Rides."[5]

A pilgrim, a veteran, a troublemaker, an All-American: Jackie Robinson was many things to many people. While the United States girded for its postwar confrontation with the Soviet Union and the specter of global communism—a struggle quickly dubbed the Cold War, although plenty of hot wars were fought on its behalf—Robinson was saddled with a new role. Like many Black American athletes, willing or otherwise, Robinson became part of a narrative, propagated by the US government, to prove that the American way of life was superior to the rival alternatives modeled by communist states like the Soviet Union, China, and Cuba. The crises that erupted during the Cold War era sprung largely from ideological differences that too often the United States considered existentially threatening. Government officials and the country's business community concluded that the American way of life—which above all else meant free enterprise—required extensive defense internationally. In Korea, Cuba, Vietnam, and elsewhere, US Cold War ideology hyperventilated into wars and armed conflict that only destabilized the international system further. But as an all-consuming kind of war, the Cold War depended on other channels to sow its discord and stoke tensions among rival powers. More so than any other geopolitical struggle of the twentieth century, the Cold War was one in which governments considered propaganda and the cultivation of national identities paramount to the outcome of the war.

This chapter explores how sport and sport diplomacy in the early Cold War proved effective at channeling national ideology on both sides of the Iron Curtain. In America, a postwar economic boom brought about a consumer's paradise that helped turn more professional sports, especially the NFL, into legitimate, lucrative operations. The popularization of professional sport also forced a broader swath of the country to reckon with the racial barriers that had long governed US sporting culture. Sport became an early battleground in the Civil Rights Movement that transformed mid-century America. Abroad, the nation's long history of racist violence and inequality became an obvious liability to US foreign policy. The government learned quickly that sport had unique value as a form of public diplomacy, and began to lean heavily on American sporting culture, and the athletes it bore, to address its national shortcomings before the world.

Among the many important figures who challenged structural prejudice in this era, Black athletes, as they had earlier in the century, played a critical role in advancing the country's consciousness of its racism. This chapter highlights several prominent African Americans, including Jackie Robinson, Bill Russell, Wilma Rudolph, Muhammad Ali, Kareem Abdul-Jabbar, Mal Whitfield, Tommie Smith, and Althea Gibson, to show how sport, race, gender, and politics became inextricably bound together in the Cold War era, and in the process redefined what it meant to be an American athlete. Competing against communist governments to win hearts and minds throughout the international community, the United States began earnestly harnessing sport and athletes as forms of soft power to advance its national interests. Doing so helped craft a message about the possibilities of a democratic society, but also left America open to obvious and biting criticisms about the limitations of a political system that, despite what it might pretend to be globally, treated non-white Americans more like subjects of an empire than citizens of a democracy.

Postwar Professional Sport in America

Historian Lizabeth Cohen's brilliant study on postwar America, *A Consumers' Republic*, posits that a novel strategy "emerged after the Second World War for reconstructing the nation's economy and reaffirming its democratic values through promoting the expansion of mass consumption."[6] An unprecedented emphasis on consumerism as a defining trait of the American identity triggered wholesale changes in US society, from how businesses looked at customers to how citizens looked at their government. Cohen shows how government policies like the G.I. Bill, the expansion of college admissions, a tax structure favoring the middle class, and the arrival of sophisticated and targeted marketing strategies built this new consumers' republic.

These and other developments drove a postwar economic boom resulting in a massive expansion of the American middle class and, with it, entirely new ways of living in a material world. A technological link to many of these forces was television, what Cohen calls "a beckoning new frontier for advertising" that allowed companies to cultivate loyal audiences, and, with that knowledge, construct marketing campaigns designed to maximize their appeal to segments of American consumers. By 1953, at which point color televisions were hitting the market, two-thirds of Americans had a television in their homes. A decade later it was 94 percent.[7]

Sport was one of many American consumer-based industries that flourished in the postwar era, and television was a major reason why. Beaming into family rooms in full color for the first time came America's heroic athletes, competing at their game's highest levels, courtesy of major broadcast companies like the Columbia Broadcasting System (CBS), the American Broadcasting Company (ABC), and the National Broadcasting Company (NBC). In-game attendance and player salaries also rose in these years, although players earned only a whisker of what awaited them once the era of free-agency began. All three of America's major professional leagues today—the NFL, NBA, and MLB—enjoyed growing fortunes between 1945 and 1970, but the postwar boom times were felt all around. Even leagues that depended heavily on international audiences, like the NHL and PGA, welcomed higher profits and greater visibility in the early Cold War era.[8] But for the major American sports in particular, the twenty-five years after the Second World War were crucial to their maturation and future success.

The NFL Sets the Edge

The professional leagues that survived the Second World War found upgraded living in the consumers' republic, and the NFL grabbed a corner lot. In 1950, the NFL was only slightly behind both the AL and NL in per-game attendance; in 1960 it had surpassed the AL; and by 1970, the NFL averaged more fans per game than MLB, the NBA, and the NHL combined.[9] Cultural attitudes toward American football had changed since the prewar era, regarding both the game's reliance on aggression and physicality and its role in the professional world of sport. College campuses, the cradle of American football, nourished the game early in the century, ostensibly free from the undue influence of money and where its physicality could be justified as abetting the formative development of young collegiate men. "Pro football," writes the historian David Surdam, "long the ignored stepsibling of college football, began to rival, if not surpass, the amateur game" beginning in the late 1940s.[10] Even the Soviet Union took note of America's growing thirst for football, claiming in 1952 that the sport was "designed to brutalize American youth and prepare it to take its place in an 'army of bandits and haters of mankind' under the United States' policy of militarization."[11]

With the league's popularity climbing by 1950, the expansion of televised NFL games brought the sport to new audiences and helped build out a national fanbase for the game. Journalist David Zirin explains that professional football, "a fringe sport for decades, was tailor-made for television like nothing else on the landscape."[12] Broadcast rights for league championship games brought in tens of thousands of dollars by the 1950s, and by 1952 every NFL franchise was making $70,000 a year from television broadcast revenue. The NFL and CBS reached an agreement in 1956 to carry a selection of regular season games to various regional markets in the United States. Then, in 1958, following one of the most famous and thrilling championship games in American football history—when the Baltimore Colts, led by the Hall of Fame quarterback Jonny Unitas, nipped the New York Giants in overtime before a sold-out Yankee Stadium and a huge national television audience—NFL league officials grasped "professional football's enormous appeal to a televised audience as an alternative to the game's broadcasts on the radio."[13]

A change in commissionership in 1960, when Pete Rozelle succeeded Bert Bell, signaled an inflection point in NFL history. Rozelle leveraged the league's growing popularity and renegotiated with CBS, who agreed to pay $4.6 million for the rights to broadcast the NFL's regular season schedule. Rozelle told the owners that the "NFL has been credited with harnessing television and using it to greater advantage than any other sport activity." But whatever edge football enjoyed, he warned, "will be lost without planning for the future."[14] Rozelle continued to press his sport's advantage with the networks, and in 1963 he got CBS to agree to pay $14.1 million for regular season games, plus $2 million for the championship game. When Rozelle told the owners the terms of the deal—"fourteen million a year. Twenty-eight million for two years," he boasted—a dubious Art Modell, owner of the Cleveland Browns, told him "Pete, you gotta stop drinking at breakfast."[15]

But Rozelle was neither drunk nor wild-eyed about the profits the NFL stood to make thanks to television. Indeed, by 1969, the television network ABC worked out a deal to air regular season games on Monday nights, thus starting the tradition of Monday Night Football in America.[16] Rozelle also authorized the licensing of NFL Films, the league's video production wing that canonized its legendary teams and players beginning in 1962. Using high-quality editing, dramatic music, and polished narration, the crew behind NFL Films "told stories about pro football in a self-consciously epic mode," writes former NFL lineman-turned-English professor Michael Oriard.[17] "Through the montages of violent collisions and the close-ups of bloodied fists and contorted faces spraying sweat drops in super slow motion," he adds, "NFL Films lets the viewer see and feel more intensely the thrill and power and struggle of professional football."[18]

Under Rozelle, the NFL began its evolution into a media-savvy, consumer-focused, national sport giant. But these years were not without their challenges. The league's policy toward Black players reflected professional football's fraught history of racism, as well as the reactionary white identity politics of the day, all dating back to the prewar years. Sport historian Louis Moore has argued that one thing unique about the NFL "is that it's a full-fledged league and it starts off integrated" in the 1920s.[19] Indeed, as sportswriter Jack Silverstein writes, from "the league's inaugural season of 1920 until 1933, black players not only played—they dominated." Black professional football players topped early league record books and led their teams to league championships—that is, until 1933. That year, partly under the direction of the NFL's oft-credited founder George Halas, professional football quietly instituted a ban on Black players that lasted until 1946.[20] It took Halas's own Chicago Bears six years after the NFL reintegrated before they signed the first Black player in franchise history. The most egregious example of the lingering racism was, of course, the Washington Redskins, who, under their proudly white supremacist owner George Marshall, became the last NFL team to integrate—and only when the league mandated they do so in 1962. With an overtly racist team name to boot, the Washington club made clear they wanted to be "the South's team," and signed exclusive broadcast contracts with southern media companies and drafted the majority of their players from southern schools.[21]

Another challenge for the NFL came from competition with the American Football League (AFL), which formed in 1960 and drew considerable national attention. The AFL boasted some of the country's best talent, including the legendary New York Jets quarterback Joe Namath. Both leagues battled throughout the 1960s over talent and media attention as the AFL scooped up lucrative television contracts with NBC, which had lost out on broadcasting the NFL. In 1964, NBC agreed to a five-year contract with the AFL worth $36 million.[22]

Competition between the leagues culminated in 1967 when they agreed to host an interleague championship game, played by the respective winners of each league. The event marked the first official Super Bowl in professional football history. The NFL's Green Bay Packers, coached by the legendary Vince Lombardi, defeated the AFL's Kansas City Chiefs by a score of 35–10. Four years later, the leagues finally merged under the NFL's name. The AFL's ten teams, along with Baltimore, Cleveland, and Pittsburg, became the American Football Conference (AFC), and the remaining thirteen NFL teams became the National Football Conference (NFC). The Superbowl highlighted the NFL's rapid ascent to the top of US sporting culture after the Second World War. The NFL exemplified how professional sport leagues could harness consumer-driven media to generate unprecedented financial gain. Baseball was still considered America's national pastime, but as Oriard writes, there was no doubt that "[p]rofessional football became Americans' favorite spectator sport in the 1960s."[23]

The Making of the NBA

By the early 1940s, the outline of a sustainable, popular professional version of basketball was coming into focus. The various regionalized professional leagues—like the American Basketball League and the Midwestern

League—that had come and gone in the early 1900s helped solder together a fledgling professional circuit that two leagues, the NBL and the BAA, used to bring the sport one step closer to sustained profitability. Formed in 1937, the NBL attracted the best talent, yet commercially the NBL struggled marketing its product. Dependent on business sponsors, after whom NBL teams were named, and arena access that proved difficult to secure, teams constantly relocated to different cities. Untethered to a consistent fanbase, the NBL still attracted quality professional basketball players thanks to the money brought in by its business partnerships, which gave them an advantage in an era of depleted talent pools due to the Second World War. Gene Scholz, who played in the NBL in the 1940s, recalled that "I didn't even know we were in a league. I didn't know what was going on. I was just picking up a few bucks on the side playing basketball."[24]

The NBL's search for the country's best talent even included integrating team rosters in 1942—five years before Jackie Robinson broke baseball's color barrier. The historian Robert Peterson writes that integration "came without fanfare or fuss, either because of the NBL's obscurity or because the nation was at war and had more pressing concerns—perhaps both."[25] Here one has to wonder about the history that preceded the integration of the NBL—the profusion of basketball at the local level, its suitability for urban space, its low equipment costs, its pace and emphasis on teamwork, its importance to immigrants, women, and ethnic minorities—the things about the sport that hinted at its wide appeal to diverse audiences, and how that might have conditioned a more democratic atmosphere within the game. It was never unanimous, and the racial animus of white players, coaches, owners, media, and fans was an urgent problem throughout the twentieth century and beyond. But certainly, there was widespread respect within the game of basketball for Black players early in the twentieth century.[26]

The BAA, formed after the war in 1946, suffered from an opposite set of symptoms: arena access and a local identity were the essence of the league, but players were reluctant to leave the NBL, and so the BAA's talent pool was shallow. "Unlike the NBL," writes Peterson, "which had grown out of the desire of basketball managers and promoters to formalize competition, the BAA was born because arena managers wanted seats to fill."[27] The majority of BAA owners, in fact, also owned NHL hockey teams. The hope was basketball games could pad the bottom line when their hockey teams skated out of town. In its first season, the BAA's connection to hockey also brought professional basketball across the border, as one of the BAA's franchises, the Huskies, played their home games in Toronto, Canada. The Huskies, however, struggled to stay afloat, and by 1947 they were out of the league. According to Charley Rosen, basketball in Canada flailed initially "because college and amateur basketball had not been developed in the area," and Toronto specifically "was such a hockey town that high school skaters drew more attention than the Huskies."[28] It would be several decades before professional basketball would return to Toronto, but over that time Canadian interest in the game grew considerably.

The NBL and BAA sparred for talent and attention until the NBL suggested a merger in 1949. Ten BAA teams joined with seven from the NBL in a new league named the National Basketball Association.[29] The NBA's charter franchises adopted the BAA's tradition of naming teams after local cities, including the Minneapolis Lakers, the Philadelphia Warriors, and the Waterloo Hawks as well as others that remain intact today, such as the Boston Celtics, the New York Knickerbockers (Knicks), and the Denver Nuggets. The league integrated in 1950 when the Celtics drafted Chuck Cooper out of Duquesne University and the Washington Capitals drafted Earl Lloyd from West Virginia State University. "The color line had fallen for good," writes Peterson, but "it would be another decade, though, before black players were in the NBA in appreciable numbers."[30]

The NBA's early years were slow going, and one immediate challenge it faced was competing with college basketball for national notoriety. The NCAA and NIT tournaments inaugurated earlier in the century had helped market college ball to a national audience. But in 1951, a point-fixing scandal involving players on the Bradley Braves in Peoria, Illinois, who were caught taking money in return for manipulating game scores to reward bettors and bookies, rocked the world of college basketball and dirtied its image as a pure, amateur game.[31] The sport scholar Albert Figone argues that the "quest for profits had caused college administrators, coaches and the NCAA to develop a purblind attitude toward the problem of gambling in college basketball," leading some disillusioned fans to go looking for alternative versions of the game.[32] "The college scandal opened the way for the major professional league to take top billing in the basketball world," adds Peterson, "after all the years as second banana."[33]

Even with college basketball reeling, the NBA remained marginally popular in the 1950s and 1960s. Over those years, NBA franchises rose, fell, and relocated at a striking rate. In the 1960s, the number of teams dropped from seventeen to eight and the total number of league regular season games was cut in half. Attendance was slightly better than it had been for both the NBL and BAA prior to the merger but still well below what MLB, the NHL, and the NFL enjoyed through the 1970s.[34] Nonetheless, some great NBA teams formed over these early years, and by the 1960s its first legendary dynasties were born. Four of the first five NBA championships went to the Minneapolis Lakers, led by the dominant big man George Mikan. In 1957, the Boston Celtics became the new force in the NBA. Thanks to the brilliance of their best player, the Hall of Famer Bill Russell, the Celtics captured eleven titles in fifteen years, including a record eight straight championships between 1959 and 1966.

Finally, important structural changes in the game—most critically, the introduction of a twenty-four-second shot clock that cut down on tactical stalling and resulted in the league's points-per-game (PPG) average jumping from 79.5 to 93.1—and a new style of shooting called the "jump shot" enlivened the sport, enhanced its athletic grace, and helped set the table for a much rosier landscape that awaited in the 1970s and beyond. Fraught though they were, these formative years of the NBA were nonetheless essential to its eventual growth into a globally popular sport. By the end of the 1960s, writes Peterson, at "long last basketball was on its way to full acceptance as a major sport." Success for the league "did not come all at once," he adds. "There were still some rocky times ahead, but the corner had been turned."[35]

Jackie Robinson, the Black Press, and Baseball's Integration after the Second World War

Baseball, like other major professional sports, benefited from television's mass adoption after 1945. Baseball's postwar history also highlights the essential role of the Black press in American sport culture and US society at large. African American newspapers date back to the New York-based *Freedom's Journal*, first published in 1827. Other Black-run newspapers, like the *New York Amsterdam News* and the *Pittsburg Courier*, proliferated at the turn of the twentieth century. News coverage ranged from persistent injustices in American life and global patterns of inequality caused by imperialism to the achievements of prominent Black Americans, including athletes. A major conduit for the Black press formed in the Northeast in the 1930s when the *Boston Guardian* launched the National Negro Newspaper All-American Association of Sports Editors. Coming out of the Second World War and emboldened by the country's fight against Nazism, the Black press became the leading voice for an emerging social consciousness in American sport. Moore argues that "black sportswriters knew that their fight for fairness in sports helped push for democracy outside of sports," and that "it was black sportswriters who challenged black athletes to get involved in the movement."[36]

Sport integrationists, particularly those in the Black press, had long targeted Jackie Robinson as the ideal candidate to break baseball's color barrier, thanks to his inimitable collegiate career, his highly regarded character, and his personal toughness. After his discharge from the military, Robinson signed with the Kansas City Monarchs of the Negro Leagues in 1945, batted over .300 for the season, and earned a spot in the All-Star game.[37] That same year, thanks to the prodding of a *Pittsburg Courier* journalist named Wendell Smith, the Boston Red Sox invited Robinson to a tryout. Two other Negro League players joined Robinson in Fenway Park on April 16, where they went through drills in front of Red Sox management. Sam Jethroe, one of the players who tried out with Robinson and later premiered as the first Black player for the Atlanta Braves, told friends the tryout was "a joke." Jethroe accused Red Sox general manager, Joe Cronin, of hanging out "in the stands with his back turned most of the time. He just sent some of his men out there and told them to throw some balls, hit balls to us, and then come back and say we had ability."[38] The tryout, which only happened because local politicians and the Black press pressured the team into doing so, was a con. Boston's brass had no intention of signing any of the players. The indignity was not lost on Robinson or other African Americans in baseball who, according to the scholar Glen Stout, "held the Red Sox in disdain more so than any other team in the game."[39]

Several months after the Red Sox ruse, Robinson got his break. In August 1945, he met with the Brooklyn Dodgers' general manager Branch Rickey, whom Robinson assumed wanted to speak about Brooklyn's all-Black affiliate team known as the Brown Dodgers. Instead, Rickey informed Robinson the plan was for Jackie to star for the major league franchise. Robinson would start with their minor league club in Montreal, but the goal was Brooklyn. Rickey, with the help of Wendell Smith, spoke honestly to Robinson about what he would face being the first Black player since the 1880s to play in the majors. Historian Thomas Zeiler recounts how Rickey "roleplayed taunting fans, insensitive managers, and racist, spike-sliding players" in an attempt to coax a rise out of Jackie.[40] When Robinson asked if Rickey expected him to endure the abuse in silence, Rickey said that what he most wanted was "a ballplayer with the guts *not* to fight back." Rickey promised Robinson he would support him if one day he did "come up swinging" but cautioned that doing so "would set the cause back twenty years."[41]

By the end of his historic ten-year MLB career, Robinson suffered every indignity, and more, that Rickey warned him about, and rose above them all. He won Rookie of the Year after his debut season in 1947, notched a league MVP in 1949, and brought Brooklyn its only World Series championship in 1955. Robinson maintained his cool on the field, but off it he was willing to speak out about the realities he faced as MLB's lone Black player. In a recurring column called "Jackie Robinson Says" that he wrote with his friend and journalist Wendell Smith for the *Pittsburg Courier*, Robinson noted that for all the "nasty letters I've received," support from his fans, particularly in the Black community, "have helped me a lot and I'm not worrying about a few 'small' people who can't make up their minds whether or not they like living in a Democracy."[42]

Historians often note how difficult it can be to properly describe the impact Robinson made on America, and particularly his importance to African Americans. Without a doubt, the integration of baseball ranks among the most important early gains of the postwar Civil Rights Movement, given the sport's centrality to the nation's identity. Much like Joe Louis and Jesse Owens, Robinson was a symbol of hope and happiness to Black Americans. His success suggested that wholesale change of American society might be possible, though the brooding of angry whites pointed at the enormous structural obstacles that still needed to be overcome.[43]

Robinson's impact on the game of baseball is also challenging to summarize, but simply quantifying the growth of non-white players in the game gives a sense of his importance to democratizing the major leagues.

When he retired in 1957, the number of African Americans in MLB had grown from 0.9 percent in 1947 (the year he broke in) to 6.7 percent. Ten years later, when he was inducted into MLB's Hall of Fame, that number had doubled. And by 1975, Black players constituted 18.5 percent of major leaguers. The 1970s and 1980s reflected the height of African Americans in professional baseball, followed by several eras of a decline in those percentages.[44]

Baseball's integration after 1947 also included steady growth in the number of Latino ballplayers in the majors—some of whom became the first athletes of color signed by a major league team. Latino players were very much, as Adrian Burgos describes them, "integration pioneers" who helped knock down baseball's color line for good. And, as the number of Latinos in professional baseball grew, so too did MLB's connections with and dependence on Latin American countries with burgeoning baseball cultures.[45] In 1947, 0.7 percent of MLB players were Latino; in 1957 that number was 5.2 percent; and by 1967, it was 10.7. By 1993, there were more Latino players in MLB than Black players, and by 2016 Latino players

FIGURE 3.1 *Jackie Robinson (right), Satchel Paige (middle), and Larry Doby (left) chat before a game in 1948. After Robinson broke MLB's color line in 1947, Doby became the second African American to sign with an MLB team, and the first in the American League, when he joined the Cleveland Indians a few months later. Paige, one of the greatest pitchers in baseball history, signed with the Indians for the 1948 season at the age of forty-two after a legendary career in the Negro Leagues. (Photo by Sporting News via Getty Images).*

accounted for 27.4 percent of MLB's rosters, compared to just 6.7 percent of Black players—down to exactly the same percentage as when Robinson retired in 1957.[46]

Even after players like Robinson proved their tremendous value on the diamond, several of the league's white owners refused to integrate. The Red Sox, now having struck out on two baseball legends in their franchise history—famously trading Babe Ruth to the Yankees in 1920 and then passing on Robinson after his Fenway workout—were the last team to sign a player of color, waiting until 1959. The great Satchel Paige signed with the Cleveland Indians in 1948, as did several other Negro League stars from around the country. In 1951, the same year the Chicago White Sox landed the dazzling Cuban third baseman named Minnie Miñoso (affectionately nicknamed the "Cuban Comet"), the New York Giants debuted one of the very greatest baseball players ever: a dynamic, five-tool center fielder from Alabama named Willie Mays.[47] The Major Leagues in the 1950s and 1960s sported some of the finest ballplayers to ever put on an MLB uniform, including Mickey Mantle, Ted Williams, and Henry "Hank" Aaron (the African American power-hitting outfielder who broke Babe Ruth's career home run record in 1974). But by several measurements, Mays was the greatest of an all-time great generation.[48] Talented as Robinson was, Mays was the superior player, both defensively and offensively. Although they both captured headlines and helped turn the page on baseball's segregated past, Mays took a different view of the role of Black athletes as promoters of social justice and civil rights. Whereas Robinson was predisposed to challenge and speak against racial oppression, Mays was uncomfortable in the activist-athlete role.

Mays, "the greatest player of his generation, ducked his responsibilities throughout his career," writes Louis Moore. In his book *We Will Win the Day*, Moore shows how Mays hoped that just "being himself, the likeable 'Say Hey Kid,' would be enough" to change the attitudes of racist Americans.[49] Mays once said that whenever he was asked "why I don't sit-in or demonstrate for civil rights," his response was that "I try to make my contributions for racial harmony in the best way I know how—on the baseball field."[50] Striking a neutral tone on the pressing civil rights issues of the day did not always endear Mays to other Black athletes or to the leaders of the Civil Rights Movement. It also contrasted sharply with the positions Robinson and other prominent African American athletes took, despite the enormous personal risks that came with being a Black activist in America. Still, Mays reflects an important tension that African American athletes were beginning to wrestle with more frequently, and one that would only intensify as the Cold War wore on: should athletes stick to sports, or should they use their platforms to advocate for causes they believe in?

With MLB's history of racism finally at its reckoning, the infusion of Latino talent also highlighted the fraught legacies of baseball's connection to American empire. The territories America wrangled from Spain and usurped from indigenous control at the turn of the century were now part of a sprawling international baseball community. The rise in Latino ballplayers on MLB rosters, such as the Puerto Rican phenom and humanitarian Roberto Clemente and the Dominican star Juan Marichal, underscored baseball's growing dependence on the Caribbean and Central America for its elite talent. In the case of Cuba, the history of baseball and American empire converged in revolution in 1959, when the baseball-loving Cuban nationalist leader, Fidel Castro, overthrew the US-backed Batista government. Castro, whose own Los Barbudos (the Bearded Ones) baseball team went on a barnstorming tour of Cuba to help shore up popular support for his political movement, was initially open to maintaining some diplomatic and cultural ties with the United States. In the earliest days of revolution, it seemed plausible the transnational connections forged by baseball might survive. But after the United States imposed an economic embargo on the island in 1960, Castro responded by cutting off Cuban players from MLB and reducing all Cuban baseball to amateur status.[51]

The freeze in US-Cuban relations affected the baseball world in several ways. Burgos writes that the "turbulent political climate made a trying time even more difficult for Cuban professional ballplayers" who remained on MLB rosters after 1960. Dozens of Cuban players wrestled with the "life-changing decision of whether to stay in Cuba and give up their US professional career," Burgos explains, "or leave the island without knowing whether they would be able to return."[52] Meanwhile, MLB looked to deepen its international ties with other Latin American countries after Cuba's revolution, culminating in the development of the Dominican leagues as a talent pipeline for MLB clubs and premier destination for US ballplayers who wanted to hone their skills in the winter.[53] With more Latino players making their way onto MLB rosters, the game's relationship with countries like Cuba and the Dominican Republic, as well as Venezuela, Colombia, and Mexico, evolved into the baseball ecosystem that exists throughout the western hemisphere to this day.

Sport Diplomacy and the Cold War

In the middle of his MVP season in 1949, Jackie Robinson traveled to Washington, DC, to sit before Congress and speak on racial attitudes in America as part of a session of the House Un-American Activities Committee (HUAC). The committee's investigation stemmed from an incident involving Paul Robeson, the famous African American actor, singer, and, in his youth, highly touted American football player. Robeson was publicly critical about the threat of racism in America, and, most grievously, insinuated that African Americans might hold nuanced views on the Soviet Union, and toward the Cold War's broader ideological struggle, due to the persistence of white supremacy in America and the nation's exploitative foreign policies. Robeson was a hugely popular figure with a worldwide audience. US officials knew his words carried weight, and so they set out to tarnish his credibility. In July, HUAC arranged for several prominent Black Americans to speak before the committee. Along with Robinson, the committee invited Black veterans, academics, and members of the media, such as the editor Thomas Young, to share their views on the state of race relations in America. Young, for his part, described what Robeson had said as "a great disservice to his race."[54] Not all the witnesses were as sharply critical of Robeson, but the consensus was that African Americans, although unsatisfied with their status in the country, were nonetheless proudly American. The committee, of course, chose not to extend Robeson the chance to explain or defend himself.

Jackie Robinson was the final speaker of the session. Historian Damion Thomas writes that while Robinson "took as harsh a stance against Jim Crow as Paul Robeson had ... what distinguished Robinson from Robeson was that he continued to identify the American capitalist, democratic system as the vehicle through which African Americans would achieve full equality."[55] Robinson told the committee that while "I can't speak for any 15,000,000 people any more than any other one person can," he had "too much invested for my wife and child and myself in the future of this country ... to throw it away because of a siren song sung in bass."[56] Robinson was referring to the communist ideology, which he later told the committee had nothing to do with African Americans pressing for equal rights. The white press and most Black newspapers hailed Robinson for his bravery. Robeson, for his part, refused to criticize Robinson for what many saw as one Black celebrity publicly shaming another. According to Moore, "Robinson later regretted these words and the fact he let Congress use him for its own political agenda."[57] What mattered most to US government officials was that Robinson, a world-famous example of a Black man making it good in America, had validated the US way of life in the court of public opinion.

Robinson's 1949 HUAC testimony is just one example of Black athletes becoming political agents, willing or otherwise, on behalf of the United States in the early Cold War. While the HUAC hearings principally served a domestic audience, the global implications of someone like Jackie Robinson reaffirming the American Dream were not lost on the government or the press. Other African Americans, including members of the Harlem Globetrotters, Wilma Rudolph, Bill Russell, and Muhammad Ali, faced similar expectations of their own. Their stories reveal several key facets of American history in the early Cold War. Together they embody the evolution of the Civil Rights Movement, the US government's conceptualization of soft power and sport diplomacy, and the intensifying politicization of the global sporting community.

The Harlem Globetrotters and Cold War Civil Rights

In her book *Cold War Civil Rights*, the historian Mary Dudziak draws out the connection between US Cold War strategy and the progress made on civil rights reform over several presidential administrations. Soviet leaders were quick to point out their enemy's brutal legacy of racism as evidence of an exploitative ethnocentrism they claimed defined the United States—and many foreign audiences found this framing persuasive. According to State Department estimates in the 1950s, the Soviet Union devoted nearly half of its propaganda to hammering the United States over its record of racism.[58] "US government officials realized that their ability to promote democracy among peoples of color around the world was seriously hampered by continuing racial injustice at home," writes Dudziak. "In this context, efforts to promote civil rights within the United States were consistent with and important to the more central US mission of fighting world communism."[59]

More recently, sport historians have dug further into the history Dudziak uncovered to show how sport became a means of public diplomacy used to advance the message that America was the land of opportunity. Damion Thomas argues that sport was an especially attractive tool to US officials. For one, it was easier for the government to counter communist critiques by pointing to figures like Jackie Robinson than embracing the heavy structural reform that was actually needed to repair America. Second, as Thomas writes, sport was "one of the few places where the two nations competed head-to-head." Consequently, "the symbol of the black athlete became contested terrain" during the Cold War.[60]

One of the US government's initial targets to conduct its sport diplomacy was the Harlem Globetrotters: a professional team made up of some of the best African American basketball players in the country that had been around since 1926. Throughout their early history, the 'Trotters, as they were called, were anything but global, sticking to regional markets in the United States until their first world tour in 1950. Yet their dominance and style of play made them a popular attraction by the late 1930s. In 1940, the Globetrotters won the WPBT and twice after the war they beat George Mikan's Minneapolis Lakers in exhibition games—a Lakers team, it is worth noting, that won championships in the NBL, BAA, and NBA between 1947 and 1950. When the NBL integrated in 1942 it tried to compete with the Globetrotters for talent; however, the 'Trotters were a major draw for elite Black basketball players. A few Globetrotters jumped to NBL teams after 1942, such as Bernie Price, Roosevelt Hudson, and, most famously, Wilt Chamberlain, but the 'Trotters remained a show unto themselves well in the early Cold War years.[61]

The Globetrotters' audacity was its primary commercial advantage. But as Thomas has shown, it came at a price. The 'Trotters were known for their ostentatious brand of basketball, using stunts, tricks, and gaffes to turn the sport into performative spectacle, even as they often pummeled their opponents. They would sneak in weighted basketballs, play hide-and-seek on the court, and run up into the stands all in the middle of a game. Thomas links the Globetrotter's style to the minstrel tradition that emerged as a degrading representation of Black culture in the Jim Crow era. Another term for it was "clowning," a type of unserious play that baseball leagues popularized early in the century. Black ballplayers would "bat one-handed, run the bases on their knees, and circle the bases in the wrong direction" in order to "keep the crowd amused." A famous all-Black team named the Indianapolis Clowns became so popular in the 1930s that they could draw upward of 40,000 fans. Members of the Black press, such as Wendell Smith, who worked tirelessly toward the integration of American sport, discouraged performances like the Clowns. Yet to many white Americans, the Clown's brand of sport presented a lush blend of profits, entertainment, and racial stereotyping that padded their worldviews perfectly.[62]

Indeed, as Secretary of State Dean Acheson saw it, the Globetrotters worked as "ambassadors of goodwill" in part because they were a laugh—at least for some people. Acheson wrote that the team's "attraction consists not only in superb skill but also showmanship and broad humor," which he believed created "unlimited possibilities for racial understanding and good will in the visits of these teams as already demonstrated in Latin America, North Africa, the Near East and Europe." Acheson hoped that deploying an attraction like the Globetrotters on America's behalf "may provide an effective answer to Communist charges of racial prejudice in the USA."[63] Thomas explains that "while emphasizing the notion that African Americans had opportunity in American society, the image that the Globetrotters portrayed suggested that African Americans were still capable of handling only limited tasks and responsibilities." The 'Trotters thus helped "reinforce prevalent stereotypes of black men as infantile, shiftless, irresponsible, inept, 'inadequate souls, who longed for the guidance of white men.'"[64]

The Harlem squad's first genuine globe-trotting experience came in 1950 when they visited nine countries in Europe and Africa and played seventy-nine games. For US officials, the tour was a huge success and led to more initiatives. In 1951, they traveled to West Berlin and played before a crowd of 75,000 and then later visited East Germany and competed in the Third World Festival of Youth and Students. The next year, they visited 85 cities across four continents.[65] The team continued to tour, globally and domestically, throughout the 1950s and 1960s, by which point the US government had found ways of enlisting other Black athletes to advance the message that racism was a thing of the past. Thomas concludes that the "Globetrotters traveled throughout the world as examples of the State Department's evolutionary theory of improving race relations, which suggested that opportunity in America was available to talented and motivated African Americans, even under segregation."[66]

Wilma Rudolph, Femininity, and the Cold War

Not many Olympic legends could boast of beating both polio and scarlet fever as a child—but Wilma Rudolph could. Rudolph was born in 1940 in Saint Bethlehem, Tennessee, and due to polio, she wore a leg brace until she was five. "My doctor told me I would never walk again," she once famously remarked. "My mother told me I would. I believed my mother."[67] After overcoming illness, Rudolph grew into an incredible young athlete. She was named a high school All-American in basketball, but soon track became her primary passion. Throughout high school, Rudolph ran competitively for the Alabama Tuskegee Institute and then, later, the Tennessee State Tigerbelle track team.

The Tigerbelles were coached by a man named Ed Temple, who noticed Rudolph's prodigious talent and invited her to join the Tennessee State team during AAU competitions where she was eligible to compete as a high schooler. She led the Tigerbelles to the 1955 AAU national championship as a fifteen-year-old, and a year later won a bronze medal in the 4X100 meter relay for the US Olympic team in Melbourne, Australia. As Rudolph's fame within the sport world grew, the press and the US government became enamored with her good looks and feminine charm. According to historian Cat Ariail, Rudolph's "achievement, attractiveness, and racial identity made her a powerful representative of the possibilities for progress in a democratic society."[68] Most Black women in sport were called brutish or un-ladylike by white observers; however, Rudolph's beauty became fodder for cold warriors looking to degrade Soviet female athletes for their muscularity. Ariail writes in her book *Passing the Baton* that when confronted with "the double burden of blackness and femaleness, Wilma Rudolph most evocatively and effectively demonstrated the imagined inclusivity of American democracy."[69]

Rudolph got an official taste of the Cold War when she competed as part of a dual track meet held in 1958 between the United States and the Soviet Union. The two superpowers arranged the event "to foster friendship and understanding throughout sport," Ariail explains, "albeit while trying to assert the athletic superiority of their respective nations."[70] The event proved a striking sign of the times with the Soviets outpacing the United States in total points (172–170), yet some of the best individual performances came from America's Black athletes, particularly Rudolph and the Tigerbelles, who won four of their ten events. "US officials intent on demonstrating that the nation was fulfilling it democratic values," argues Ariail, "viewed Temple's Tigerbelles as a powerful counter to accusations of American racism."[71] When preparations began for the 1960 Olympics in Rome, Rudolph became one of the most popularly showcased African American athletes the US Olympic team had to offer.

Once in Rome, Rudolph transformed into an Olympic icon. Although she twisted her ankle before the first stage of the 100-meter sprint she had no problem advancing to the finals where, in spectacular fashion, Rudolph won the race going away. She captured a second gold medal in the 200-meter dash, and then a third in the 4X100-meter relay, despite a botched handoff between Rudolph and her teammate Lucinda Williams. The Olympic stadium rocked as onlookers chanted her name. The press thronged her, as did adoring fans who could not get enough of the beautiful American track sensation. A *New York Times* article titled "World Speed Queen" came wrapped around two large photographs of Rudolph and gushed about her athletic prowess and her feminine allure, with quotes about how "Boys seem to like her, and every so often she seems to have a new one."[72]

Rudolph became an international sensation after the 1960 Olympics. She accepted invitations to visit track and field associations in Australia, Israel, and Trinidad. Her exploits remained of acute interest to sportswriters throughout Europe.[73] A flushed *Daily Express* article from London, for instance, described her as the "flamingo-legged American heroine" who "won with feet that seemed to caress the track," among other things.[74] In 1961, she returned for another confrontation with the Soviets as part of an AAU summer tour that carried Rudolph to Russia, Poland, West Germany, and Great Britain. Like they had in 1958, the Soviets won the most points at the event. And again, Rudolph delivered a memorable performance. She tied the world record in the 100-meter sprint and led a dramatic come-from-behind win over the Soviets in the 4X100 relay. When the tour moved to West Germany, she outdid herself and set a new women's world record with an 11.2-second 100-meter dash. She won races in Poland and Britain, in front of as many as 70,000 spectators who, according to the *New York Times*, "cheered her lustily for many minutes."[75]

For obvious reasons, Rudolph was a prime candidate for the State Department's sport ambassador initiative. The government initially arranged for Rudolph to visit East Asia and India until those plans fell through. But in 1963, she became an official American Sports Specialist and traveled to Africa, where she toured Ghana, Guinea, Mali, Senegal, Upper Volta, and French West Africa. Ariail argues that "the State Department recognized that Rudolph seemed to singularly embody an idealized image of American democracy," and that while on her tour, which lasted twenty-seven days, Rudolph "fulfilled these expectations."[76] Rudolph was, indeed, a polished representative for the US government, preaching the importance of physical and mental health, as well as offering running instruction particularly to women in the various countries she visited. Her foreign hosts seemed enamored by her, while the State Department was also very pleased by Rudolph's diplomatic aptitude. "The combination of athleticism and attractiveness that had captivated so many in the United States and Europe also proved effective in West Africa," Ariail writes, adding that "Rudolph later said that she received more than fifty marriage proposals while she was in Africa."[77] In the end, Rudolph's sport ambassadorship not only reflected the US government's broader objective of using African American athletes as intermediaries to some of the Cold War's nonaligned world—one of the most important, if nebulous, targets for the Cold War superpowers. Her international career also highlighted some of the ways gender and sexuality intersected with Cold War paradigms, revealing the value many Americans continued to place on traditional measurements of femininity in their overall assessment of women in sport and politics.

Bill Russell and the Transnational Power of Sport

Bill Russell was a comparatively risky bet to play the part of sport ambassador. A child of the Great Migration and born to proud parents who preached thoughtfulness but also a willingness to stand one's ground, Russell became one of the most outspoken athletes during the era of the Civil Rights Movement. He won an Olympic gold medal for the US basketball team at the 1956 Melbourne Olympics, and then emerged as the most dominant player on the most dominant team in the 1960s, leading his Boston Celtics to eleven NBA championships, including eight in a row between 1959 and 1966. He became the first Black NBA coach— a player-coach, at that!—in 1966 for the Celtics until his retirement in 1969. His stardom as a Celtic highlighted the NBA's relative progressiveness on integration and equality in sport, particularly juxtaposed with Boston's other major sporting franchise, the Red Sox, who were the last MLB team to sign a player of color (Pumpsie Green) in 1959. Russell carved out an inimitable professional basketball career and did so in a city notorious for racist fans and media. Moore writes that "Russell was one of the few athletes who could match Jackie Robinson as an activist."[78] His assertiveness with the media and the American public stemmed from his childhood rearing, especially his mother who told him in youth, "I don't want you to ever, ever pick a fight. But always finish the fight that you're in."[79]

Russell's activist mentality was apparent early in his professional career. He sparred with the Boston press, about whom he said, "to get any recognition, I would have to change my complexion."[80] Once he told the *Saturday Evening Post* that his goal was "to make the white population uncomfortable and keep it uncomfortable, because that is the only way to get their attention." Forcing Americans to come clean on their racial attitudes would either produce "a really integrated society or we will understand, absolutely and finally, that [black Americans] will never become part of society."[81] What made Russell's words especially powerful was that, compared to some of the other prominent Black athletes of his era, Russell "got involved in the movement."[82]

His mother advised him to avoid white folks as much as possible because "you'll never know what they might do." But wherever Russell went, racists found him. When living in Oakland, California (where his family settled after leaving Louisiana in 1942), a group of white minor league baseball players accosted Russell, snarled slurs, and spat tobacco

juice at him.[83] He endured persistent racism in college and during his early
NBA career. When his teams needed lodging for the night or a bite to eat
on the road, white business owners often refused to countenance Russell
on their property. In 1963, while Russell and his wife and kids were on
vacation, someone broke into his house in Boston and covered the walls
with racial slurs. After establishing himself as one of basketball's giants,
however, Russell began to feel his oats and went beyond attacking racism
through the press. In 1964, during Freedom Summer, Charlie Evers, the
brother of slain Civil Rights leader Medgar Evers, asked Russell if he would
come down to Mississippi to support the movement and provide a morale
boost to the activists. At Charlie's suggestion, Russell hosted free basketball
clinics in Jackson, Mississippi, open to the whole community. Reflecting
on his legacy and impact on Black youth in America, Russell explained
that "in the society I live in, every time I can do something, I see it as an
opportunity."[84]

Russell's participation in the 1964 Freedom Summer initiative was not,
in fact, the first time he had used basketball to connect with Black youth. In
1959 the US State Department enlisted Russell as a goodwill ambassador
and deployed him to Africa, where he traveled to Ethiopia, the Ivory Coast,
Liberia, and Libya and met with local communities. Thomas calls Russell
"an intriguing choice for a goodwill ambassadorship because he had a self-
acknowledged reputation for being grouchy, opinionated, and ungrateful
to the White Establishment."[85] Before long, Russell learned his government
handlers were no different than the fans and media back in Boston. "The
State Department representatives who greeted me were seedy, alcoholic
types," Russell recounted, a group of "arrogant louts, almost competitively
eager to be racist."[86]

The encounters with his African hosts, however, left an entirely different
impression on Russell. Touring Northern Africa, running basketball clinics,
and meeting with children, community leaders, and government officials,
Russell had an emotional breakthrough of his own. In one particularly
evocative moment with school children from Liberia, Russell was asked
the question, "why are you here?" According to Thomas, Russell diverged
from the diplomatic response he was expected to give, and instead "became
choked with emotion," and explained that "I came here because I believe
that somewhere in Africa is my ancestral home. I came here because I am
drawn here, like any man, drawn to see the land of his ancestors."[87]

Russell's "co-option of the tour for his own personal growth and sense
of identity," writes Thomas, "had not been the desired outcome that the
[US] government had anticipated."[88] Rather than reify his Americanness
and, by extension, his patriotism, Russell had instead landed on a deeper,
more intimate, and, ultimately, more human emotion. Shooting hoops with
children in Africa, he said, awakened him to the fact that he could "go out
under the sky in a foreign land, with nothing but a hundred words and a
basketball, and communicate so well with kids that within a half hour I'd

see the same looks of joy that I'd felt with my first high leap." His African tour, he said, "made me feel like a magician."[89]

Despite his official capacity as a sport ambassador, Russell was tapping into a power structure beyond the US government's control—one that modern sport had helped spawn over the twentieth century. Sport was becoming more global, and athletes more socially conscious. Experiences like the one Russell had in Liberia illuminated the power that athletes like him had to call attention to larger issues. Among its many consequences, the Cold War helped entrench popular athletes at the center of an emerging nexus between a solidifying global sport community and high-level geopolitics.

Muhammad Ali v. United States

Muhammad Ali, born Cassius Clay in 1942, was the athlete of his generation and one of the most important human beings of the twentieth century. Clay (as he was known until he was twenty-two) grew up in Louisville, Kentucky, and began boxing at age twelve. At eighteen, Clay became one of ten US amateur boxers to compete at the Rome Olympics, where he won the gold medal in the light heavyweight division. The newly minted Olympian, charismatic and brimming with pride, returned to Louisville expecting a hero's welcome. "I went downtown that day, had my big old medal on and went in a restaurant," he recalled later in an interview, "I said, 'cup of coffee [and a] hotdog,' and the lady said 'we don't serve negroes.'" Ali said he "had to leave that restaurant, in my hometown, where I went to church and served in their Christianity, my daddy fought in world wars, I just won the gold medal and couldn't eat downtown. I said 'something's wrong.'"[90]

Clay grew increasingly vocal over the 1960s about the abuse people of color suffered in America and around the world. Compared to other Black boxers like Jack Johnson and Joe Louis, Clay was unflinching about calling out a system that worked against people like him. He could be emotional, even abrasive, when he spoke on social issues. But he became more poignant and eloquent the older he got and the more he spoke up. Through it all, of course, was his famous wit. For instance, once during an interview he joked that as a child, after asking his mother why there were no Black angels in any of the pictures he saw in church, he told her, "Oh I know, if the white folks are in heaven too, the black folks are in the kitchen preparing the milk and honey."[91] Even before his religious awakening and turn toward political activism, it was clear Clay was simply not wired to be quiet about much of anything, and certainly not when it came to his greatness or the inequalities he noticed around him. "Boxing is just a stepping stone to introduce me to the audience," he told reporters. "If I was still in Louisville, Kentucky and never was a boxer, I might get killed next week in some type of freedom struggle and you'd never read the news. Now if I even say the wrong thing, it makes the news."[92]

Clay's style set him at odds with many white fans and journalists—even after he started dominating the boxing world and his unique greatness became indisputable. His antics also rubbed several prominent Black athletes the wrong way. When Clay signed a fight contract to challenge Sonny Liston for the heavyweight title in 1964, Joe Louis was on hand for the televised press conference. A reporter tried asking Liston how he felt about the upcoming fight but Clay interrupted, shouting, "I'm not going to get knocked out .... I move so fast, slow-motion cameras can't catch the speed .... I'm loaded with confidence, I can't be beat!" As Clay continued shouting things like "I don't get hit, I'm so pretty," Joe Louis stood behind Liston, staring daggers at the young, brash contender. Just before the fight, Clay predicted he would knock out Liston in eight rounds. To the astonishment of almost everyone in the boxing world, Clay bested his own prediction when Liston's team threw in the towel after round six. "I'm a bad man," roared the new heavyweight champion, "I shook up the world!"

Sitting ringside at the Ali–Liston fight was Malcolm X, the radical civil rights activist and member of the Nation of Islam (NOI). The appearance of Malcolm X at the fight raised questions about a swirling rumor that Clay had secretly converted to Islam. Shortly after becoming champion, he announced he was, in fact, a member of the NOI and in March declared he had a new name: "Muhammad Ali," he told to the press, adding that the NOI leader Elijah Muhammad had chosen the name for him and that "Muhammad means 'worthy of all praises' and Ali means 'most high.'" Ali also told reporters that he was planning a world tour where he hoped to pray with other Muslims and learn about other cultures.[93] In what became the first of many international tours that Ali took beginning in 1964, he visited Ghana, Nigeria, and Egypt, where he at one point he was photographed riding a camel and holding up the Black Power salute.[94] Zirin writes that at the moment Ali broke into world of sport, the "politics of black power was starting to emerge, and Muhammad Ali became the critical symbol of this transformation."[95]

Ali fought Liston for a rematch in May of 1965 and knocked him out in less than two minutes—still one of the most controversial fight endings in boxing history.[96] Over the next two years, he fought and won eight more matches to retain his title as world heavyweight champion. But by March 1967, the month he dispatched Zora Folley in seven rounds at Madison Square Garden, Ali's bristly relationship with the state reached a breaking point. At a time when the US government was actively enlisting Black athletes to travel the world on America's behalf and sing the praises of their country, Ali declared he was refusing military service after he had been drafted to fight in the Vietnam War. For his actions, Ali was stripped of his title, barred from professional boxing, and faced with a possible five-year prison sentence. Ali refused to be conscripted on religious grounds and proved that he had been ordained as a minister in the NOI. However, he also rooted his opposition in the very narrative the US government was desperate to dispel. "Why should they ask me to put on a uniform and go ten thousand miles from home and drop bombs and bullets on brown people in Vietnam," he asked the press, "while so-called Negro people in Louisville are treated like dogs?"[97] Ali's criticisms mirrored those of other Black civil rights leaders, from Stokely Carmichael to Martin Luther King Jr., with whom Ali developed a friendship. King vehemently opposed the war in Vietnam, calling America "the greatest purveyor of violence in the world today."[98] King rallied to Ali's defense as the criticism surrounding him intensified.[99]

By contrast, the tepidness of some Black athletes toward Ali as a public figure exposed an important generational rift in how Black sport stars understood their role in society. Joe Louis, for one, was quick to denounce Ali's draft dodging. Louis had served in the US military during the Second World War, mostly boxing exhibition matches to keep up morale among the troops. When asked by a friend why he would fight in a "white man's Army," Louis told him there were "[l]ots of things wrong with America, but Hitler ain't going to fix them."[100] Robinson, too, emerged as an outspoken critic of Ali in 1967. Robinson's fraught military background, his legendary career as the pioneer of sport integration, and his continued deference to the American Dream meant Robinson's words carried enormous weight in America. Robinson sat for a televised interview and said Ali's actions were "hurting ... the morale of a lot of young Negro soldiers" fighting in Vietnam. "And the tragedy to me is, Cassius," Robinson said, forcefully emphasizing what Ali called his "slave name," has "made millions of dollars off of the American public, and now he's not willing to show his appreciation to a country that's giving him, in my view, a fantastic opportunity."[101]

But the times were changing and not everyone was so quick to pile on Ali. Several younger Black athletes wanted to hear for themselves if Ali's objections to the war were sincere. A group that included Bill Russell, UCLA basketball superstar Lew Alcindor (who would later convert to Islam and change his name to Kareem Abdul-Jabbar), as well as the legendary NFL running back Jim Brown arranged a meeting with the champ in June 1967, known afterward as the Cleveland Summit. Some of the meeting's participants admitted their original goal was to convince Ali to change his mind and accept a deal they had brokered with the US military where, like Louis, Ali would spend his enlistment boxing in exhibition matches. After several hours, Ali prevailed. When they met the press, Ali told reporters there was "nothing new to say," at least for his part. Other athletes, including Russell, walked away convinced that Ali was not seeking publicity, but genuinely opposed the war based on his religious beliefs.[102]

Shortly after the meeting, Russell penned an article for *Sports Illustrated* in which he explained that the group was "there to give him an out if he wanted one, but [Ali] never wavered for a moment." Russell stated that Ali "has one of the quickest minds I have ever known. At the meeting in Cleveland all of us found out thoroughly that he knew a great deal more

FIGURE 3.2 *Muhammad Ali talks to the media after the famous Cleveland Summit in 1967, where he defended his opposition to the Vietnam War among a group of prominent Black athletes and professionals. Sitting to Ali's right is Bill Russell of the Boston Celtics, a vocal social activist and sport ambassador for the State Department. Listening at the other end of the table is Lew Alcindor, whose activist politics led to him boycott the 1968 Olympics. After joining the NBA, Alcindor converted to Islam and changed his name to Kareem Abdul Jabbar. (Photo by Robert Abbott Sengstacke/Getty Images).*

about the situation than we did." Toward the end of his essay, Russell concluded that the "hysterical and sometimes fanatical criticism of Ali is, it seems to me, a symptom of the deeper sickness of our times .... I'm not worried about Muhammad Ali," he added. "He is better equipped than anyone I know to withstand the trials in store for him. What I'm worried about is the rest of the us."[103]

Three days after Russell's *Sports Illustrated* article hit newsstands, a court convicted Ali of draft evasion, which cemented his ban from professional boxing, imposed a $10,000 fine (a pittance compared to the millions of dollars he lost due to the boxing ban), and carried a five-year prison sentence. Ali appealed the ruling and eventually his case reached the US Supreme Court in 1971. Based on a legal technicality involving the Justice Department's handling of the case, eight justices ruled unanimously to reverse the initial conviction. Shortly afterward, the New York State Supreme Court reinstated Ali's license, though he was no longer the heavyweight champion.

Ali's boxing career was far from over, and many of his most incredible accomplishments were still ahead of him. However, his efforts in the 1960s to oppose the Vietnam War and shed light on the injustices suffered by Black Americans were enough to earn him legendary status in American sport history. After his own conversion to Islam, Kareem Abdul-Jabbar spoke directly about Ali's impact on him and the broader world of sport. Abdul-Jabbar chose to boycott the 1968 Olympics—an important moment in international sport history the next section in this chapter explores—and credited Ali for inspiring him to make that decision. He wrote:

> In 1968, I boycotted the Olympics because I didn't feel I could represent a country that was actively suppressing the civil rights of black people while beating, jailing and murdering those who spoke out against it. I was in part inspired by my involvement in the Cleveland Summit the year before during which myself and several other famous athletes debated the sincerity of Muhammad Ali boycotting the draft as a conscientious objector. Ali's decision cost him his heavyweight title, millions of dollars and threatened his imprisonment …. Ali's choice, and to a much lesser extent my own, gained us nothing and cost us a lot. But in speaking out, in taking direct actions, we both focused the nation's eyes on the disparity in our country and nudged the boulder of civil rights a few feet farther up the mountain.[104]

Cold War Competitions and the Arrival of the Activist Athlete

The Statue of Liberty stares back wearily, and on her face splashed in tears of blood the image of police-led lynch mob seizing a terrified Black man. Along the bottom of the poster, right at the lady's neckline, read the words "The Stigma of American Democracy." Victor Koretsky, the artist who designed the harrowing image in 1963, was one of many Soviet propagandists who understood how to attack the emotional center of the American paradox. A country founded on ideas of liberty and opportunity and that claimed to stand for those same principles during the Cold War, the United States had made sure that its sordid history of racist violence and discrimination would be the softest of targets for its communist adversaries. And that is precisely what the Soviet Union wanted propagandists like Koretsky to do: to call out American hypocrisy and discredit its claims as the morally righteous superpower.

The previous section explored how America went to great lengths and relied heavily on prominent Black Americans to undermine Soviet messaging—with varying degrees of success. But their stories reflect only part of this history. The entire sport landscape became a seedbed for anti-communist rhetoric and epics of national greatness. According to sport historian Toby Rider, US propagandists, like their Soviet counterparts, "used

America's sporting culture to project the vitality and merits of the American way of life and the nation's earnest commitment to liberty, democracy and international peace." Sport became one of several tools "in a broad US propaganda strategy that evolved after 1945," he adds, "as the White House strove to counter the threat of communist expansion in the destabilized conditions of the postwar world."[105]

With US foreign policy becoming more dependent than ever on propaganda, government agencies that had their roots in the Second World War, such as the Central Intelligence Agency (CIA) and Voice of America (VOA), helped carry America's anti-communist messages all over the world. The US government also launched new initiatives to spread its propaganda. In 1953, the Eisenhower administration created the United States Information Agency (USIA) and tasked its agents to coordinate the US propaganda strategy against the Soviet Union. The USIA featured sport heavily in its efforts. Its publications played up President Eisenhower's golf enthusiasm; framed sporting culture in America as evidence of a healthy, active, and happy society; and touted the civic mindedness of athletes and sporting organizations like the YMCA.[106] With so much of the world at play for the Cold War superpowers, capturing sport victories before an increasingly attentive world audience became an around-the-clock job.

Packaging sport as propaganda was an obvious, almost natural, fit, given how it constantly manufactures stories of conflict, struggle, and victory over one's opponent. The theatrical elements of highly competitive sport worked perfectly with the Cold War, which depended so much on an "us versus them" mentality to maintain popular support for the conflicts and crises it wrought. But the arrival of the activist athlete threw open the question of who could control the message in the arena of international sport. Between 1945 and 1970, the global sporting community that had formed over the first half of the century changed considerably. The muscular nationalism that Hitler and Mussolini introduced to the 1936 Olympics in many ways intensified but cast against the flags and anthems were rising calls for social justice from a new generation of athletes. The tension between sport as soft power versus a transnational form of human rights advocacy broke clearer into view, culminating in the iconic 1968 Olympic Games in Mexico City.

Sport across the Iron Curtain

Prior to the Second World War, the Soviet Union disparaged the Olympic movement as a vestige of bourgeois, materialist culture with roots in international capitalist competition and war. Russians in the early twentieth century embraced sport and physical rigor as important vehicles for national rejuvenation and community building. The state, however, made sure to distinguish between communal athletic pursuits and the type of sport Western capitalist countries enjoyed. But like it did for other countries, the

Berlin Olympics in 1936 redefined how Russians, including Joseph Stalin, understood the relationship between sport and national power. According to Toby Rider, after the Second World War the Soviet Union migrated "into the 'imagined community' of globalized sport" which meant expanding its "contacts and exchanges with capitalist countries."[107] In 1945, the Soviet Union joined the International Amateur Athletic Federation (IAAF), and three years later the Politburo announced new measures "to spread sport to every corner of the land" and "help Soviet athletes win world supremacy in major sports in the immediate future."[108] At the IOC's Vienna session in 1951, the Soviet Union formally applied for and received Olympic recognition.[109] In their first Olympic appearance, at the 1952 Helsinki Games, the Soviets nearly nipped the United States in the medal count, coming up just five points short (although well behind in the gold). Four years later, competing against a record seventy-four nations in Melbourne, Australia, the Russians walked away with the most gold, silver, and bronze medals of any country, beating the United States in the total medal count 99–74.[110] The Soviets had surpassed the Americans as Olympic favorites in four short years.[111]

Although the medal table pointed to a changing guard in international sport, another set of headlines out of Melbourne delivered the United States a major Cold War victory. Thirty-eight Eastern European athletes, many from the communist country of Hungary, defected to the United States citing political oppression at home and their desire for personal freedom. The drama involved the new magazine *Sports Illustrated* that in 1954 became another appendage of Henry Luce's sprawling print media empire, which included magazines like *Time*, *Life*, and *Fortune*. Luce was a devotee of America's Cold War mission and used his vast influence to advance US interests in myriad ways.[112] Luce's companies sometimes coordinated efforts with the CIA, and, as Rider shows, "the Melbourne Olympics indicate that *Sports Illustrated* was part of Luce's 'private war' against communism, and that this war was not isolated by any means from the US government."[113]

One of Luce's reporters went to Melbourne with instructions to communicate with the Hungarian National Sports Federation through a Cold War intelligence cutout known as Radio Free Europe (what was, in fact, a useful mouthpiece for the CIA). A Hungarian émigré became the point of contact, established residence near the Olympic festivities in Melbourne, and before long his lodging became, as Rider describes it, "a second home for Hungarian Olympians [who were] welcomed at all hours of the day and night."[114]

The Melbourne defections occurred amid an unfolding crisis in Hungary, a country that had fought for the Allies during the Second World War, occupied by Russia after the war, and folded into the Warsaw Treaty Organization in 1955. Between 1945 and 1956, the USSR established a communist, Soviet-led Hungarian government that stifled democratic politics and struggled to provide materially for the people. Shortly after the start of the 1956 Melbourne Olympics, student protests in Hungary mushroomed into full-scale revolution. By October, a new Hungarian government announced its withdrawal from the Warsaw Pact. In November, the same month the Melbourne Olympics kicked off, Soviet leader Nikita Khrushchev intervened by sending tanks into Budapest and launching airstrikes and artillery bombardments against the new government and dissidents. Over 2,500 Hungarians died in the fighting which ended with the Soviet Union reestablishing control over the country. Tens of thousands of political prisoners were arrested and imprisoned, hundreds executed, and an estimated 200,000 Hungarians fled as political refugees.[115]

At the Olympics, operatives involved in the plan estimated somewhere between 20 and 50 percent of the Hungarian team was looking to defect. Preparations began in Washington near the end of the Games to coordinate the transport of the Eastern European athletes to the United States, who were intimating to the press their intentions not to return home. Reports surfaced of Eastern European athletes "vanishing" across Melbourne, hiding in the Hungarian intermediary's house or in other secure locations waiting for what they hoped would be safe passage to the United States. Eventually, the US government granted asylum to the athletes. In the end thirty-four Hungarian athletes, plus four Polish athletes, boarded a Pan-American aircraft and arrived in the United States in December 1956. Newspapers and, of course, *Sports Illustrated* carried stories of their arrival, including extensive coverage of the athletes' "Freedom Tour" of the United States in 1957.[116] In one article, the magazine bragged that the tour, "successful in America, had apparently been a sensation across the Iron Curtain."[117] Despite losing its inside position as an Olympic power, the story of the Hungarian defections represented a significant propaganda win for the United States.

Still, the Soviet teams' accruing victories became a major dilemma for US athletic and government officials. Hockey, for instance, although a marginal professional sport in America, was a cause of endless embarrassment for the United States in the 1950s and 1960s, punctuated by a disastrous performance in the 1963 World Ice Hockey Classic when the United States lost five of seven games including a humiliating 17–2 drubbing to Sweden. The outcome spurred President John F. Kennedy to direct an aide, David Hackett, to investigate why American hockey was so far behind the Soviets. Hackett wrote back that "unless we can generate more interest, support, and most important of all, financial backing, there is every possibility" the US national team would continue its slide in the world of hockey.[118]

In addition to the defections in Melbourne, sport also played a more general role in East–West cultural exchange during the early Cold War. The Minister to Romania, Robert Thayer, noted the effect the soft power of sport was having in Eastern Europe, telling Secretary of State Dulles in 1957 that "if you had seen as I did the rising stands of thousands of Rumanians acclaiming three United States athletes marching behind the American flag at an International Track Meet in Bucharest last fall you would appreciate the adulation which these people have for our country and our people."[119] Around the same time, another US diplomat named William Macy marveled at how sport, as a "cultural field," created possibilities for "communication to take place between many thousands of citizens of both countries [East and West]."[120]

However, Americans were becoming more aware of their competition in the field of sport diplomacy. In 1958, US officials warned the National Security Council that the Soviets were promoting sport, especially soccer, "to gain added prestige in Latin American opinion and to diminish the significance of Latin America's traditional cultural ties with and dependence on the United States and Western Europe."[121] Government intervention across US sport intensified over the 1960s, and as it did, Americans found other ways to discredit Soviet sport success. When they could not beat them, Americans found impugning the personal integrity of Soviet athletes an effective way to self soothe.

Drugs, Sex, and Gender

Rumors that Eastern European athletes were using illicit drugs began making headlines at the 1952 Olympics, the first ever to include the Soviet Union. Although they came up just short in the medal count, the Soviets performed very well, particularly in weightlifting where they won three of seven competitions and came in second in two others. Historians John Gleaves and Matthew Llewellyn, who write about performance-enhancing drugs (PEDs) and the Cold War, explain that prior to the 1952 Games, the "Soviets mobilized for success on an unprecedented scale ... implementing an elaborate, scientific system replete with pioneering training methods and professional practices."[122] When US officials were asked to comment on the surprising success of Soviet weightlifters, one American claimed he saw Russian athletes using "a drug, or a stimulant or something," implying that the Soviets were guilty of doping. "Before each lift," he said, "a bottle of the stuff would be put under the competitor's nose and he'd take a deep wiff then his eyes would become glassy and he'd start lifting like a maniac." The US weightlifting coach Bob Hoffman also claimed that the Soviets "were taking that hormone stuff to increase their strength."[123] Speculation in the press about a Soviet doping program intensified after their first Olympics medal count victory in 1956 and then again after they trounced the competition four years later in Rome, where they won five of seven weightlifting events.[124]

Americans openly accused the Soviets of using steroids to cheat; however, US athletes were often guilty of doing the same. The 1956 US hammer-thrower Hal Connolly admitted to drug use during his Olympic competitions, as did the Olympic shot-putters Dalls Long and Randy Matson. The US gold medalist in the 1968 decathlon, Bill Toomey, claimed to have used PEDs. One US physician stated that "more than one-third of the US track and field team was using anabolic steroids" at the pre-Olympic workout camp in Lake Tahoe in 1968. Over time, Americans dropped the conceit that only the Soviets used PEDs. The real problem, they began admitting, was that the Soviets had the better dope. In 1971, US weightlifter Ken Patera told the *New York Times* that "when I hit Munich next year, I'll weigh in at 340, maybe 350 pounds. Then we'll see which are better—[the Soviet's] steroids or mine." Another US team physician later admitted that "if every member of the US Olympic weightlifting team who took non-therapeutic drugs was disqualified, the United States would not have a team at Munich" for the 1972 Games.[125]

In 1976, the US government allotted $2 million to the US Olympic Committee (USOC) "to establish a major sports medicine program in the hope that 'American athletes can start utilizing the same complex medical data that has benefited athletes in Communist-bloc countries.'" Dr. Irving Dardi, chair of the USOC sports medicine program, stated plainly that "we want to go into blood doping, steroids and all these other areas that have sprung up in the athletics. Our purpose is to leave no stone unturned."[126] Even after US athletes were busted for doping—which occurred several times—the US press continued to paint the Soviets as the only country guilty of steroid use. Americans were the pure, authentic athletes, so the story went, while Soviets were pill-riddled state agents who performed more like machines than men. Or, in the case of Soviet female athletes, more like men than women.

Indeed, with few exceptions, Soviet women dominated international sport in the early Cold War and sent the United States in search of new answers to explain away American losses. US women like Wilma Rudolph and the Lady Tigerbelles were famous exceptions, as were others, like the 1957 US women's national basketball team which won that year's World Basketball Championship held in Brazil. But as historian Kevin Witherspoon writes, when Soviet women began winning international basketball tournaments, "American officials elected to minimize the significance of the women's [national basketball] games and eventually to discontinue them altogether."[127] Witherspoon adds that sportswriters typically "emphasized the feminine qualities of the US players" compared to their Soviet counterparts "as a way of dismissing [American] defeats."[128] This gendered approach to covering women's sport in the Cold War extended to other arenas, particularly the Olympics, where harsh judgments about femininity eventually led to accusations of sex deception by Soviet athletes.

The fact that Soviet women were pivotal to the USSR's medal count victories "set off alarm bells in the United States," writes historian Lindsay Pieper. Insistent "that masculinized Soviet female competitors unfairly skewed the medal count, the US public condemned the Soviet athletes and advocated for the introduction of sex testing."[129] At the 1952 Games, where Soviet women earned twenty-three medals compared to eight won by US women, rumors swirled that the athletes were men disguised as women. The pattern repeated at the 1956 and 1960 Games. Despite what Americans wanted to believe, in truth Soviet women had no restrictions on their training which was a huge Olympic advantage. By comparison, the USOC discouraged women from building their muscles because of how it might affect their femininity. One US journalist wrote that "most of the Russian athletes are far from pretty. They're masculine looking, big-limbed, hard-faced girls, with legs and biceps of an all-American fullback."[130] Meanwhile, US government and athletic officials, all men, debated barring American women from competing in the more "masculine" events like shot-putting because those were not appropriate for the female form.

American paranoia about Soviet sex deception precipitated the use of sex testing at the Olympics starting in 1966. The British athlete Mary Peters recalled "being ordered to lie down, pull up her knees, and remain still while doctors scrutinized her body." It was, she said, "the most crude and degrading experience I have ever known in my life."[131] Canadian women also reported unwanted genital and breast exams. "Ignoring the athletes' humiliation and declaring the technique effective for detecting imposters," writes Pieper, Olympic officials continued performing intrusive physical examinations of female athletes through the 1960s. The dominance of Soviet women, combined with repressive gender norms in the United States, created a toxic mix of sexism and personal degradation that hung over Cold War Olympics. Watching Soviet women capture medals in events like shotput and discus throwing led many Americans to believe that "individuals who excelled in athletics could not be real women."[132]

In 1967, at the bequest of US officials, the IOC began using chromatin tests, which evaluate athletes' X chromosomes, and stipulated that only the athletes with two true X chromosomes could participate in the women's Olympics. Almost immediately some women with incomplete or inconclusive tests (which are common with such testing) were barred from the Olympics. Predictably, US officials only wanted Soviet athletes to be subject to the testing, saying it was ludicrous to test American women. Even as scientists and health experts criticized chromosome testing as a wildly imperfect method to determine a person's sex, the practice persisted thanks largely to US insistence. Only when the Cold War ended did Americans begin to rethink the necessity of sex testing in sport. Several international sporting organizations banned chromosome testing in 1992 and in 1999 the IOC ended the policy. "The strong, powerful Soviet women became the primary targets because they did not embody US notions of conventional femininity," Pieper concludes. "From the US perspective, sex testing was a necessary tool for defending American gender norms in sport."[133]

American Credibility, Mal Whitfield, and the 1968 Olympics

While America's preeminence in international sport slipped away, its reputation as a champion of personal freedom and self-government became harder to defend. The intensification of the Civil Rights Movement between 1964 and 1968 undermined US propaganda in the Cold War and created a wider space for US athletes to bring attention to the movement. The year 1968 proved a breaking point in a long history of whitewashing the violence and oppression that had underpinned American democracy for almost two centuries. In that year, deployments to Vietnam topped 500,000; protests against the war intensified and grew violent; major civil rights leaders, including Martin Luther King Jr. and Robert Kennedy, were killed by assassins; riots erupted in most major US cities; and a calamitous Democratic National Convention broadcast on television featured tear gas and clashes between protesters and police. Heading into the Mexico City Olympics in October 1968, the United States had not looked more divided and vulnerable since the era of the Civil War.

Even the most patriotic Americans, like the Olympic champion Mal Whitfield, were losing patience watching their country tear itself apart. Whitfield served as a Tuskegee Airman during the Second World War and flew again for the US Air Force in the Korean War, where he kept up on his Olympic training by exercising in between sorties with a .45-caliber on his hip.[134] Between 1948 and 1952, Whitfield cemented himself as one of America's greatest Olympic track stars by winning five Olympic medals, including two golds in the 800-meter run and one gold in the 4X400 relay. Whitfield was also one of the US government's favorite sport ambassadors. He toured internationally as part of the AAU in the 1940s. In 1955, after retiring from Olympic competition, he headlined a State Department goodwill tour of Africa. Whitfield once said that his tour, scheduled to last just three months, "turned out to be more than a quarter century of involvement in African sports programs." Whitfield became a leading architect of African track and field training, in part by securing a huge grant from Mobil Oil Company to train young athletes in West Africa. Witherspoon, who credits Whitfield for starting the tradition of world-class runners coming from Africa, writes that Mal "perfectly represented the idealized racial vision [the US government] sought to portray abroad." An Olympic gold medalist and military veteran, Whitfield "demonstrated that he had the restraint and discipline to follow orders but also that he was accustomed to working in an integrated environment and under white leadership."[135]

Whitfield, like Jackie Robinson and Joe Louis, embodied a generation of Black athletes who could be critical of race relations in America, but still supported US national interests abroad. Therefore, it came as a surprise when ahead of the 1964 Tokyo Games, Whitfield penned an article for

Ebony magazine titled "Let's Boycott the Olympics." More than a decade removed from his last Olympic appearance and still deeply involved in sport diplomacy in Africa, Whitfield had watched from afar as the reactionary politics of white supremacists clashed against African Americans demanding their civil rights. The breaking point for Whitfield was the repeated use of the Senate filibuster—a legislative procedure that proponents of Jim Crow had used throughout the twentieth century to block debate and legislation on civil rights reform—which was keeping the Civil Rights Act and Voting Rights Act from advancing through Congress. "I advocate that every Negro athlete eligible to participate in the Olympic Games in Japan," he wrote in *Ebony*, "boycott the games if Negro Americans by that time have not been guaranteed full and equal rights." He speculated that "if every single Negro athlete ... simply decided to stay at home and not compete because adequate civil rights legislation had not been passed by Congress," their actions "would seriously dampen American foreign policy" and thus convince "sensible" US politicians "that freedom means a great deal more to Negroes than nice-sounding promises."[136]

According to Thomas, many Olympic-eligible Black athletes sympathized with Whitfield but were "unwilling to seriously consider forfeiting their Olympic dreams."[137] Yet as social unrest intensified over the 1960s, and as more African Americans like Muhammad Ali began to use their platforms to speak out about the injustices of their own country, the mood started to change. In 1967, a group of amateur Black athletes created the Olympic Project for Human Rights (OPHR) and called for a mass boycott of the 1968 Games. "Their goal was nothing less than to expose how the United States used black athletes to project a lie," Zirin argues, "both at home and internationally."[138] Lew Alcindor was a leading OPHR activist and one of the few who actually did boycott the 1968 Games. "White America seemed ready to do anything necessary to stop the progress of civil rights, and I thought going to Mexico would seem like I was either fleeing the issue or more interested in my career than in justice," he explained.[139] The momentum behind the OPHR rankled many prominent white politicians, including then-governor Ronald Reagan who accused the Black athletes of "contributing nothing toward harmony between the races."[140] Influential Black athletes were divided over the idea of a boycott. Jackie Robinson voiced his support for the OPHR, while Jesse Owens and Joe Louis disavowed the movement for what Owens called "political aggrandizement."[141]

The OPHR's most prominent spokesperson was Tommie Smith, whom Moore calls "the greatest sprinter of his generation," and soon-to-be one of the most iconic sport figures in US history.[142] Smith had grown up experiencing both sides of America. He came from a biracial family of farm workers in California and witnessed the destructive power of racism as a child. But due to his prodigious athletic talents, Smith had also tasted opportunity and the fruits of personal excellence. He earned a college

scholarship to San Jose State, was drafted by the professional football team
the Cincinnati Bengals, and, later, earned a master's degree from Goddard
College. As much as any athlete of his day, Smith understood that sport,
while an imperfect measurement for social progress in America, was one of
the most powerful tools Black Americans like himself had to change public
perceptions about race relations in the United States.

Smith was a fierce advocate of the OPHR's plans, but when momentum
for the boycott waned as the 1968 Games neared, he decided to participate
and use the platform the Olympics provided to signal to his country and
the world his state of mind. After winning the gold medal in the 200-meter
sprint, Smith and his bronze-winning US teammate, John Carlos, ascended
the medal podium and stood waiting for the "Star-Spangled Banner" to play.
When the music began, Smith and Carlos, each wearing a single black glove,
raised their fists and bowed their heads in solidarity with the Black Power
movement.[143]

In his book *The Revolt of the Black Athlete*, sociologist Harry Edwards
describes how years after the 1968 Games, Smith told Edwards that "the
gesture of the bowed head was in remembrance of the fallen warriors in
the black liberation struggle in America—Malcolm X., Martin Luther King
Jr., and others."[144] In fact, nearly everything about the protest had been

FIGURE 3.3 *Tommie Smith (gold podium) and John Carlos (bronze podium)
raise their gloved fists in solidarity with the Black Power movement during the US
national anthem at the 1968 Olympics in Mexico City. (Bettmann/Contributor via
Getty Images).*

carefully orchestrated, down the Olympians' socks. Smith explained to the famous broadcaster Howard Cosell:

> I wore a black right-hand glove and Carlos wore a left-hand glove of the same pair. My raised right hand stood for the power in black America. Carlos' raised left hand stood for the unity of black America. Together they formed an arch of unity and power. The black scarf around my neck stood for black pride. The black socks with no shoes stood for black poverty in racist America. The totality of our effort was the regaining of black dignity.[145]

Carlos said afterward that he believed to most whites, Black men like him "were not supposed to think." He and Smith wanted "people to know that we are not animals ... We wanted all the black people in the world—the little grocer, the man with the shoe repair store—to know that when that medal hangs on my chest and Tommie's chest, it hangs on his also."[146] For their actions, both were kicked out of the Olympic Games and faced incredible backlash when they returned home. Although the Black press largely supported the Olympians' actions, white Americans were irate. Brent Musberger, the legendary American sports announcer, called them "dark-skinned storm troopers" and the Los Angeles Times accused the athletes of making a "Nazi-like salute" during the national anthem.[147]

Both men struggled to find work afterward and suffered social ostracization because many whites saw them as deviant radicals who did not sufficiently love their country. But over time, the iconic image of both men raising their fists atop the Olympic podium became an enduring symbol of Black pride. Moore writes that "Smith and Carlos were heroes in their community. Blacks greeted each other with clinched fists in the air, hung the famous photo of Smith and Carlos on their wall, and invited them to campus to speak." Although structural changes were still desperately needed, their efforts, Moore adds, created for Black athletes "a new platform from which to speak, a stage to challenge the status quo, and an atmosphere to demand change."[148]

The 1968 Olympics popularized the tradition of politicizing national anthems during sporting events. Anthem protests became a worldwide phenomenon in the early twenty-first century, but in fact they have a much longer history. A few weeks after the 1968 Games, the college basketball star Chris Wood lost his scholarship for protesting the anthem before a game by refusing to stand with his team.[149] Perhaps most surprisingly, Jackie Robinson disclosed in his autobiography that he too had a hard time feeling pride in his country when he heard the "Star-Spangled Banner" or saw the American flag. "As I write this, I cannot stand and sing the national anthem," he admitted. "I cannot salute the flag; I know that I am a black man in a white world. In 1972, in 1947, at my birth in 1919, I know that I never had it made."[150] With those words, Robinson, who embodied so much of the nation's history in the early Cold War, revealed the depths of the rupture that had formed in the landscape of sport. Although many white observers would continue to demand otherwise, the time of compliant athletes sticking to sports and turning down the platform their athletic greatness had given them was over. The era of the activist athlete had arrived.

Notes

1   Jackie Robinson, *I Never Had It Made: An Autobiography of Jackie Robinson* (New York: Ecco Publishers, 2003), 18.

2   Ibid., 13.

3   Ibid., 20.

4   Ibid., 22–3.

5   Martin Luther King Jr., "Hall of Famer," *New York Amsterdam News*, August 4, 1962.

6   Lizabeth Cohen, *A Consumers' Republic: The Politics of Mass Consumption in Postwar America* (New York: Vintage Books, 2003), 11.

7   Ibid., 302.

8   George B. Kirsch, *Golf in America* (Chicago: University of Illinois Press, 2009), 188.

9   Josza Jr., *American Sports Empire*, 2.

10 David Surdam, *Run to Glory and Profits: The Economic Rise of the NFL during the 1950s* (Lincoln: University of Nebraska Press, 2013), 5.

11 "Russians Find US 'Futbol' Rough Game, Designed to Create 'Bandits and Haters,'" *NYT*, November 19, 1952, 9 quoted in ibid., 8.

12 Zirin, *A People's History of Sports in the United States*, 127.

13 Josza Jr., *American Sports Empire*, 122.

14 Pete Rozelle quoted in Surdam, *Run to Glory and Profits*, 246.

15 Rozelle quoted in ibid., 253.

16 Ibid., 123.

17 Michael Oriard, *Brand NFL: Making and Selling America's Favorite Sport* (Chapel Hill: University of North Carolina Press, 2010), 16.

18 Ibid., 18.

19 Louis Moore quoted in Jack Silverstein, "Throwback: The Truth about George Halas and the NFL's Ban on Black Players," *Windy City Gridiron*, December 5, 2019, URL: https://www.windycitygridiron.com/2019/8/28/20836166/chicago-bears-100-throwback-1936-jersey-truth-about-george-halas-nfl-12-year-ban-on-black-players [accessed 2.27.21].

20 Ibid. As Silverstein notes, Halas once claimed that "the game didn't have the appeal to black players at the time. Probably they didn't realize the possibilities of the game at the time"—a statement that is both ludicrous and undermined both by the league's own early history and the enormous success of Black collegiate football players during the era of the NFL's color line.

21 Surdam, *Run to Glory and Profits*, 127.

22 Oriard, *Brand NFL*, 20.

23 Ibid., 10.

24 Peterson, *From Cages to Jump Shots*, 125.

25 Ibid., 130.

26 Zirin, *A People's History of Sports in the United States,* 56; 152. For more on the obstacles Black basketball players faced, see Kuska, *Hot Potato*, 161–3.

27 Peterson, *From Cages to Jump Shots*, 130.

28 Charley Rosen, *The First Tip-Off: The Incredible Story of the Birth of the NBA* (New York: McGraw-Hill Education, 2008), 128.

29 Peterson, *From Cages to Jump Shots*, 167.

30 Ibid., 173.

31 Phil Luciano, "After 65 Years, Should Bradley Forgive Squeaky Melchiorre?" *The Peoria Journal Star* (October 1, 2016), URL: https://www.pjstar.com/news/20161001/luciano-after-65-years-should-bradley-forgive-squeaky-melchiorre [accessed 2. 25.2021].

32 Albert J. Figone and Albert G. Figone, "Gambling and College Basketball: The Scandal of 1951," *Journal of Sport History* 16, no.1 (1989): 44.

33 Peterson, *From Cages to Jump Shots*, 176.

34 See Table 1.2, "Per Game Attendance, by Sport League, for Selected Seasons" in Josza Jr., *American Sports Empire*, 2.

35 Peterson, *From Cages to Jump Shots*, 182.

36 Louis Moore, *We Will Win the Day: The Civil Rights Movement, the Black Athletes, and the Quest for Equality* (Denver, CO: Praeger, 2017), xiv.

37 Baseball's statistical repositories lack uniformity when it comes to Robinson's Negro League numbers. The statistics used by this study come from Jackie Robinson's *Baseball Reference* career statistics page, URL: https://www.baseball-reference.com/register/player.fcgi?id=robins002jac [accessed 3.1.2021].

38 Sam Jethroe quoted in Glen Stout, "Tryout and Fallout: Race, Jackie Robinson, and the Red Sox," *Massachusetts Historical Review* 6 (2004): 22.

39 Ibid.

40 Thomas Zeiler, *Jackie Robinson and Race in America: A Brief History with Documents* (New York: Bedford/St. Martin's, 2014), 17.

41 Rickey quoted in ibid., 19.

42 Ibid., 98.

43 For excellent treatments on Jackie Robinson's impact on American sport and society, see: Thomas Zeiler's *Jackie Robinson and Race in America*; Robert Peterson's *Only the Ball was White*.

44 Mark Armou and Daniel Levitt, "Baseball Demographics, 1947–2016," *Society for American Baseball Research*, URL: https://sabr.org/bioproj/topic/baseball-demographics-1947-2016/ [accessed 3.4.2021]. The data in this article point to some remarkable conclusions based on their demographic analysis of MLB. For instance, even though only about 18.5 percent of the league was Black between 1975 and 1985,

African Americans contributed 25 per cent of the total WAR over those ten seasons, which suggests at just *how much* above average Black players had to be to get a shot in the majors. Less than 20 percent of its manpower, they were generating 25 percent of all league wins. As Armou and Levitt show, African Americans continued to overperform their demographic representation in the game through the twenty-first century.

45   Burgos, *Playing America's Game*, 212.

46   Armou and Levitt, "Baseball Demographics, 1947–2016." See also Louis Moore, "Major League Baseball Had a Chance to Stop the Drain of Black Players from Baseball," *Global Sport Matters*, October 6, 2021, URL: https://globalsportmatters. com/culture/2021/10/06/major-league-baseball-drain-black-players-darryl-strawberry-bill-lucas-eric-davis/ [accessed 10.10.21].

47   A "five-tool" baseball player refers to someone who excels at hitting for contact, hitting for power, throwing, fielding, and running. By any metric, Mays could do it all.

48   Many baseball fans regard Mays as the greatest of his era, and several advanced statistics bear that out. The metric called "Wins Above Replacement" (or WAR) attempts to measure how many wins a player adds to their team. Based on WAR, Mays stands alone, with a career WAR of 156.2, compared to Mantle's 110.2, Williams 121.9, and Aaron 143.1. Robinson, who played in MLB for a much shorter time than the others in this list, ended with a 61.7 career WAR. For more information on the WAR statistic, see "Baseball-Reference.com WAR Explained," *Baseball Reference*, URL: https://www.baseball-reference.com/about/war_explained.shtml [accessed 3.3.21].

49   Moore, *We Will Win the Day*, 150.

50   Mays quoted in ibid.

51   Burgos, *Playing America's Game*, 213–15.

52   Ibid., 215.

53   Elias, *The Empire Strikes Out*, 197–8.

54   Young quoted in Damion Thomas, *Globetrotting: African American Athletes and the Cold War* (Champaign: University of Illinois Press, 2012), 30.

55   Thomas, *Globetrotting*, 35.

56   "Annual Report of the Committee on Un-American Activities for the Year 1949," prepared and released by the Committee on Un-American Activities, US House of Representatives (Washington, DC, March 15, 1950), 13.

57   Moore, *We Will Win the Day*, 146.

58   Thomas, *Globetrotting*, 4.

59   Mary Dudziak, *Cold War Civil Rights* (New Jersey: Princeton University Press, 2000), 12.

60   Thomas, *Globetrotting*, 10.

61   Peterson, *Cages to Jump Shots*, 105–7; 130–1.

62   Thomas, *Globetrotting*, 57.

63   Letter from Dean Acheson to American Legation—Damascus, July 28, 1952 quoted in ibid., 47.

64 Thomas, *Globetrotting*, 48.

65 Ibid., 45–8.

66 Ibid., 74.

67 Wilma Rudolph quoted in Arlisha R. Norwood, "Wilma Rudolph (1940–1994)," National Women's History Museum, URL: https://www.womenshistory.org/ education-resources/biographies/wilma-rudolph [accessed 5.1.2021].

68 Cat Ariail, "'One of the Greatest Ambassadors that the United States Has Ever Sent Abroad': Wilma Rudolph, American Athletic Icon for the cold War and the Civil Rights Movement," in Toby C. Rider and Kevin B. Witherspoon, eds., *Defending the American Way of Life: Sport, Culture, and the Cold War* (Fayetteville: University of Arkansas Press, 2018), 141.

69 Cat Ariail, *Passing the Baton: Black Women Track Stars and American Identity* (Champaign: University of Illinois Press, 2020), 157.

70 Ariail, "'One of the Greatest Ambassadors that the United States Has Ever Sent Abroad'," 143.

71 Ibid.

72 "World Speed Queen," *NYT*, September 9, 1960, 20.

73 Ariail, "'One of the Greatest Ambassadors that the United States Has Ever Sent Abroad'," 147–8.

74 *Daily Express* quoted in ibid., 147.

75 *NYT*, quoted in ibid., 149.

76 Ibid., 151, 152.

77 Ibid., 153–4.

78 Moore, *We Will Win the Day*, 151.

79 Bill Russell interview with Taylor Branch for the Civil Rights History Project Collection, Archive of American Folk Culture, American Folklife Center, Library of Congress, Washington, DC, May 12, 2013, URL: https://www.loc.gov/ item/2015669187/ [access 5.1.2021].

80 Ibid.

81 Russell quoted in Moore, *We Will Win the Day*, 153.

82 Ibid., 152.

83 Russell interview with Branch, Civil Rights History Project Collection.

84 Ibid.

85 Thomas, *Globetrotting*, 1.

86 Russell quoted in ibid., 2.

87 Russell quoted in ibid.

88 Ibid., 2–3.

89 Ibid., 2.

90 Muhammad Ali interview with Michael Parkinson, BBC Archive, URL: https://www.bbc. co.uk/archive/muhammad-ali-why-is-everything-white/z3v4ydm [accessed 4.16.21].

91 Ibid.

92 Ibid.

93 Jim Axelrod, "The Life of 'The Greatest,'" *CBS News*, June 5, 2016, URL: https://www.cbsnews.com/news/the-life-of-the-greatest/ [last accessed 4.20.21].

94 "In Pictures: Muhammad Ali's Love Affair with Africa," *BBC News*, June 9, 2016, URL: https://www.bbc.com/news/world-africa-36469288 [accessed 4.20.21].

95 Zirin, *A People's History of Sports in the United States*, 139.

96 For more on the accusations of a fixed fight, see Richard O'Brien, "Remembering One of Boxing's Most Controversial Fights: Ali Liston II," *Sports Illustrated* [hereafter *SI*], May 21, 2015, URL: https://www.si.com/boxing/2015/05/21/ali-liston-ii-neil-leifer-50-years-later [accessed 5.1.2021].

97 Ali quoted in Louis Moore, *We Will Win the Day*, 170.

98 Martin Luther King Jr., "Beyond Vietnam," The Martin Luther King Jr., Research and Education Institute, Stanford University, URL: https://kinginstitute.stanford.edu/king-papers/documents/beyond-vietnam [accessed 4.20.21].

99 Moore, *We Will Win the Day*, 171.

100 Ira Berkow, "Joe Louis Was There Earlier," *NYT*, April 22, 1997, URL: https://www.nytimes.com/1997/04/22/sports/joe-louis-was-there-earlier.html#:~:text=When%20he%20knocked%20out%20Max,emblematic%20of%20a%20powerful%20America.&text=Louis%20looked%20at%20him%2C%20and [accessed 4.24.21]. As this article also explains, in the 1970s, Louis told Berkow that "Jackie was my hero. He don't bite his tongue for nothing. I just don't have the guts, you might call it, to say what he says." In the same interview Louis said that Paul Robeson was more important than Martin Luther King Jr. to the advancement of civil rights— an astonishing assessment considering the fallout from Jackie Robinson's HUAC testimony and, more critically, the fact that Louis's defense of Robeson centered on the actor's stance toward the Soviet Union.

101 Robinson quoted in Krishnadev Calamur, "Muhammad Ali and Vietnam," *The Atlantic*, June 4, 2016, URL: https://www.theatlantic.com/news/archive/2016/06/muhammad-ali-vietnam/485717/ [accessed 4.24.21].

102 "June 4, 1967: Muhammad Ali Summit," *Zinn Education Project*, URL: https://www.zinnedproject.org/news/tdih/muhammed-ali-summit/ [accessed 10.14.21].

103 Bill Russell, "I Am Not Worried about Ali," *SI*, June 19, 1967, 19–22, URL: https://vault.si.com/vault/1967/06/19/42943#&gid=ci0258beed701b278a&pid=42943—027—image [accessed 4.24.21].

104 Kareem Abdul-Jabbar, "Republicans Want Black People to Disappear. Sport Leagues Can Help Stop Them," *The Guardian*, April 23, 2021, URL: https://www.theguardian.com/sport/2021/apr/23/republicans-want-black-people-to-disappear-sports-leagues-can-help-stop-them [accessed 4.23.21]. For more on Abdul-Jabbar's activism in the 1960s, see John Matthew Smith, "'It's Really Not My Country': Lew Alcindor and the Revolt of the Black Athlete," *Journal of Sport History* 36, no. 2 (Summer 2009): 223–44.

105 Toby C. Rider, "Projecting America: Sport and Early US Cold War Propaganda, 1947–1960," in Toby C. Rider and Kevin B. Witherspoon, eds., *Defending the American Way of Life: Sport, Culture, and the Cold War* (Fayetteville: University of Arkansas Press, 2018), 14–15.

106 Toby C. Rider, *Cold War Games: Propaganda, the Olympics, and US Foreign Policy* (Champagne: University of Illinois, 2016), 9–29.

107 Rider, *Cold War Games*, 42.

108 Communist party resolution quoted in ibid., 43.

109 Ibid., 42–7.

110 See *Olympic.org*, URL: https://www.olympic.org/helsinki-1952; https://www.olympic.org/melbourne-stockholm-1956 [accessed 3.17.21].

111 For more, see Jenifer Parks, "Verbal Gymnastics: Sports, Bureaucracy, and the Soviet Union's Entrance into the Olympic Games, 1946–1952," in Stephen Wagg and David Andrews, eds., *East Plays West: Sport and the Cold War* (Oxfordshire: Routledge, 2007), 27–44.

112 Henry Luce "American Century," *Diplomatic History* 23, no. 2 (1999): 159–71. URL: http://www.jstor.org/stable/24913736 [accessed 6.9.2021].

113 Rider, *Cold War Games*, 113.

114 Ibid., 112–15.

115 Immerman and Goedde, *The Oxford Handbook of the Cold* War, 177.

116 "Hungarians Discover America," *SI*, April 8, 1957, URL: https://vault.si.com/vault/1957/04/08/45737#&gid=ci0258bfa2b02326ef&pid=45737—009—image [accessed 5.6.21].

117 Richard Neale, "Across a Free Land," *SI*, April 8, 1957, URL: https://vault.si.com/vault/1957/04/08/across-a-free-land [accessed 5.6.21].

118 David Hackett, Special Assistant to the Attorney General, to President John F. Kennedy, Memorandum titled "Why Sweden Beat the United States 17–2," March 14, 1963, John F. Kennedy Presidential Library, Cold War International History Project, URL: https://digitalarchive.wilsoncenter.org/document/122519 [accessed 5.8.21]. See also John Soares, "Cold War, Hot Ice: International Ice Hockey, 1947–1980," *Journal of Sport History* 34, no. 2 (2007): 207–30; John Soares, "'Very Correct Adversaries': The Cold War on Ice from 1947 to the Squaw Valley Olympics," *International Journal of the History of Sport* 30, no. 13 (2013): 1536–53.

119 Letter from the Minister in Romania (Thayer) to Secretary of State John Foster Dulles, February 6, 1957, *FRUS* 1955–1957, Eastern Europe Volume XXV 1955/1957, 564, URL: https://search.library.wisc.edu/digital/AYZR7KXU5KUQO487/pages/A6HSGJNLKROLAV8Q.

120 Letter From the Secretary of State's Special Assistant for East-West Exchanges (Lacy) to Secretary of State Dulles, July 25, 1958, *FRUS* 1958–1960. Eastern Europe; Finland; Greece; Turkey Volume X, Part 2 1958/1960, 13, URL: https://search.library.wisc.edu/digital/AZXLZEKXYACOXA8O/pages/A2LJQH3ITRDJEJ85.

121 Special Report by the Operations Coordinating Board to the National Security Council, November 26, 1958, *FRUS*, 1958–1960. American Republics Volume V 1958/1960 57, URL: https://search.library.wisc.edu/digital/A3BMVEFFZCJK6F8E/pages/AKE3KPNJATWZZU83.

122 John Gleaves and Matthew P. Llewelyn, "The Big Arms Race: Doping and the Cold War Defense of American Exceptionalism," in Rider *Defending the American Way of Life*, 52.

123   Quoted in ibid., 53.

124   Seymour Topping, "Soviet Chief Sets 2 Olympic Goals," *NYT*, August 10, 1960, p. 40.

125   Gleaves and Llewelyn, "The Big Arms Race," 56–7.

126   Ibid., 60.

127   Kevin Witherspoon, "America's Team: The US Women's National Basketball Team Confronts the Soviets, 1958–1969," in Rider, *Defending the American Way of Life*, 100.

128   Ibid., 110.

129   Lindsay Parks Pieper, "'Wolves in Skirts?' Sex Testing in Cold War Women's Sport," in ibid., 91–2.

130   Quoted in ibid., 92.

131   Quoted in ibid.

132   Ibid.

133   Ibid., 98.

134   Frank Litsky, "Mal Whitfield, Olympic Gold Medalist and Tuskegee Airman, Dies at 91," *NYT*, November 19, 1945, URL: https://www.nytimes.com/2015/11/20/sports/mal-whitfield-olympic-gold-medalist-and-tuskegee-airman-dies-at-91.html [accessed 5.11.21].

135   Kevin Witherspoon, "'An Outstanding Representative of America': Mal Whitfield and America's Black Sports Ambassadors in Africa," 135.

136   Mal Whitfield, "Let's Boycott the Olympics," *Ebony*, March 1964, p. 95.

137   Thomas, *Globetrotting*, 164.

138   Zirin, *A People's History of Sport in the United States*, 161.

139   Kareem Abdul-Jabbar, *Coach Wooden and Me: Our 50-Year Friendship On and Off the Court* (New York: Grand Central Publishing, 2017), 139.

140   Ronald Reagan quoted in Zirin, *A People's History of Sport in the United States*, 165.

141   Ibid., 169–70.

142   Moore, *We Will Win the Day*, 175.

143   Harry Edwards, *The Revolt of the Black Athlete: 50th Anniversary Edition* (Urbana: University of Illinois Press, 2017), 76–93.

144   Ibid., 86.

145   Smith quoted in ibid.

146   Quoted in Moore, *We Will Win the Day*, 182.

147   Quoted in Zirin, *A People's History of Sports in the United States*, 171–2.

148   Moore, *We Will Win the Day*, 183–4.

149   Zirin, *A People's History of Sports in the United States*, 176.

150   Robinson, *I Never Had It Made*, 27.

Athlete Spotlight #3:
Althea Gibson

FIGURE 3.4 *Althea Gibson stretches for a backhand at a tennis tournament in 1956. Gibson was a multi-sport athlete who helped integrate professional women's tennis and golf, while also serving the State Department as a sport ambassador during the Cold War. (Photo by ullstein bild/ullstein bild via Getty Images).*

Althea Gibson was born in 1927 in Silver, South Carolina, the child of sharecroppers who moved to Harlem, New York, amid the Great Migration when Althea was three. Although she had escaped the South, her childhood was nonetheless violent and unmoored. Her father was abusive, she rarely attended school, and spent her days on the streets. Sport became a refuge of its own for Gibson, and she quickly proved to be a gifted athlete. Gibson excelled in many sports, but her talent in tennis shone brightest early in life.[1]

Initially, Gibson could only play segregated tournaments. She soon proved herself the best African American woman in tennis and in 1950 she became the first Black woman to compete in the US Open. By 1953 she was the seventh-ranked women's tennis player in the world. She won her first Grand Slam title in 1956 at the French Open and then went on to win consecutive US Open and Wimbledon titles in 1957 and 1958—all firsts for a Black woman in tennis. The Black press cheered her meteoric rise, while critics eventually acknowledged her greatness. The Associated Press named her the Female Athlete of the Year in 1957, the same year she became the first Black woman to appear on the cover of *Sports Illustrated*. The *Chicago Defender* called her triumphs "a victory for Uncle Sam, for democracy," while *Ebony* magazine titled her "the most significant black athlete in America."[2]

The accolades belied the financial hardship Gibson faced as a woman in tennis. In 1958, Gibson decided to leave the sport she loved and do what only the rarest of great athletes can do—pick up another sport and excel again. Like Babe Didrikson Zaharias before her, Gibson migrated to golf, where, as she had in tennis, she became a trailblazer for Black women. "After Althea applied for her [LPGA] card in 1963," explain her biographers, "she singlehandedly integrated courses" throughout the country.[3]

Integration, however, came slowly to the LPGA, and some Southern tournaments refused to allow her to compete. "There were a lot of tournaments that wouldn't accept me," she once quipped. "I don't know if they thought I was going to eat the grass. All I wanted to do was hit the ball off it." She was prohibited from staying at the same hotels as her white peers and segregated from the locker rooms at certain courses. "Despite the racial barriers," Louis Moore writes, "Gibson found instant success. Known for her long drives and athletic shots, by the mid-1960s she ranked as one of the top women golfers in the nation."[4]

The prejudice she endured in sport did not drive her toward activism as it did for some Black athletes in the 1960s. Gibson instead believed that competing and winning were all she needed to do to prove her worth in society. "If my being out here and playing golf can be of some stimulation to other young ladies of my race," she explained, "then I feel I've made my contribution."[5] She was, however, willing to serve as a sport ambassador for her country. In 1955, the US State Department sent her on a six-week tour of Asia that included Burma, India, Pakistan, and Ceylon. As an official US representative, she played in regional championship tournaments during the tour. Not only did it broaden her worldview, but the tour served as critical preparation in advance of her historic run of tennis victories between 1956 and 1958.

In later life, Gibson returned to hardship. Her financial woes persisted, and she struggled with depression until her death in 2003. Gibson's stellar career, one of the most consequential in US history, embodied the dynamics of her generation. She overcame impossible odds and achieved more in her profession than most anyone else. But in her era, fame and accomplishment in sport did not always translate to a sufficient standard of living. Gibson straddled a line in athlete history, between the midcentury social pioneers and the commercial mavens who followed.

Notes

1   Moore, *We Will Win the Day*, 12.
2   Ibid., 15; Frances Clayton Gray and Yanick Rice Lamb, *Born to Win: The Authorized Biography of Althea Gibson* (Hoboken: John Wiley & Sons, 2004), 135.
3   Ibid., 153.
4   Moore, *We Will Win the Day*, 67.
5   Gibson quoted in ibid.

4

New Frontiers in Player Empowerment

The Globalization of US Sport at the Close of the American Century

Introduction

What began as individual defiance in the early twentieth century evolved into concerted activism by the 1960s, and over the rest of the century US athletes launched a crusade for player empowerment that presses on today. Between 1970 and 2000, US sport embarked on a new era where athletes had more agency over their careers and where professional leagues, teams, and stars became big-time global businesses. Yet amid all this change, sport continued to show its capacity to mirror the times.

When the Cold War ended, and President George H. W. Bush promised a "new world order ... in which the nations of the world, east and west, north and south, can prosper and live in harmony," the United States for a moment stood alone at the top of world politics.[1] Few could have anticipated how fleeting American hegemony would be—that what looked like the onset of a US-led world order was actually the high watermark of American power. But as the twentieth century closed and new problems emerged in an unpredictable post–Cold War world, US sport captured the intensity, struggle, and dynamism of these years as well as any institution or cultural medium.

This chapter attempts to make sense of this era by focusing on three themes that together reflect the direction America and the world of sport were headed as the twentieth century closed. The first is the conclusion of the Cold War and the role sport played in its final decades. As a means of fracturing Sino-Soviet relations, a sign of US vulnerability, and a political bellwether of a culture shift in American politics, sport attended several key moments of the late Cold War era. The second section traces the thread of athlete activism into the 1970s and 1980s by focusing on international tennis. Thanks to the professional success and individual heroism of both Arthur Ashe and Billie Jean King, tennis became a testing ground for a new wave in athlete empowerment that focused as much on economic gains as social ones. Advancements in athlete earning power in other major US sports began around the same time Ashe and King launched their crusade in tennis. This chapter's third section explores how the birth of free agency in baseball fueled MLB's globalization, followed swiftly by athletes and other leagues— most importantly, Michael Jordan and the NBA—who likewise found their fortunes in global markets. The years 1970–2000 saw the realization of US sport becoming more politicized, professionalized, and globalized, a process dating back to the prior century and that continues apace today.

Sport and the End of the Cold War

American power, like American sport, was adrift in the 1970s. The Vietnam War was coming to its disastrous conclusion; the chaos of the late 1960s still rattled the nation; and the new Nixon administration came to power promising law and order but delivered mostly crime and punishment of a democracy. Aside from the domestic crises they caused, ignored, or mismanaged, Presidents Nixon, Ford, and Carter each attempted to stabilize US foreign relations, with mixed results. Normalization and a retreat from the aggression that produced the Vietnam War was a common mantra, but little could be done to stop the global forces shaping up as retribution for decades of US-caused exploitation and injustice in various parts of the world.

In sport, the country likewise struggled to regain the mantle it once wore. China emerged as a powerful factor in international athletics, while the Soviet Union and its satellites continued to ambush the United States and its Western allies at the Olympics. America even witnessed its supremacy in basketball, a sport it had carried from birth, surpassed by a Soviet sport program that poured enormous resources into national athletics. The brume over US sport darkened with President Carter's decision to boycott the 1980 Olympics in Moscow after the Soviet Union's invasion of Afghanistan the prior year.

The 1980s proved a major turning point in American history. The election of Ronald Reagan reignited the engine of nationalism left idling in the prior decade. He convinced Americans to ignore the warnings President Carter had made about the dangers of excessive consumption, environmental degradation, and cavalier foreign policies. Reagan promised to "Make America Great Again" by cutting taxes, spending billions on the military, antagonizing the Soviet Union, and growing the national debt by more than 30 percent. The "Reagan Revolution" tuned American politics to a different key and charted a new trajectory for the global capitalist economy. Once again, many of these changes were also visible in sport. Although the Eastern bloc dominated the international scene until the Cold War ended, signs of a rejuvenation in US national sport appeared in the 1980s, setting the stage for much larger global sport gains at the end of the century.

Diplomacy and Sport in Cold War China

Sport served several purposes within the sprawling Chinese diaspora of the early twentieth century. Games like baseball and basketball became important social pastimes and vehicles of assimilation for Chinese migrant communities in the Philippines, Hawaii, and California. In China itself, a country under siege from foreign aggression and hamstrung by national political failures, a sporting culture evolved unevenly between 1900 and 1950. Reformers debated whether traditional Chinese physical education or a westernized sport culture would better strengthen Chinese society. "Modern sport, which represented modern Western industrial civilization, and Chinese traditional culture, which embodied the feudal patriarchal system, were constantly in conflict in the late nineteenth and early twentieth centuries," write historians Fan Hong and Tan Hua. By the 1920s, however, even Mao Tse-tung began to advocate for new forms of athletic and physical competitions in China to help prepare it for the rigors of national regeneration. "The modernization of China provided a suitable climate for the growth of modern sport," Hong and Hua argue, "and the development of modern sport stimulated the process of modernization of Chinese society at the turn of the twentieth century."[2]

Owing to groups like the YMCA, signs of Western sport influence in China were evident by the time of the 1911 Xinhai Revolution that toppled the Qing dynasty and founded a national government named the Republic of China (ROC). Progress toward a more developed sport culture in the new nation continued into the 1930s. In 1932, the ROC sent its first Olympic athlete to the Los Angeles Games. Around that same time, a major Chinese newspaper hosted a contest to decide which modern sport should be the country's national pastime. Among thousands of votes cast, soccer and basketball were the runaway favorites. Historian Andrew Morris writes that soccer and basketball were logical choices, "perfect both for cultivating notions of collective struggle and sacrifice in the Chinese masses and for developing a stronger athletic tradition and deeper talent pool that would be reflected in international competitions."[3] National basketball tournaments in China drew tens of thousands of spectators throughout the 1930s, while other sports, like volleyball, also became increasingly popular.[4]

The Chinese Civil War (1927–49), which bookended the Second Sino-Japanese War (1937–45) and the Second World War, marked the brutal finale to China's "century of humiliation." Mao's Chinese Communist Party (CCP) in 1949 at last prevailed over the nationalist government. Mao established the People's Republic of China (PRC) on the mainland the same year. Sport became an early flashpoint between Mao and the exiled ROC government that had fled to the island of Taiwan. The ROC was the established member in the world of sport, so initially international organizations like the IOC treated the ROC as the legitimate representative of the Chinese people. Mao, however, was determined to achieve international recognition of his new China which meant the IOC became a target for his disruptive brand of geopolitics.[5]

The PRC sent a small delegation to the 1952 Games in Helsinki, but because of the IOC's policy, Mao chose not to send PRC athletes to the 1956 Games and withdrew from the Olympic movement entirely in 1958—a move that lasted until the 1984 Olympics in Los Angeles. In the meantime, Mao set off to reorder the world of Asian sport, starting with the Asian Games Federation (AGF), which began hosting large-scale sporting competitions in 1951. Within a decade, Mao's pressure campaign compelled the AGF to expel Taiwan from its ranks. Next, Mao announced his support for an alternative to the Olympic Games known as the Games of the New Emerging Forces (GANEFO). Fan Hong and Lu Zhouxiang explain that "the GANEFO movement intended to divide and fragment the Olympic movement, to emphasize the political realities of the new world structure, and to fan the political ambitions of the new and nonaligned states."[6]

For China, "GANEFO provided an ideal stage upon which the PRC could project its image, extend its influence, and unite with the countries of the Third World." Additionally, the new games "enabled Beijing to compete with the other two power blocs ... for influence within international sport."[7] Indeed, by the mid-1960s, China and the Soviet Union were already showing signs of distrust and the notion of a global communist bloc was losing viability. When Richard Nixon won the White House in 1968 and anointed Henry Kissinger as his foreign-policy soothsayer, the two men decided it would be useful to irritate the chaffing Sino-Soviet alliance. Nixon and Kissinger reshuffled US foreign relations by giving the PRC a much higher status, which helped accomplish their goal of reducing Cold War tensions while weakening their greatest adversary all in the name of détente.[8]

In the end, it was table tennis, or ping pong, that created the space for the normalization of diplomatic relations between China and the United States. In 1971, China's foreign minister, Chou En-lai, persuaded Mao to send China's best table tennis players to Japan for the Thirty-First World Table Tennis Championships. Chou defined China's objective as "friendship first, competition second. Politics is the most important thing." Mao agreed, and while in Japan, the Chinese invited the US team to travel to China for a table tennis exhibition in the spring of 1971, making them the first Americans welcomed back to China since the PRC's founding. The move was also aimed at facilitating more delicate communications between heads of state, culminating in Henry Kissinger's secret trip to China just a few months later. Kissinger worked with Chou to arrange the details for President Nixon's surprise arrival in Beijing in February of 1972. With the help of sport, argue Hong and Lu, the United States and China both advanced national interests, alienated the Soviet Union, "and subsequently changed the direction of world politics."[9]

US National Sport before and after the 1972 Munich Games

What contemporaries called "Ping Pong Diplomacy" was a bright spot in an otherwise bleak period of US sport history—at least at the national level. Sport scholars Nevada Cooke and Robert Barney, who study the White House's enhanced role in US national sport after 1970, explain that while the "Olympics Games had been dominated from the outset of their recent history by US athletes," by the late 1960s, "American Olympic supremacy was severely challenged by athletes from the Soviet Union." The 1972 Munich Olympics—an event forever marred by the murder of eleven Israeli athletes by Palestinian terrorists—put a fine point on America's declension. Between 1952 and 1968, the United States tallied 418 Olympic medals at the Summer Games, compared to the Soviet Union's 459 medals. Those numbers looked even worse for the United States if other Eastern bloc countries were added to the Soviet's, totaling 842 medals won by communist athletes over those years. At Munich in 1972, the Soviet Union stunned the world by winning fifty gold medals and finished first in the overall count. The "results of the 1972 Games in Munich caused considerable alarm" for Americans, write Cooke and Barney, and "seemed to symbolize the general malaise the United States faced" as the Cold War rolled on. Perhaps the single most surprising outcome in Munich was the US men's basketball team's loss to the Soviet Union in the gold medal round, revealing just how far American sport had fallen in the world.[10]

The shock of losing the Olympic gold in basketball—which the United States had won without interruption since the game's inaugural Olympic tournament in 1936—was especially painful for Americans. Like in other sports, Soviet competitiveness in basketball was evident well before the 1972 Munich upset.[11] Going back to the 1952 Helsinki Olympics, where the Russians fell to the United States in the gold medal game, the Soviet Union began a concerted effort to improve their national basketball teams. "Defeating the Americans in their 'own' sport, basketball," Witherspoon writes, "was the ultimate representation of Soviet organizational, physical, and mental acumen."[12]

In 1958, the Soviet Union invited the AAU to send a team to Russia. The Americans agreed and swept the Soviets in all six games they played. The next year, at an international tournament in Chile, the Soviet team trounced the Americans in the final game, winning 62–37. A year after that, the Soviet national team came to the United States, where it defeated various iterations of a US squad in four of six contests. The US teams were entirely amateur, made up largely of AAU players, compared to Soviet lineups comprising grown men who trained like professionals under the direction of USSR athletic programs. After watching second-tier American basketball players lose to the Soviets on US soil, one coach admitted "the propaganda value to the Russians ... is tremendous. If we lose, the rest of the world won't know who was or who wasn't on our team, all they'll know is that the Russians beat us."[13]

The simmering US-Soviet basketball rivalry became a rolling boil at the 1967 world championship games in Uruguay. The Soviets overcame a contentious defeat to the Americans during the preliminary rounds to win the tournament, while the United States finished in fourth place. Then, just a year before the infamous showdown in Munich, the Soviet Union sent a team consisting of former and future Olympians to the United States, where they played against US teams made up of "top local AAU talent, with the occasional college player thrown in." Witherspoon writes that "while everyone professed to have a good time during this tour, and the Soviet players took in movies, listened to Elvis, and bought blue jeans and records, the Soviet team also went on an unexpected winning streak."[14] The Soviets ripped off eight straight victories before losing the ninth and final game of the tour "after thoroughly gorging themselves on American food and exhausting themselves with all manner of American entertainment."[15]

Heading into the 1972 Munich Games, US basketball was ripe for major embarrassment on the Olympic stage. Both the Russians and Americans were undefeated when they faced off for the gold medal. From the jump, the Americans played poorly. The Soviets scored first and controlled the pace of play throughout the game, leading by eight points late in the second half. In the waning minutes, the Americans rallied and with seconds on the clock, guard Doug Collins was viscously fouled on a layup and knocked unconscious. Several moments later, Collins stood and steadied himself, stepped to the line, and sank two free throws, giving the United States a 50–49 lead with only three seconds left. After Collins swished his second free throw, the Soviets attempted an inbound pass just as the buzzer sounded, signaling the game was over. But quickly officials announced the Soviet coach had called a timeout prior to the inbound and gave the Soviets another chance. On the second inbound attempt, the Soviets again failed to score and this time, when the horn blared, the American team erupted in celebration and stormed the court. Yet IOC officials once again called for a re-do. The scorer's table had not given the Soviets the full three seconds they deserved, so the teams reassembled for one last play. This time, the Soviet inbounder—who appeared to step on the baseline before releasing the ball, which is a violation and turnover of possession—launched a pass the length of the court that landed in the hands of Soviet big man Aleksandr Belov, who elbowed aside an American defender and laid the ball in the hoop as time expired.

In the end, the US team skipped the medal ceremony, refusing to accept in silver something they believed they won in gold. "United States supremacy in Olympic basketball was ended early today at Munich," reported a despondent *New York Times*. Sportswriter Hedrick Smith added that "Cold War competitiveness may be mellowing in other fields, but it still runs strong in sports." In his article summarizing the Soviet Union's impressive overall Olympic performance, Smith noted "Moscow's obsessive concern with besting the Americans, who were chided for being poor losers in basketball and unmannerly in other competitions."[16]

Accusations of doping, sex deception, and other skullduggery might have satiated Americans after faltering in events like weightlifting or the hammer throw, but to lose in their own sport to their Cold War nemesis forced US athletes and officials to confront the inadequacies of their once-unrivaled national sport system. Bob Cousy, the Hall of Fame Boston Celtics point guard who became a coach for the US national basketball team after the Munich debacle, stated plainly that Americans "have to send our best players to the Olympic Games .... The Russians are capable of beating any amateur or college team in the United States under international rules." At the heart of the matter was what Cousy called "the battle between the AAU and the NCAA" over who ultimately controlled amateur athletics in America.[17] Historians Cooke and Barney explain that while the United States Olympic Committee (USOC), formed in 1951 to replace the AOC, technically had "the authority to select the country's Olympic teams," the "problem was that the majority of the prospective Olympic participants were under the jurisdiction of the AAU or the NCAA" both of which "still had the authority to revoke an athlete's amateur status."[18] The result was that throughout the Cold War "each organization failed to work harmoniously with the other in mustering the best American Olympic team possible," leaving the USOC "caught in the middle of this persistent problem."[19]

Eventually, the combination of US national sport failures and the squabbling between the AAU and NCAA provoked the federal government to take action. The challenge of reforming US national sport was particularly knotty for a country that had long prided itself on a privately run, amateur sport movement that took little direction or money from the federal government. But because "the USOC was a federally chartered organization, Congressional action was necessary if reform measures were to be enforced by law." This arrangement wound up pitting prominent US senators, many who believed the time for a Soviet-style federal sport program had arrived, and a Nixon/Ford White House that continued to insist on the merits of privatized amateur sports. Both men worked to quash the Senate's attempt at a reform bill, arguing it "represented unnecessary federal intervention into an area that [they] construed as decidedly non-federal."[20]

After Nixon resigned in 1974, Ford signed an executive order establishing the President's Commission on Olympic Sport. The commission labored throughout Ford's entire short presidency. Its chief recommendations became part of the Amateur Sports Act of 1978, which Ford's successor, President Jimmy Carter, signed into law. The act streamlined US national sport by empowering the USOC over the AAU and NCAA, but more important was how it "stymied those who flirted with the idea of emulating the Soviet bloc."[21] Within a decade, the IOC dropped its ban on professional athletes, and the question of amateurism at the Olympics was finally put to bed.

Ice and Mortar

Olympic frustrations persisted through the 1970s, a period of acute international strain for the United States. There is some tragic irony to the global crises Carter encountered while in office, considering his conscientiousness as a leader. Indeed, in 1977, Carter brokered a deal to return the Panama Canal to the Panamanian Government while acknowledging American duplicity in the history of the region.[22] He warned against excessive consumption, particularly of foreign oil, and gestured at the unsustainability of American empire.[23] Carter beseeched Americans to think more seriously about the consequences of their actions, only then to watch an Islamic revolution overthrow Iran's last shah, Mohammad Reza Pahlavi, whom the CIA helped install in the 1950s in return for favorable access to Iran's vast oil reserves.

The Iranian Revolution and its leader, the Ayatollah Khomeini, were fiercely anti-American, and the hostage crisis involving the US embassy in Tehran that began in November of 1979 saw that rhetoric turned into action. Adding to the international turmoil, a month after Iranians stormed the US embassy and captured its occupants, the USSR invaded Iran's neighbor Afghanistan, a country on the outer ring of the Soviet Union's orbit. The Soviet-backed, communist government that had run the country since the early Cold War faltered and became embroiled by an insurgency led by Islamic fighters known as the Mujahideen.[24] When the Soviets intervened militarily, the US applied sanctions, embargoed grain exports, and sent covert funds to the Afghan fighters. The president's Republican opponents, sensing blood in the water, framed Soviet aggression and Carter's hesitancy to provide more extensive military aid to the insurgents as proof of the need for new leadership in Washington.[25]

Carter escalated his response in March when he announced a boycott of the 1980 Moscow Olympics—the first-ever Summer Games held in Russia. He initially believed that "if many nations act in concert" an Olympic boycott would "be the most severe blow to the Soviet Union."[26] Because he made the move unilaterally, however, the president struggled to line up international support for the idea. Carter remained steadfast and insisted to the press "[n]either I nor the American people would support the sending of an American team to Moscow with Soviet invasion troops in Afghanistan."[27]

Initially, a majority of the US public agreed with his position. But not everyone was happy. The US fencer and Olympic hopeful John Nonna captured the ambivalence other US athletes felt toward Carter's decision. "I don't like using the Olympics as a foreign policy tool," he told the press, "I'd like to think there are other ways to show our displeasure and put pressure on the Soviets."[28] In the end, Carter managed to forge a boycott that included sixty-five teams. As a stand-in for the 1980 Summer Olympics, the White House organized the Liberty Bell Classic, a track and field event that attracted twenty-nine teams to come to Philadelphia three days before the Moscow Games kicked off. Compared to the impact the 1980 Lake Placid Games had on international sport, however, Carter's Olympic machinations did little to inspire Americans or shame the Soviets.[29]

The famous US-Soviet hockey game defined Lake Placid's place in American sport history, yet Eastern bloc athletes were the ones who dominated those Olympics. The Soviet Union won ten golds and twenty-two medals overall, and East Germany secured nine golds and twenty-four total medals. The United States came in third with twelve total medals, six of them gold. But the surprise win in hockey seemed to capture a shift in the mood of Americans in the early 1980s. Through politics and the media, historian Mary McDonald writes, "the puckish resolve of the victorious US hockey team was narrated in such a way that both anticipated and helped promote the broader sentiment, which eventually became known as the 'Reagan Revolution.'"[30] To her point, the notorious Reagan operative Oliver North insisted the "Miracle on Ice" portended a sea change underway in American politics. The US hockey team, North puffed, "illustrated a belief shared by Ronald Reagan: Leadership is the courage to defy the fatalism of the quitters and so-called 'experts.' From Plymouth Rock to the Moon, we are an intrepid people not made for defeat. The Soviet skaters learned that lesson on a rink in Lake Placid."[31]

US national hockey had struggled ever since its surprise 1960 gold medal victory at the Squaw Valley Games in California—the first hockey gold in US history. The United States finished fifth, sixth, second, and fifth at the next four Winter Games, while the Soviet team took the gold at each event. The 1980 team that US hockey coach Herb Brooks assembled represented the best of collegiate hockey in America, but they "were by far the youngest, most inexperienced team when it came to the Olympic Games," Brooks acknowledged. "We were just college kids playing flat-out professional, older, stronger, better … athletes, so it was a real formidable task."[32]

The Soviets were the undisputed favorites to win their fifth consecutive gold medal, and the pressure their players faced back home was tremendous. The USSR's sport program made athletic training a full-time occupation for the country's best athletes, and to those rigors came the expectation that in hockey the Soviet team should never lose. They had world-class talent on every line, and one of the most dominant goalies ever in Vladislav Tretiak. Underscoring the disparity in talent, at an exhibition just a few days before Lake Placid Games opened, the United States and the Soviets squared off in Madison Square Garden, and the USSR waxed the young Americans 10–3. "The goals they scored, you could have filmed them they were so beautiful," remembered US forward Mark Johnson, who admitted he and his teammates felt more like "spectators" than opponents, "ready to stand up and applaud" as they marveled at the USSR's talent and teamwork.[33]

The Soviets breezed through the qualifying rounds when the 1980 Olympic hockey tournament began, outscoring their opponents 33–4. The United States, however, played Sweden and Czechoslovakia, respectively considered the third and second-best teams behind the Soviets. The Americans tied Sweden and pounded the Czechs, which got them into the playoffs. Then they defeated Norway, Romania, and Germany to advance to the medal round where, in the semifinals, they drew the Soviets.

When the puck dropped, it was clear the Americans came ready to play. The teams exchanged goals over the first few minutes and with time running out in the first period, Mark Johnson snuck in a goal to tie up the game 2–2. Before the second period started, the USSR coach made the shocking move of replacing Tretiak at goal, and it seemed to steady the Soviets. Heading into the final period, the United States trailed 3–2. But then Johnson struck for his second goal and tied the game up. Moments later, with ten minutes left in the game, the US captain Mike Eruzione fired a shot past the right shoulder of the Soviet goalie and gave the United States the lead. "That's when sound had feel," remembered Al Michaels, the famous American broadcaster who called the game. "It was like an earthquake."[34] Long minutes dragged on, and the Americans clung to their one-goal lead. The Soviets launched a frenzied, final assault but could not put the puck in the net. As time expired, Michaels asked his audience the famous question "Do you believe in miracles?" and answered himself: "Yes!" A few days later, the United States defeated Finland for the gold medal, completing one of the unlikeliest Olympic victories in US history.

"Us winning the gold medal didn't solve the Iranian crisis, didn't pull the Soviets out of Afghanistan, but people felt better," Eruzione later claimed. "People were proud, people felt good about being American, because they could relate to who we were, working-class, lunch-pail, hard-hat kids who represented them in an athletic event that was far greater than a hockey game."[35] To what extent the 1980 US men's hockey team represented the American public is debatable, but certainly those Winter Games helped rejuvenate the country's interest in the Olympics. After Carter's boycott of the Moscow Games a few months later, the United States began preparing for the Olympics' return to Los Angeles in 1984. The Soviets orchestrated a boycott of their own for those Games, joined by thirteen of their allies

FIGURE 4.1 *America's Rob McClanahan fends off a Soviet defender during the semifinal hockey match at the 1980 Winter Olympics in Lake Placid, New York. The US shocked the Soviets by winning 4–3 to advance to the gold medal round where they defeated Finland to cap off what became known as the "Miracle on Ice." (Photo by Tom Sweeney/Star Tribune via Getty Images).*

who declined to send athletes to California. Without the Eastern bloc in its way, the US rolled to an Olympic victory reminiscent of the 1904 Games in St. Louis. Against forty-six other countries, the United States won 181 total medals, including eighty-six gold.[36]

The final US-Soviet Olympic showdowns happened in 1988, at the Winter Games in Canada and the Summer Games in South Korea. For the last time, Eastern bloc athletes overwhelmed the medal count, while the United States came in ninth and third, respectively. Reflective though it can be of a society's well-being, a robust sporting culture is not always a sign of a viable, healthy polity. By the next Olympics, in 1992, the Soviet Union was no more. The eruption of political dissidence throughout Eastern Europe culminated in the fall of the Berlin Wall in November of 1989. Over the next two years, the remaining Soviet satellite states became independent countries while Russia embarked on a foggy, bumpy recovery as a fallen empire.[37]

The Cold War both reaffirmed and altered the way sport functioned in the world, and in the United States specifically. At the center of the storm, argues historian Andrew Johns, "Washington and Moscow—and their allies—used sport as part of a broader propaganda offensive to certify and promote the superiority of their respective systems without the fear of a real ('hot') war or nuclear destruction."[38] Meanwhile, countries "outside of Europe and North America also attempted to use sport in their efforts to assert their prerogatives, negotiate the international environment dominated by Cold War considerations, and enhance the international standing of nonaligned and newly independent states."[39] The way states used sport as soft power was not new, but no doubt the relationship between states and sport strengthened between 1945 and 1991. For the United States, while the government became more familiar with the diplomatic and propagandistic value of a vibrant sporting culture, perhaps the most salient change occurred among American athletes themselves. With performances that demanded the spotlight, and causes close to their hearts, US sport stars of the Cold War era completely remade what it meant to have agency as an athlete. As much as it was a vessel for US foreign policy amid a major geopolitical struggle, American sport during the Cold War became a means of advancing the influence of US athletes across the country and around the world.

Social Justice Takes Center Court

The Soviet Union's sudden implosion caught many Americans, not to mention Russians, by surprise. The rise of the activist athlete, however, occurred more gradually and gave observers plenty of time to weigh its merits. Certainly, some Americans doubted or wished away the permanence of sport as an engine of social justice after the 1960s. But as the century rolled on, athlete activism only became sharper and more pronounced. The fact that athletes like Kareem Abdul-Jabbar and Muhammad Ali remained planted in the headlines through the 1970s provided a bridge between the activist athletes of the 1960s and the new frontiers in athlete empowerment that opened in the decades after.

Achievements in the racial integration of professional sport in America were soon followed by watershed developments in the struggle for gender equality. The landmark 1972 Title IX legislation, which stipulated that organizations receiving federal funds could not discriminate on the basis of sex, opened up the tap for athletic opportunities at public schools and universities for women. The number of young women playing school sports grew sevenfold between 1971 and 2015, from fewer than 30,000 to more than 211,000.[40] However, as historian Susan Ware argues, the law's success has been uneven. Serious improvement toward gender parity was made in the mid- to late-1970s, then due to "a variety of historical, political, and legal reasons, little progress occurred in the 1980s, but in the 1990s there was another surge forward." Along the way, sexist reactionaries misleadingly characterized the law as "increased opportunities for women ... coming at the expense of decreased opportunities for men."[41]

There was no better venue in all of sport to observe athlete activism evolve into an offensive for individual empowerment than professional tennis in the 1970s. The sport was not only surging in popularity, but some of its leading lights came of age, including Americans Tracy Austin, Jimmy Connors, Chris Evert, John McEnroe, Martina Navratilova, and Stan Smith—not to mention a host of international stars like Björn Borg, Margaret Court, and Ilie Năstase. The careers of two other professional tennis players of that era—Arthur Ashe and Billie Jean King—exemplify the game's rising stature in the world of sport as well as the ways athletes sought to affect change on a global scale. Whether it was fighting apartheid, advancing athlete economic power, challenging sexism, or redefining gender norms, Ashe and King created legacies that remain vital for understanding modern sport.

Arthur Ashe, Apartheid, and the ATP

Arthur Ashe Jr. was born in 1943 in Richmond, Virginia, the former capital of the vanquished Confederate States of America. A young Black man in the Jim Crow South, Ashe gained a unique perspective on the world through his affiliation with tennis. The sport dates back at least to the sixteenth century and had professionalized early in the 1900s. It was among the most international of all games by the time Ashe started playing. He once remarked that "the life we lead in tennis is most unlike any other sport ... and it's spectacularly international. I don't really live anywhere ... we have no real home."[42] By the 1970s tennis had also caught the commercial breeze that other leagues, like the NFL and MLB, were riding to greater profits and popularity. Indeed, in 1972, the World Championship Tennis (WCT) finals outdrew both the NBA and NHL for television viewership—and that was during basketball and hockey's playoff seasons.[43] Ashe won the 1968 US Open as an amateur and quickly became one of several unforgettable tennis stars of the 1970s who helped grow the sport's audience all over the world.

Ashe's evolution as an activist athlete took longer than others of his era. Through the mid-1960s, he tacked himself to the path carved by more moderate Black athletes. Ashe once said, "I feel the way Joe Louis does. When somebody asked why he wasn't active in the civil rights fight, he said 'Some people do it by shouting, some march, some give lots of money.' I do it my way—behaving. All ways help."[44] Like Willie Mays and Althea Gibson, Ashe initially maintained that his performance on the court was all he needed to make his point, once telling Jesse Jackson that "I don't do it with my mouth, I do it with my racket."[45] Moore writes that "the black press loved Ashe and celebrated his accomplishments for what they meant for black advancement; however, they wanted him to show more consciousness about the civil rights movement."[46] To his point, Harry Edwards, the famous sociologist who led the OPHR during the buildup to the 1968 Olympics, admitted he thought Ashe was an "Uncle Tom"—a reference to the titular character in Harriet Beecher Stowe's *Uncle Tom's Cabin*. Edwards, who later wrote the seminal book on this era titled *The Revolt of the Black Athlete*, added that when he first met Ashe, he was "not a radical, not even a liberal."[47]

Ashe's transformation into an activist athlete was, as Moore writes, indicative of "the transition a number of leading black athletes went through as individuals trying to come to terms with their special privileges as superstars and their people's plight as second-class citizens."[48] Like Joe Louis, Ashe eventually began to appreciate the more radical elements of the Civil Rights Movement, admitting that what "was liberal five years ago may be moderate now."[49] His emerging activism became evident in the early 1970s, then turned into a crusade in 1973 when Ashe collided with the deeply racist South African government.

South Africa was a former British colony and had existed under a state of racialized segregation known as apartheid dating back to 1948. South African society resembled the Jim Crow South but in ways more stringent and absolute. The white ruling class and their National Party used state power to dominate and brutalize Black South Africans, seeking to hide Blacks from public sight as much as possible. Historian John Nauright explains that for "most whites their sole contact with blacks was to bark orders at their servants; few experienced direct cultural links." He adds that both "the psychology and geography of apartheid meant that whites tucked blacks out of sight and most whites lost all 'feeling for human fellowship with blacks.'"[50] South African liberation groups that opposed the National Party—including the African National Congress, led by Nelson Mandela—were outlawed and those who were found guilty of organizing against the government were imprisoned, or worse. Mandela himself was arrested and sentenced to life in prison for conspiring to overthrow the National Party in 1964.[51]

The annihilation of Black South African persons and culture from white society extended to sport, which had long been a vital part of the country's history. Rugby was preeminent, but other sports, including tennis, also carried cultural significance in South Africa. The segregation of white and Black bodies reached everywhere and, like fascism in Europe and Jim Crow in America, depended on contrived theories involving scientific racism to justify its existence. To explain why no worthy Black swimmers competed on the South African national team, for instance, the president of their national Olympic committee alleged that "the African is not suited to swimming: in swimming, the water closes their pores so they cannot get rid of carbon dioxide and they tire quickly."[52]

The Olympic movement banned South Africa in 1964, ten years after a global cultural boycott had formed seeking to alienate South Africa from the international community. Historian Eric Morgan writes that the "first signs in the United States of a movement toward a cultural boycott against South

Africa appeared in 1965" when a "notable group of American artists agreed with the liberation movement's strategy and embraced cultural isolation of South Africa as a legitimate tool in the struggle against apartheid."[53] It was only in 1967, once international rugby tours began to exclude South Africa from their competitions, that the National Party softened some of their laws to allow small numbers of non-whites to play in their country, beginning in 1970.[54] That was also the year Arthur Ashe applied for a visa to compete in the South African Open—only to be denied. The move cost South Africa admission to the Davis Cup, one of the most prestigious events in the tennis world, thus compounding the growing anti-apartheid sport boycott.[55]

Ashe, meanwhile, kept applying for his visa, and with the help of the Nixon administration in 1973 the South African government agreed to let him in. Once admitted, he refused the restrictions the National Party had imposed on other non-whites visiting the country since 1970. Ashe demanded fully integrated tennis facilities, the freedom to visit any part of the country, and "that he would not be given honorary white status by the South African government (as many visiting African Americans, such as Percy Sledge and Eartha Kitt had been)."[56]

Ashe lost in the 1973 South African Open finals against Jimmy Connors, followed by repeat performances in two other visits to South Africa in 1974 and 1975. Ashe spent his final 1977 visit touring the country to evaluate its commitment to making social progress. Afterward he told the press that "he opposes the total sports boycott" that others were calling for. "I know the Africans would kill me for saying this, and probably the militant blacks at home as well, but I know I'm right in saying that if you isolate them completely, the progress will come to a stop, a dead stop." Ashe, instead, believed sport could create opportunities for Black South Africans, and held up as an example the million-dollar Arthur Ashe Tennis Center and Library he had built in Soweto, a township in South Africa's largest city of Johannesburg.[57]

Ashe's legacy extends beyond his fight against apartheid and his general brilliance as a tennis star. He became passionate about promoting tennis in American inner cities, and founded the National Junior Tennis League in 1969, a program that "teaches tennis while also emphasizing leadership and academics" for underserved young Americans.[58] Ashe wrote prolifically for a professional athlete, including a sweeping, three-volume history of African American athletes he titled *A Hard Rode to Glory*. His career is loaded with examples showing the direction athlete activism was headed in the 1970s. While he came of age as a critic of racial oppression in America and cut his teeth as a global activist challenging apartheid in South Africa, Ashe simultaneously led a war against the barons of professional tennis and became one of the pioneers of the economic empowerment movement that was gaining speed in professional sport. As historian Eric Allen Hall puts it, Ashe's "leaderships skills, nurtured in civil rights and antiapartheid activism, had blossomed into the drive for player unionization."[59]

Before the Association of Tennis Professionals (ATP)—the players' union for men's tennis that Ashe helped found—two organizations governed professional men's tennis: the WCT and the International Lawn Tennis Federation (ILTF). Through 1973, "the WCT and the ITLF," writes Hall, "clashed over player contracts and the rights of players to compete in open tournaments." However dysfunctional its operations, professional tennis nonetheless flourished over those years. In 1971, the WCT paid out more than $1 million to tournament winners. The next year, it was $5 million, and Ashe alone earned around $100,000. That was also the year the WCT finals outdrew the NBA and NHL playoffs with a television audience over 21 million. The sport's growing dependence on television resulted in networks demanding to know if the tournaments they were paying to telecast would include the best players. But because of the infighting between the WCT and the ILTF, those assurances were never guaranteed. Moreover, huge stars were liable to skip major events like Wimbledon and the US Open, run by the ILTF, because the WCT was offering them better prize money to play in their less prestigious tournaments. Just as both organizations began to hammer out the terms of a more fruitful relationship, Ashe and the other stars of men's tennis aligned to shake the money from the sport themselves.[60]

Ashe asserted that neither the WCT nor the ILTF should have the power to dictate player earnings or influence tournament selection. He believed if the best players in tennis "banded together, the players could dictate the distribution of prizes, tournament schedules, and allocation of pensions and insurance."[61] Corralling a generation of tennis legends that included characters like Ilie Năstase was not easy, but with Ashe pushing the group, fifty-six professional tennis players met in New York shortly before the 1972 US Open and drew up bylaws and a provisional constitution. Within a week, the ATP was official.[62] Ashe became an officer and later served as ATP president. His emergence as a voice for athlete's labor rights coincided with some of the greatest years of his tennis career. In 1975, Ashe became the first African American man to win Wimbledon. He retired in 1980 with more than a thousand combined wins, more than forty titles, three Grand Slam singles titles, two Grand Slam doubles titles, and $1.5 million in career earnings.[63]

The reason for his retirement also set in motion Ashe's tragic death thirteen years later. Ashe suffered from cardiac trouble that required two heart bypass surgeries: the first in 1979 after he suffered a heart attack, and the second in 1983. It was after the second operation, in the hope of expediting his recovery, that Ashe consented to a blood transfusion during which, unbeknownst to him or his medical team, Ashe contracted HIV. By the time doctors discovered what was wrong, five years had passed, and the HIV had become AIDS. Yet Ashe, with the steely resolve that defined his personal style and tennis career, remained an activist to the end. In his final months, he was arrested in Washington, DC, for protesting the George H. W. Bush administration's treatment of Haitian immigrants. He established the Arthur Ashe Foundation for the Defeat of AIDS and the Arthur Ashe Institute for Urban Health "to help address issues of inadequate health care delivery to urban minority populations."[64] Somehow, amid this final flurry of personal excellence, he penned an autobiography titled *Days of Grace*. In an interview once, before he was sick, Ashe told a reporter that "a long time ago, I was standoffish about everything. I wasn't aware that what I said carried any weight." Eventually, however, those views changed, and Ashe learned he could make a real difference in the world. By the end, he believed "it would be almost sinful not to throw [my weight] around in the right direction."[65]

Billie Jean King and Gender Boundaries in Sport

"We had parallel careers, there's no question," Billie Jean King once remarked about her relationship with Arthur Ashe. "Of all the players who played in our era, he and I were people who had a cause, not just on the court but off the court."[66] Historians have compared King to other activist athletes as well, including "sports stars such as Muhammad Ali, Jackie Robinson, and Joe Louis," writes Susan Ware, "who grabbed national attention to become icons of their individual sports and ambassadors of sport in general."[67] King was a genuine force of nature on and off the tennis court, stringing together one of the finest professional careers of any American athlete around some of the most assertive and successful social activism of anyone in the twentieth century. King forced the international game of tennis to bend itself to the cause of women's rights while in the process making tennis one of the most popular foreign sports in America. "Billie Jean King won a following for her role in transforming amateur tennis into a successful professional sport with broad national appeal," Ware argues. "Soon after, she emerged as one of the nation's most prominent and outspoken champions for the female sex—'Mother Courage with a backhand.'"[68]

King, born Billie Jean Moffit, was named after her father who in 1943 was in Virginia drilling for war in Europe when her mother gave birth in Long Beach, California. She grew up in a blue-collar, union family with a brother, Randy, who also became a professional athlete, pitching for twelve years in the major leagues. Her parents encouraged their daughter's obvious passion for sport and athletics. After her first tennis lesson, King recalled driving home and declaring to her mother that she would become the greatest female tennis player in the world—a revealing anecdote that illustrates both her competitive spirit and immediate awareness that athletic accomplishment provided the rare path to social agency for women. "Unless I was number one," she recalled thinking, "I wouldn't be listened to."[69]

A tennis sporting culture shaped by wealth and privilege—and she had neither—left a mark during King's formative years. Bespectacled and stocky, she had a hard time fitting in, even as she walloped the competition. The

FIGURE 4.2 *Billie Jean King displays her incredible athleticism at the 1972 Wimbledon Championships in London, England. King won the women's singles and doubles titles at that year's tournament, two of twenty Wimbledon titles that King racked up during her illustrious career. (Photo by Evening Standard/Hulton Archive/ Getty Images).*

Moffits were not country club folks and "her parents always felt much more comfortable in a baseball crowd cheering Randy than at a tennis match watching Billie Jean."[70] Throughout her career, King strove to make tennis more accessible and less snooty, while redirecting some of that country club cash in her direction. By fifteen she was competing as an amateur in Grand Slam events. Two years later, in 1961, she won the women's doubles championship at Wimbledon—the first of twenty Wimbledon titles King won over her career.

International tennis stardom carried with it very few economic perks, particularly for women in the 1960s. So, in 1961, King enrolled at California State University (Cal State). She soon dropped out, however, in part at the suggestion of her fiancé and fellow Cal State tennis player, Larry King. Larry made a huge impact on Billie Jean King's career trajectory. "He was the one who made me a feminist," she stated. Not only did Larry encourage her activism, perhaps most importantly, "he was the one person who gave me the courage to go back to being a [tennis] bum." After she left Cal State in 1964, King began a meteoric rise and by 1966 she achieved her childhood ambition of becoming the top ranked woman in all of tennis.[71]

Her maturation as a tennis star coincided with other changes, including how she felt about her sexuality. Ware suggests that "Billie Jean welcomed the respectability of being married, in effect, using Larry as her beard." The two maintained an open marriage, as Larry "looked the other way when she had relationships with women, and she did the same when he had affairs." For many years, Ware argues, "both concluded that on balance there were benefits to their public charade, even as their personal lives diverged."[72] In 1971, King discreetly began a seven-year affair with her hairdresser, Marilyn Barnett. "King kept her relationships with women a secret," the kinesiologist Jamie Schultz explains, "fearing that they would hurt the women's tour and her own reputation."[73] Indeed, in 1981, Barnett outed Billie Jean by suing her, "contending she was entitled to share in Mrs. King's assets because of the relationship."[74] The lawsuit forced King to come out publicly as a lesbian, after which she "lost nearly all her endorsement deals within twenty-four hours."[75]

Like Ashe, King was angry with the financial restrictions governing competitive tennis, which kept professionals from competing on the biggest stages. Stars like King sometimes earned appearance payments under the table, but mostly the money flowed to tournament organizers, not the players. Before she turned professional, King was part of the United States Lawn Tennis Association (USLTA) which paid her $196 a week to cover expenses "so I could help draw crowds that put money into its pot," she said, "and where that money went, your guess is as good as mine."[76] The era of Open Tennis started in 1968 when Wimbledon became the first Grand Slam tournament to welcome amateurs and professionals alike. Women still earned far less than the men; organizers paid Rob Laver three times more than King got for winning her third consecutive Wimbledon singles title. Having "won round one to take the sport professional," Ware writes, "women now found out that they had to fight a second battle: to get gender equity for women professionals."[77]

Her frustrations with the tennis world mounting, King worked with Gladys Heldman, the founder of *World Tennis* magazine, to pressure tennis officials to address the sport's pay gap. The breaking point came in 1970, after the Pacific Southwest Championship announced that its prize money would favor the men by an eight-to-one margin. King and Heldman protested by arranging a tournament of their own in Houston, Texas, sponsored by Phillip Morris and its Virginia Slims cigarette brand. A few days later, King and eight others—known as the "Original Nine"—signed one-dollar contracts as professional members of the Virginia Slims Tour.

The 1971 tour consisted of fourteen tournaments and $300,000 in prize money, well beyond what women were winning through the USLTA. Yet not everyone was ready to make the leap to the women's tour. The young prodigy Chris Evert, still under the firm guidance of her parents, remained in the USLTA. With "her two-fisted backhand and icy composure," writes Ware, Evert was not well liked by other women on the tour. But King saw greatness in Evert, and greatness meant more publicity for women's tennis, even if Evert ducked the professional circuit. "Billie Jean King went out of her way to befriend her," Ware explains, because she knew having "such an attractive and appealing star, especially when television was beginning to discover that tennis could be profitable ... was going to help them all."[78] Never one to pass up an opportunity to broaden tennis's appeal, King kept women's tennis in the spotlight and on the sports page. She also pocketed more than $100,000 in prize money in 1970, becoming the first woman in sport to achieve six-figure earnings. "Money is everything in sports," King once said, "and making women's tennis, particularly, into a legitimate big-league game was a crusade for me and I threw my whole self into it in ways that exhausted me emotionally as much as they did physically."[79]

Between 1972 and 1973, King went on a brilliant run of tournament championships, winning nine Grand Slam titles and becoming *Sports Illustrated*'s first Sportswoman of the Year in 1972. King's personal life remained in the spotlight, including a maelstrom when her name appeared on a petition with other famous women admitting to having an abortion. The details of who signed Billie Jean's name to that petition—she or Larry— are disputed; nonetheless, Billie Jean charged forward as a champion for women's rights. After the US Open became the first Grand Slam tournament to equalize prize money for men and women, King pressed the initiative to form a union for women tennis players. At the 1973 Wimbledon, King locked sixty-three of her peers in a room and convinced them to support the Women's Tennis Association. They did—and then King promptly won the tournament's singles, doubles, and mixed doubles.[80] "It is hard to believe," King wrote in her book *We Have Come a Long Way*, "but in 1973 many women professionals still did not want, or think we needed, a union." But King stood firm because she "did not want the USLTA and the ILTF making decisions about women's tennis without our input."[81]

In September 1973, King accomplished one of the most symbolically important achievements of her career when she defeated Bobby Riggs in the "Battle of the Sexes." Riggs had been a tennis star in the 1940s and developed an insatiable gambling habit to go along with a reputation as a braggart and sexist. Riggs tried to coax King into a match earlier in 1973, but she refused, so he instead played the Australian tennis phenom Margaret Court, who rivaled King as the best female tennis player in the early 1970s. Court accepted the offer and, as King feared, she lost to Riggs badly. "The match, played during the height of the women's movement and promoted by Riggs's endless chauvinistic blather," King wrote, "took on political overtones that made it bigger that any women's match had ever been." Yet Court, "who hated women's liberation and embraced everything gracious and traditional in tennis, had unwittingly walked into a circus carrying the banner of women's rights."[82]

To avenge the name of women's tennis—and, by extension, women's sport more broadly—King accepted Riggs's offer to play in September at the Houston Astrodome for $100,000, plus another $200,000 in television royalties. The television network ABC paid $750,000 for the rights to the match and was rewarded with a viewership that topped forty-eight million

Americans. Despite the likes of *Sports Illustrated* and Chris Evert picking Riggs to win the match, King rose to the occasion, defeating Riggs in straight sets. She recalled:

> When I led 2-1, in the first set I knew I would win. I could see that Bobby was sweating profusely and hyperventilating, and I could tell that he had underestimated me. I played him just as I had planned: I did not hit my hardest, I did not rush the net at every opportunity, and I did not always end the point when I had the chance. I moved him from side to side, played his backhand, and gave him plenty of junk, which forced him to generate the pace. When I did put the ball away, I smashed away his lobs and angled away volleys he could only watch and admire.[83]

The symbolism of a woman defeating a former male tennis champion carried huge significance at the time, yet as Ware shows, "King seemed most proud to have brought tennis to a far greater national audience than traditionally followed the game."[84] After her victory, King explained that "as an athlete my victory over a man twenty-six years my senior was no great feat." What she had accomplished, however, was "shown thousands of people who had never taken an interest in women's sports that women were skillful, entertaining, and capable of coming through in the clutch. The match legitimized women's tennis. It was the culmination of an era."[85]

King's overall importance to international sport stems from both her athletic brilliance and her social activism. She retired in 1983 after one of the most decorated careers of any athlete in the world. She won thirty-nine Grand Slam titles, was elected to the International Tennis Hall of Fame in 1987, and went on to coach several famous tennis players, including all-time tennis legend Martina Navratilova. As an activist, King sought to make women an equal partner in the tennis world while, simultaneously, enhancing the game's popularity in the United States and abroad. For herself, her fellow women tennis stars, and the sport itself, she wanted more money, more fame, and broader participation. Tennis "has always been reserved for the rich, the white, the males," King remarked after winning the Battle of the Sexes, "and I've always pledged to change all that."[86]

Global Sport Capitalism

In other professional sports, the end of the century brought more attention, bigger profits, and increased pressure to reach global audiences. Following the success of US hockey at Lake Placid came an impressive run of US-born hockey players making a name for themselves in the NHL. The NHL's history from 1970 to 2000 is defined by the inimitable career of the Canadian Wayne Gretzky, but the United States generated home-grown stars of its own. Legends like Neil Broten, Chris Chelios, Pat LaFontaine, and Mike Modano emerged as all-stars and future Hall of Famers. Attendance at NHL games grew by over 700 percent between 1950 and 2000, better than MLB and comparable to the NFL, though only half of the growth the NBA saw (1,400 percent).[87]

In sheer numbers, however, no one was competing with the NFL for the eyes and wallets of American sport consumers. In 1970, ten million fans paid tickets to watch NFL games live; by 2000, it was up to twenty million. Television audience numbers were even gaudier. The NFL, already the king of TV by 1970, saw its broadcast rights grow from $200 million in 1973 to $4.4 billion by 1997. As Jousza Jr. writes, when it came time to renegotiate with the networks after 1997, "six television companies prepared to bid on the rights to broadcast the league's regular season games and playoffs. In total, media industry analysts estimated the deal to be valued at $7 billion."[88] Cozy at home, the NFL nonetheless failed to internationalize on the scale that other major US sports achieved. Certainly, the NHL showed the potential of a multinational league, and by 2000, MLB and the NBA became major benefactors of the new era in global sport capitalism.

This section looks squarely at the NBA's and MLB's international commercial growth in the late twentieth century. Doing so presents a complex picture where individual athletic greatness, free-trade market pressures, and the adoption of new media technologies elevated both leagues as exports of American culture and capitalism. Additionally, both reflect the emerging story of player economic empowerment, which other sports like professional tennis encountered around the same time. The leagues' response to athlete demands for more money also helped push MLB and the NBA toward the global possibilities available in the 1980s and 1990s. By the century's close, American baseball and basketball players were some of the wealthiest and most famous people in the world.

MLB, Globalization, and the Making of the Free Agent

Baseball's history from 1970 to 2000 is a departure from the tidy narrative that preceded it. Once a story of steady, tightly managed growth, by 1970 the major leagues watched as football became America's sport of choice, while control over its game slipped from the owners and teams to a new generation of assertive ballplayers riding the wave of athlete activism. The sport remained popular around the country, but its primacy was gone. Baseball's headlines also read differently than they had earlier in the century. Legends like Hank Aaron, Bob Gibson, Pete Rose, and Nolan Ryan captivated fans and rewrote the record books. However, internal strife and a series of bitter labor disputes at times overshadowed the product on the field. The turmoil that resulted from the players' efforts to reshape the economics of baseball muddied MLB's brand, yet the ramifications of its labor wars were some of baseball's most significant contributions to the history of professional sport in America. Meanwhile, abroad, the game's growth continued apace as the sinews that had formed in Latin America and the Pacific Rim earlier in the century hardened into one of the most sprawling sporting communities in the world.

The revolution in baseball began on Christmas Eve 1969, when the St. Louis Cardinals' all-star centerfielder Curt Flood wrote a letter to MLB commissioner Bowie Kuhn objecting to his team's decision to trade him to the Philadelphia Phillies. He told Kuhn he was not "a piece of property to be sold regardless of my desire," that he had "the right to consider offers from other clubs," and requested the commissioner "make known to all the major leagues clubs ... of my availability for the 1970 season."[89] Alas, Commissioner Kuhn did not oblige. Flood understood the fact that he was a Black athlete invoking the memory of slavery would cost him support in and out of the game, and he was not wrong.[90] He was also attacking the heart of baseball's economic infrastructure—the hallowed reserve clause—that had guided MLB's growth since the late nineteenth century, thus ensuring the owners would come after him, too. Flood was a dynamic offensive and defensive player—some contemporaries believed he had surpassed an aging Willie Mays as the premier defensive centerfielder in the game—and prior to challenging baseball's reserve clause he was known as the "Rembrandt of Baseball." After he launched his crusade, however, white sportswriters admonished him as a "spoiled ingrate" and mocked him as the "ninety-thousand-dollar-a-year slave."[91] Black writers, meanwhile, defended Flood, and so did Jackie Robinson, who publicly supported Flood and privately told him: "you can't be out there by yourself."[92]

Flood also had the support of the new head of the Major League Baseball Player's Association (MLBPA), Marvin Miller. The MLBPA originated in 1953, but initially did little to champion players' rights. A major league official once described the MLBPA as a "house union" under the direction of "a member of the commissioner's office and the most influential owner at the time."[93] But when Miller took over, the "MLBPA transformed itself ... into an assertive force that set the whole new pattern for labor relations in baseball .... and the goals for unions in other sports."[94] Miller had a background with the Steelworker's Union and instituted what the historian Charles Korr calls a "playing for keeps" approach to negotiations with the league that meant using "every legitimate weapon in the arsenal of labor law."[95]

With Miller pushing the players to think more collectively and aggressively about their stake in the business of baseball, Flood focused the conversation on the central matter: with the reserve clause in place, ballplayers had virtually no control over their contracts or where they lived and played. Flood filed suit with MLB in January 1970, on the grounds that the reserve clause violated antitrust laws and the Thirteenth Amendment.

Miller later credited the Civil Rights Movement for creating a generation of activist athletes that made possible Flood's fight against MLB. Sport "now had at least some people who were able to think in terms of what was wrong with society," Miller said.[96] One of the lessons of the 1960s was that power structures really could change, but major change required courage and, sometimes, a martyr. In the end, Flood provided both.

While Flood's case made its way through the courts, the owners blackballed Flood for the 1970 season to send the players a message. Flood returned briefly in 1971, appearing in just thirteen games for the Washington Senators, before retiring for good. Finally, in 1972, the US Supreme Court ruled against Flood by upholding MLB's exemption from antitrust laws and reaffirmed the reserve clause.[97] "No matter how the courts ruled," writes Korr, "the sense of unity that existed among the players and their recognition that something had to be done were Curt Flood's legacies."[98] Over that decade, the MLBPA continued to challenge the league's monopoly over players, including a thirteen-day strike at the start of the 1972 season that coaxed the owners into putting more money in the MLBPA's pension fund and agreeing to salary arbitration.

Finally, in 1976, a neutral arbitrator ruled in favor of Andy Messersmith, who had challenged the Dodgers' right to renew his contract using a team option without his consent. Korr writes that the "owners were still convinced that they could never lose" while the league's attorneys "assumed that the unique status of baseball" would forever protect the sanctity of the reserve clause. But arbitrator Peter Seitz exploded those illusions and changed baseball forever. Seitz ruled in Messersmith's favor—and, in effect, in favor of all professional baseball players—and granted him free agency for the 1976 season. Law professor and baseball scholar Roger Abrams writes that Seitz's "1975 decision in baseball's Messersmith case still reverberates throughout the multibillion-dollar industry. Arbitrator Seitz set the players free."[99]

Players before free agency were not allowed legal representation when they negotiated contracts with teams; they had virtually no choice but to sign whatever contract their team offered; they could be traded without warning; and were subject to fines and suspensions without the benefit of a legitimate appeal process. After 1976, players could choose representatives for contract negotiations; players with ten years of MLB service time and at least five with the same club could refuse trades; players with two years of service could elect arbitration to settle contract disputes; and they gained a legitimate grievance process to appeal fines and suspensions.[100]

Then there was the money. After 1976, writes Abrams, "[p]layer salaries skyrocketed, increasing sevenfold in the next decade as the free market came to baseball."[101] In the late 1960s, the average player earned about $19,000 annually, and the league minimum salary was set at $6,000. By 1981, the average salary had jumped to $185,651, and the league minimum was up to $32,500. In 2000, the average was around $2 million, and the minimum had reached $200,000.[102] Although he never tasted the fruit, Curt Flood set in motion the making of the modern free agent athlete. His "refusal to whine about his defeat or to claim much credit for the [MLBPA's] later victories," Korr writes, belied the extent to which his efforts "reflected the new atmosphere between players and owners," not to mention the power of athlete activism that had erupted in the late 1960s.[103]

The dawn of free agency further spurred MLB's globalization. Robert Elias explains that "free agency for US ballplayers pushed the major leagues toward foreign sources of cheap labor."[104] By the mid-1970s, Latino players constituted about 10 percent of MLB rosters; by 2000 it was 25 percent.[105] The number of East Asian ballplayers also increased. At the end of the century, baseball's cosmopolitanism was indisputable, yet, as Elias writes, "this may have resulted more from MLB's profit-motivated neocolonial strategies than from its social leadership in integration."[106]

An important entry in this history was the debut of Fernando Valenzuela, a pitching ace from Sonora, Mexico, who signed with the Dodgers in 1980 and "became an overnight star, electrifying Mexicans on both sides of the border."[107] He became the first rookie pitcher to start opening day in Dodgers' history in 1981 when he shut out the Astros on just five hits. He proceeded to win his next seven straight games and finished his rookie season with a league-leading eleven complete games and eight shutouts, making him the only player to ever win Rookie of the Year and the Cy Young Award (the player voted best pitcher in their league) in the same year. "Within the large Mexican-American community in Los Angeles," Klein writes, "the outpouring of pride in 'someone who speaks our language, and eats our food' was a baseball and cultural second coming."[108] As great as Valenzuela was, however, the Dodgers nonetheless tried to keep his labor as cheap as possible, leading to a salary dispute in 1983 that made Valenzuela the first MLB player ever awarded $1 million in arbitration.[109] The team tried to lowball him again before the 1986 season, but Valenzuela refused to be underpaid. When legendary Dodger manager Tommy Lasorda was asked about the negotiations, he joked that Valenzuela "wants Texas back."[110] Valenzuela ultimately signed a $5.5 million contract that made him the highest-paid pitcher in MLB.[111]

Baseball also flowered in East Asia. In South Korea, where organizations like the YMCA introduced baseball earlier in the century, the game rekindled during the US occupation after the Second World War, and "officially became a national mania" in the late twentieth century. By 1980, South Korea emerged as a legitimate global powerhouse. Its national teams began beating more established baseball-loving nations like Cuba and the Dominican Republic in international tournaments.[112] In Japan, professional baseball returned in force after the Second World War. The Nippon Professional Baseball (NPB) league started recruiting internationally in the late 1980s, including future MLB stars Cecil Fielder and Alfonso Soriano.[113] Then, in 1992, the video game giant Nintendo bought a stake in the Seattle

Mariners. The move not only prevented the team's financial doom but also helped make the Mariners one of the most popular MLB franchises in Japan.[114] Two years later, Japan sent Hideo Nomo, its first true MLB star, to the Los Angeles Dodgers. "Nomo's entry into major league baseball was spectacular," Klein writes. "He delighted American audiences, winning awards and impressing his major league colleagues" with his talent as well as his unique pitching style some referred to as a "tornado delivery."[115]

Meanwhile, in Taiwan, a vibrant baseball culture had taken hold by the 1980s, a product of Japan's occupation of the island in the early twentieth century.[116] The Chinese Professional Baseball League (later renamed the Taiwan Major Leagues) started in 1989, and by the mid-1990s, two professional leagues competed on the island. At the 1992 Barcelona Olympics, the first time baseball counted as a medal event, Taiwan outperformed the United States to take the silver medal while Cuba snatched the gold and Japan won bronze. Although the US team consisted largely of second-tier professional ballplayers, the roster did include MLB stars like Nomar Garciapara, Jason Giambi, and Jason Varitek. The success of Cuba, Taiwan, and Japan over the US national team confirmed how strong baseball's international reach had become by the end of the twentieth century.[117]

Even places baseball lagged—including Great Britain and Western Europe, where the game's more established forebearer, cricket, proved difficult to displace[118]—MLB officials continued to push the game. An organization called Major League Baseball International (MLBI) hosted baseball tours and instructional programs all over the world—an organizational blueprint Klein likens to "an invader's role" in transmitting baseball around the world.[119] One of those initiatives, called Pitch, Hit, and Run, began in 1994 and before long had introduced baseball to an estimated 700,000 kids in Australia, Canada, Germany, and South Africa. Thanks to initiatives like MLBI and others, MLB broadcasts extended to nearly 200 countries by the end of the century.[120]

By the late 1970s MLB had also added two franchises in Canada: the Toronto Blue Jays and Montreal Expos. In 1992 and 1993, the Blue Jays won back-to-back World Series titles, something only two other teams not named the New York Yankees have accomplished since 1940.[121] In 1994, the Expos put together one of the most star-studded lineups in baseball history—with all-star-caliber talent like Moisés Alou, Wil Cordero, Cliff Floyd, and Marquis Grissom, plus future Hall of Famers Pedro Martinez and Canada's own Larry Walker—only to have their dream season aborted by the MLBPA's fourth strike in twenty-two years. In 2000, the Expos folded due to the machinations of their new majority owner, Jeffrey Loria, who effectively returned the Expos to the league in exchange for a new franchise in Miami nicknamed the Marlins. The Expos franchise was itself relocated to Washington, DC, and renamed the Nationals.[122] Despite losing one of its major league franchises, the "future of baseball in Canada seems bright," writes historian Colin Howell. MLB teams continue to draft "more and more Canadian players, and a solid nucleus of Canadians playing in the Minor Leagues suggests that the numbers of Canadians in the big leagues will continue to grow."[123]

Baseball's globalization also had its detractors and its downsides. Back in 1992, after Nintendo became part owner of the Mariners, some Americans, including US congressmen, claimed it was "an attempt on the part of the Japanese to 'buy up' more of Americans' national heritage."[124] When the Chicago Cubs and New York Mets opened up the 1996 MLB season in the Tokyo Dome in Japan, a few fans and players were angered by the gesture. The power-hitting, PED-using, baseball nativist Mark McGwire told the press he would refuse to play a professional game in Japan. Baseball was "already too international," he whined. "This game belongs here."[125]

On the business end of MLB's global growth, exploitation was the name of the game. To meet their owners' demand for high-quality, low-cost international talent, MLB front offices deployed specialized scouts called "buscones" (sometimes called "bird dogs" in English) throughout Latin America to scour local leagues for up-and-coming baseball phenoms. The buscones have a complicated history working on behalf of MLB teams. Some are known to steal from or exploit the players they identify on behalf of an MLB club. Yet their familiarity with the talent pool in the region is so great that teams, and players, continue to rely on their services.[126] And in Haiti, where almost all of the world's baseballs are hand-made by a few thousand workers, the economics of baseball's globalization are abundantly clear. As Elias explains, with companies like Rawlings, Spalding, and Wilson relying on Haiti's cheap labor market for their sporting goods, a "Haitian woman had to work four days to earn what million-dollar sluggers were making in forty seconds of work."[127] Curt Flood might have made things a little more expensive for the owners, but MLB continued to find ways to hold down costs and expand into new markets.

The infusion of more international talent into MLB's ranks, the rise in global participation and viewership of baseball, and exploitative foreign labor policies became a business blueprint for other US professional sporting leagues by 2000. With the help of a once-in-a-generation talent, a globally focused commissioner, and a business culture reliant on cheap international labor, in the 1990s the NBA started mirroring baseball's stride.

The Doctor, Air Jordan, and the Global Rise of the NBA

The NBA's arc between 1970 and 2000 is uniquely impressive. A professional sport that struggled since its inception for relevance and stability was, by the end of the century, proving to be America's most popular sport globally. More than a decade into the NBA's development, with legendary players like Bill Russell ringing its bell, the game was still behind baseball and football for popular national attention. And then, suddenly, it started to soar. Not everything about how the NBA changed can be attributed to one man— but almost. Michael Jordan, arguably the greatest athlete of the twentieth century, capped an incredible era of individual athletic achievement and opened a new chapter in the evolution of player empowerment.

Jordan solidified key changes in the way basketball was played to create a version of athletic spectacle that observers found otherworldly. His business acumen was almost as sharp as his shooting eye, and with the help of a like-minded NBA commissioner, Jordan reshaped how corporations, professional leagues, and athletes thought about the global possibilities of sport. Everything about Jordan was different—including what athlete activism and empowerment meant—but he was the product of a longer evolution in basketball's history that traces back to the 1960s. His style and the world of sport he took hostage were both rooted in the competition between the NBA and a rival league that formed in 1967 known as the American Basketball Association (ABA).

Through the late 1960s, the NBA floated on the perimeter of professional sport in America. It had a modest fan base—smaller than the NHL's until the 1980s—and depended heavily on a few key franchises operating in major media markets like Boston, Los Angeles, and New York.[128] With Bill Russell dominating in Boston, in California the legendary Jerry West teamed up with other future Hall of Famers Elgin Baylor and Wilt Chamberlain to turn the Lakers into perennial NBA finals contenders, while the New York Knicks, led by the crafty point guard Walt Frazier and steady big man Willis Reed, won NBA titles in 1970 and 1972. Even among the big-market teams, however, player salaries were paltry because the league was still not catching on. Consequently, players trained differently than they do today. They had to work odd jobs in the off-season to compensate for their NBA salaries, which meant they could never devote themselves entirely to their craft. Through the 1970s, professional basketball was seasonal work.[129]

The NBA, nonetheless, was ahead of its time when it came to player empowerment and unionization. In 1964, West and Baylor threatened to boycott that year's All-Star Game unless the NBA agreed to a pension plan for the players. "The game went on only after a direct confrontation between the 20 all-stars and J. Walter Kennedy, the league president," the *New York Times* reported the next day.[130] The players held firm until Kennedy agreed to the players' pension plan structure, after which they took the court. But as a sign of basketball's marginality, the players' efforts, led by the biggest stars on the greatest team, made few waves at the time.

In smaller markets, success and profitability were even harder to sustain. One of the few challengers to the major market dynasties came from the Milwaukee Bucks, who rode the shoulders of their incredible big man and indomitable activist, Kareem Abdul-Jabbar, and his Hall-of-Fame teammate Oscar Robertson to a championship in 1971 and a second finals appearance in 1974. Abdul-Jabbar shook up the NBA landscape in 1975 after he was traded to Lakers, and then proceeded to win his fourth league MVP. With Abdul-Jabbar as their anchor, the Lakers were primed for another dynastic run of their own. Yet in some ways it was a decision Abdul-Jabbar made several years prior, when he was graduating from UCLA and still went by the name Lew Alcindor, that set the course of professional basketball for the rest of the century.

Before signing with Milwaukee, Alcindor came close to joining the NBA's up-and-coming rival, the ABA, which launched in 1967 and was desperate to land a big-time player to amplify its brand. The ABA hired the NBA's original superstar George Mikan as its commissioner, hoping his presence would give the league some respectability, especially with players coming out of college. In 1969 league officials decided to put everything they had into recruiting Alcindor to play for his hometown New York Nets. The ABA's brass launched what they called "Operation Kingfish": an elaborate research and recruiting effort that involved hiring a private investigator to find anything that might help the ABA land Alcindor. Although the Milwaukee Bucks drafted him first in that year's NBA draft, and despite a $1 million offer from the Globetrotters, Alcindor was open to signing with the ABA, and agreed to meet with Mikan and one of the league's owners to hear their offer.

According to Dick Tinkham, who worked as legal counsel for the ABA, the "plan was to offer [a] million-dollar check and a mink coat to Alcindor as a signing bonus," and then negotiate the terms of his annual salary. But for reasons that are still unclear, Mikan changed the league's offer simply to $1 million spread out over four seasons, with no million-dollar signing bonus and no mink coat. Incredulous league officials erupted at Mikan afterward, while others chased Alcindor and his family to the airport to offer him the original terms of the deal. But by then, it was too late. He announced he was accepting Milwaukee's offer for $1.5 million over five years and refused to change his mind. "The Alcindor fiasco finished Mikan as a commissioner," Tinkham recalled. "Right or wrong, he was blamed for not signing Lew."[131]

Ironically, Mikan's mishap is what made the ABA so special, and what led it to change basketball's style forever. As Adam McKay explains in his terrific podcast series on the NBA called *Death at the Wing*, "without Kareem, and still looking for an edge, the ABA had no choice but to double down on their own brand—part basketball, part entertainment, all fun."[132] League officials decided on a new direction where the ABA's incredible athletes could use their athleticism and creativity to score most of the points, thus taking the game out of the hands of big men and into those of its explosive guards and forwards. The league's quirky use of a three-point line beginning in 1967 also facilitated a more run-and-gun style of play. The three-point line encouraged more long-range shooting and forced defenses to play further away from the basket, which opened up passing and driving lanes for playmakers on the wing. "A different type of basketball led by a different type of star," McKay explains. "The ABA looked for players who just needed the ball in their hands and a little bit of space on the court to get creative."[133]

It was a smart tactical decision, because what the ABA had in abundance were high-flying, fast-breaking wing players who could rattle the rims with thunderous dunks and perform acrobatic drives to the basket. Whereas college basketball had actually outlawed dunking—a decision made explicitly to weaken Lew Alcindor's dominance and laced with racist overtones[134]— and the NBA downplayed it, the ABA encouraged players to take the game that was being played on blacktops and playgrounds in America onto the hardwood courts of professional basketball. Best of all, they had the perfect ambassador for their new brand of ball: Julius "Dr. J" Erving. Erving hailed from the University of Massachusetts and carried himself with a personal swagger befitting his style of play. Telegenic and always composed, Erving eventually inked endorsement deals with Coco-Cola and Converse.

Off the court, Erving was charming, sharp, and stylish; on it, he was fast, strong, and explosive with powerful hands that seemed to swallow the ball when he palmed it for a windmill dunk or a lilting finger roll. Erving's first ABA coach, Al Bianchi, once remarked that he "was always overwhelmed by the size of Julius's hands. Then I saw all the things he did—the hanging in the air … it was amazing. Michael Jordan does much of the same stuff now and perhaps it's more dramatic because Michael is smaller, but Doc did it first."[135] Or, as the famous coach and broadcaster Johnny "Red" Kerr once put it, "a young Julius Erving was like Thomas Edison. He was inventing something new every night."[136]

In flourishing style, Erving won two championships, three MVPs, and four all-ABA awards, averaging 28.7 points, 12.1 rebounds, and 4.8 assists over his five seasons in the league, split between the Virginia Squires and his hometown New York Nets.[137] Much as Bianchi understood, what became the trademark of the modern NBA—a soaring athletic grace combined with quick playmaking from the guard and forward positions—was merely the adoption of what Dr. J and a host of talented ABA stars brought to the court every game. Dynamic players like George Gervin, David Thompson, and Connie Hawkins reconfigured what modern basketball looked like, then assimilated their style into the NBA once the ABA began its death spiral. Despite its highly entertaining product, the ABA simply did not have the cache or financial means of reaching American sport consumers on the level the NBA could—to say nothing of the more popular leagues like the NFL and MLB. They tried, but league officials could never manage to ink a national television deal, which meant that most basketball fans only knew about the ABA's stars by what they read in *The Sporting News* and *Sports Illustrated*.

The ABA employed some wild tactics and gimmicks to earn attention. The balls were painted red, white, and blue. Their jerseys were garish and artsy. They signed high school players to their rosters. They concocted outlandish ticket promotions—Halter Top Night in Denver offered free tickets to women dressed for the occasion, and in Indianapolis, promoters brought an actual bear into the arena to wrestle fans—as well as innovations like a dunk contest during their all-star games (something else the NBA copied).[138] None of it was enough. In 1976, the NBA purchased four ABA franchises—the Denver Nuggets, the Indiana Pacers, the New York Nets, and the San Antonio Spurs— and the frenetic life of the ABA was no more. According to Mick Goldberg, former legal counsel for the league, the ABA's failure ultimately came down to "the fatigue factor." It took "so much energy, so much creativity just to stay in business," he explained, "the ABA simply ran out of gas."[139]

Having absorbed the ABA's best players and teams, not to mention its style, the NBA evolved into its modern, compelling form. To pay off the costs they incurred for joining the NBA, the New York Nets sold Erving's player rights to the Philadelphia 76ers for $3 million. As a Sixer, Erving became a bridge between the leagues as well as generations within basketball history. He was voted league MVP in 1981. Then in 1983, after losing three previous NBA Finals series, Erving and the Sixers knocked off Kareem Abdul-Jabbar, Earvin "Magic" Johnson, and the Showtime Lakers to become NBA champions.[140] By the time Erving retired in 1987, the NBA was entering a golden era of great teams, dynamic players, and intense personal rivalries that helped create a sense of drama its fans craved. Magic Johnson's Lakers reignited their rivalry with the Boston Celtics, who had drafted Larry Bird out of Indiana State in 1979. Between 1984 and 1988 the two powerhouses squared off three times in the NBA Finals. Abdul-Jabbar retired in 1989, a six-time NBA champion, a six-time league MVP, and still the all-time leader in points scored (38,387).[141] The arrival of players like Dominique Wilkins, Clyde Drexler, and Isiah Thomas made more teams relevant and helped solidify the game's fluid, fast-paced style.

But it was in 1984 when the fate of basketball changed forever. With the third pick in that year's draft, the Chicago Bulls drafted a skinny, silky-smooth shooting guard named Michael Jordan from the University of North Carolina. Before long, Jordan had taken the Bulls, the league, and his own brand to heights unimaginable at the time of the ABA–NBA merger. During and after his career, Jordan acknowledged how much he owed to The Doctor—and not just stylistically. In his autobiography, Jordan stated that when he came into the league, Erving "was the king when it came to professional basketball moving to corporate America. His Coca-Cola [partnership] was like the connection I eventually had with Nike," he wrote. "In that sense, Dr. J made it possible for me to take the next step off the court. He brought so much class to the professional athlete."[142]

Jordan was born in North Carolina, where he won a national championship for the UNC Tarheels under legendary college coach Dean Smith in 1982. He won a gold medal at the 1984 Los Angeles Olympics as the leading scorer for an incredible team of college players coached by the insufferable Bobby Knight. The Bulls lucked into getting him at the third overall pick, and almost immediately Jordan showed the league where its future was headed. In his first year in 1985, he played in every regular season game, was named an all-star, the Rookie of the Year, and second team All-NBA, while averaging 28.2 points, 6.5 rebounds, and 5.9 assists a game.

He broke his foot in his second year and played in just eighteen games but returned in time for a first-round playoff bout against Bird's Boston Celtics. Jordan scored 49 points in game one, then in the second game of the series he erupted for an NBA record 63 points and confirmed his place atop the NBA's Mount Olympus. After the game, which the Celtics won, Bird was asked what he made of Jordan's performance. "I think he's God disguised as Michael Jordan," Bird said. "He is the most awesome player in the NBA.

FIGURE 4.3 *Wearing the eleventh installment of his Air Jordan brand shoes (known as Concords to sneakerheads), Michael Jordan throws down a two-hand slam over a helpless Phoenix Suns defender during the 1996–97 NBA season. Jordan and his Chicago Bulls went on to win that year's NBA championship, the fifth of six titles Jordan tallied as a player. (Photo by Brian Bahr/AFP via Getty Images).*

Today in the Boston Garden, on national TV, in the playoffs, he put on one of the greatest shows of all time."[143]

Bird was not the only one who saw wings when Jordan soared. The NBA's new commissioner, along with Nike's top executives, quickly recognized MJ's enormous potential value as a global sport icon. With Jordan as its poster boy, league-wide attendance, average ticket prices, television ratings, and media broadcast deals all skyrocketed for the NBA.[144] It still could not compete with the NFL domestically, but by the mid-1990s the NBA had surpassed the NHL and was challenging baseball at home and abroad. Indeed, under the commissionership of David Stern, the NBA made about as many international gains as it did within its home market. Stern brokered a salary-capped contract with the NBA Players' Association (NBAPA) in 1983 which not all the players loved, but it did make it easier for teams in smaller markets to compete and, thus, grow the NBA's brand in other corners of America.[145] However, Stern's vision was global, and to achieve it he modeled the league off of Walt Disney's approach to entertainment capitalism. "They have theme parks, and we have theme parks. Only we call them arenas," Stern said. "They have characters: Mickey and Goofy. Our characters are named Magic and Michael. Disney sells apparel; we sell apparel. They make home videos; we make home videos."[146]

In his book *Michael Jordan and the New Global Capitalism*, the great historian Walter LaFeber wrote that "under David Stern's guidance," the NBA sprung "toward the limitless possibilities offered by the world's love of sports—and by a new global technology that US transnational corporations and certain athletes could profit from mightily."[147] When Jordan's Bulls began a championship run in the 1990s, Stern pounced on his star's singular popularity to grow the league further. In Jordan's rookie season, the NBA sent about thirty-five telecasts a week to just a handful of foreign markets. By 1996, it was 175 broadcasts to 600 million viewers in forty different languages.[148] As the new millennium approached, and the internet began to take hold, Stern leapt on the new technology and began pushing *NBATV.com* as a beacon for NBA media and entertainment all over the world. "It was his success in the global market that set Jordan apart from the earlier commercial triumphs of Kareem Abdul-Jabbar and Magic Johnson," LaFeber writes. Stern lined up broadcasts in over seventy countries for Jordan's first NBA Finals championship, against Magic and the Lakers in 1991. From there, global media deals and mass marketing campaigns took off. "Especially remarkable was Jordan's and the NBA's popularity in such countries as Italy, Spain, and Hungary, for they had long successful basketball traditions of their own." But tradition, LaFeber adds, "seemed to be no match for communication satellites, global-minded advertising executives, the drive of David Stern's marketing powerhouse, and Nike commercials."[149]

Nike was, indeed, strapped alongside Jordan's leap to superstardom. They signed Jordan to a five-year shoe deal worth $500,000 a year in

1984, and immediately produced the iconic sneaker they called Air Jordan 1. Nike's original goal was $3 million in sales in four years. Instead, Air Jordan 1 sales topped $126 million in one year, which convinced Nike to pump out a new Air Jordan model for every season.[150] By 1997, Jordan was earning upward of $40 million a year simply from his Nike and other major endorsement deals with McDonald's and Gatorade—on top of his NBA salary of $30 million a year. That summer, Jordan and the Bulls traveled to Paris to participate in the McDonald's Championship, where they faced off against international teams and toured the city. After the Bulls won the tournament, Jordan stood for pictures in front of the Eiffel Tower, an image that seemed to timestamp Jordan's global ascent. Steve Rushin, writing for *Sports Illustrated* in the fall of 1997, set the scene:

> His work is now complete. Michael Jordan posed last week in Nikes beneath the Eiffel Tower while promoting McDonald's, and the resulting photographs were not pictures so much as pictographs: swooshes, golden arches, the monument and Michael, each emblem instantly recognizable almost everywhere on earth. In Paris, Jordan finally joined that little red man in the don't-walk sign and the white silhouette on the men's room door as the most famous of world figures—a genuine international icon.[151]

Jordan's wizardry as a marketer and shoe salesman made him fabulously wealthy but left him open to criticism over how the companies he endorsed conducted business. Nike was known for relying on sweatshop labor in Vietnam, China, and Indonesia to make shoes they were selling for nearly $100 a pop. Workers stitching Air Jordans, meanwhile, earned between $1 and $2 a day. The scholar Douglas Kelner, who writes on Jordan and Nike's "unholy alliance," contends free-trade treaties "made it even easier for Nike ... to move around its production at will, searching for the lowest labor costs and most easily exploitable working conditions."[152] Jordan faced additional criticism for the impact he and Nike were having on African American communities, particularly in America's inner cities, which accounted for over one-third of Nike's sales. Air Jordan sneakers became so popular that in parts of the country accounts about Black youth stealing and killing for a pair of Jordans became a recurring story on the evening news. Other critics pointed out that, instead of exporting the labor to sweatshops in Asia, Jordan could have pushed Nike to open factories in Black-majority cities and to hire more Black executives. But as LaFeber put it, as "charges were hurled back and forth, Jordan continued to be silent," opting instead to keep his focus on basketball and his bottom line.[153]

As he dodged criticism about his role in Nike's exploitative practices, Jordan was equally uninterested in the kind of activism Russell and Abdul-Jabbar adopted during and after their playing days. A Bulls teammate named Craig Hodges once approached Jordan about using his unmatched platform to call attention to police violence after the beating of Rodney King in 1991, but Jordan refused. Hodges then did the unthinkable and criticized Jordan in the press. Hodges accused Jordan of "bailing out" by ignoring the issue even though "he has children in the palm of his hands."[154] Hodges wanted Jordan to accept his duty as a role model for young Black Americans—but what he got was a one-way ticket out of Chicago and the NBA. Despite being one of the best three-point shooters in the league, Hodges and his agent were told after the season no one would sign him for what he did.[155]

The 1992 Barcelona Games—where Jordan seared his corporate devotion into Olympic lore by draping himself in the American flag to avoid being seen wearing a Reebok-branded Olympic sweatsuit—were among the crowning events in America's international sport history. The Cold War had been won, the world was open for business, and the ultimate cultural icon for the moment steamrolled the competition. With Magic, Bird, Wilkins, Drexler, and his Chicago Bulls teammate Scottie Pippen playing with him, Jordan led the United States to the gold medal without losing a game. The only team that challenged the United States was Croatia, led by the phenomenal shooting guard Dražen Petrović, who played for the NBA's Portland Trailblazers. The United States still pummeled Croatia twice by more than 30 points, including in the gold medal game, but that was as close as any team managed against the waves of Hall of Famers the US team deployed. In the championship game, Petrović put up 24 points, and Jordan's soon-to-be-teammate, Toni Kukoč, added 16 points in the losing effort. Croatia's performance was unheralded at the time, but in hindsight it seems as much a harbinger of the NBA's future as the Dream Team's dominant performance. Over the next few years, the internationalization of the NBA shifted into full gear, with stars like Petrović, Kukoč, and others making legendary careers for themselves in America.[156]

Jordan as both a player and a brand owned the 1990s. He won a total of six NBA titles as a member of the Chicago Bulls (1991–3; 1996–8), five MVP awards, and retired at or near the top of almost every major offensive category in league history. He was also a suffocating defensive player, named to nine All-NBA defensive teams to go along with a Defensive Player of the Year award in 1988. When he retired for good as a member of the Washington Wizards in 2003, it was headline news around the world. The Chinese newspaper the *Morning Post*'s front page blazed "Flying Man Jordan Is Coming Back to Earth." Surveys conducted around the world showed that Jordan was one of the most recognizable humans on the planet, with as many people associating him with Nike and Gatorade as with the NBA. "Parlaying his athletic triumphs into commercial product endorsements," Kelner writes, "Jordan became the highest paid celebrity advertising figure ever." He was the "perfect icon for the end-of-millennium American and global culture, combining extraordinary athletic prowess, an unrivaled record of success and winning, high entertainment value, and an ability to exploit his image into impressive business success."[157]

Notes

1   "Persian Gulf Crisis," President George H.W. Bush, Address to Joint Session
    of Congress, Washington, DC, September 11, 1990, full text reprinted in the
    Washington Post [hereafter *WP*], URL: https://www.washingtonpost.com/archive/
    politics/1990/09/12/bush-out-of-these-troubled-times-a-new-world-order/b93b5cf1-
    e389-4e6a-84b0-85f71bf4c946/ [accessed 6.28.2021].

2   Fan Hong and Tan Hua, "Sport in China: Conflict between Tradition and Modernity,
    1840s to 1930s," *The International Journal of the History of Sport* 19, no. 2–3 (2002):
    203; 189.

3   Andrew Morris, *Marrow of the Nation: A History of Sport and Physical Culture in
    Republican China* (Berkeley: University of California Press, 2004), 121.

4   Ibid., 152–66.

5   Ibid., 237–40.

6   Fan Hong and Lu Zhouxiang, "Sport and China's Foreign Diplomacy in the 1960s
    and 1970s," in Heather L. Dichter and Andrew L. Johns, eds., *Diplomatic Games:
    Sport, Statecraft, and International Relations since 1945* (Lexington: University Press of
    Kentucky, 2014, 391.

7   Ibid., 394.

8   Rana Mitter, "China and the Cold War," in Richard H. Immerman and Petra Goedde
    eds., *The Oxford Handbook of the Cold War*, 133–4.

9   Fan and Lu, "Sport and China's Foreign Diplomacy in the 1960s and 1970s," 397.

10 Nevada Cooke and Robert Barney, "Preserving the 'American Way': Gerald Ford, the
    President's Commission on Olympic Sports, and the Fight against State-Funded Sport
    in America," in Rider and Witherspoon, eds., *Defending the American Way of Life*,
    68–70.

11 Ibid., 68.

12 Kevin Witherspoon, "'Fuzz Kids' and 'Musclemen'" The US-Soviet Basketball Rivalry,
    1958–1975" in Dichter and Johns eds., *Diplomatic Games*, 300.

13 Al McGuire quoted in ibid., 302.

14 Ibid., 304.

15 Ibid.

16 "Soviet Five Tops US in Olympics," *NYT*, September 10, 1972, 1; "Three Bizarre
    Seconds End a 36-Year Reign of US Quintet," *NYT*, September 11, 1972, 49; Hendrick
    Smith, "Russians Gloat over Gold Medals," *NYT*, September 13, 1972, 37, 39.

17 Bob Cousy quoted in Witherspoon, "'Fuzz Kids' and 'Musclemen,'" 312.

18 Cooke and Barney, "Preserving the 'American Way,'" 71.

19 Ibid.

20 Ibid., 78.

21 Ibid., 82.

22 George C. Herring, *From Colony to Superpower: US Foreign Relations since 1776*
    (New York: Oxford University Press, 2008), 836–8.

23 Robert D. Schulzinger, *US Diplomacy since 1900*, 6th edition (New York: Oxford University Press, 2008), 288.

24 Herring, *From Colony to Superpower*, 847–50.

25 Ibid., 853–4; Toby C. Rider, *Cold War Games: Propaganda, the Olympics, and US Foreign Policy* (Chicago: University of Illinois Press, 2016), 110.

26 Jimmy Carter quoted in Nicholas Sarantakes, "The White House Games: The Carter Administration's Efforts to Establish an Alternative to the Olympics," in Dichter and Johns eds., *Diplomatic Games*, 329. For a more complete study of Carter's Olympic boycott strategy, see Sarantakes's book on the topic, *Dropping the Torch: Jimmy Carter, the Olympic Boycott, and the Cold War* (New York: Cambridge University Press, 2011).

27 Sarantakes, "The White House Games," 330.

28 Steven Daly, "Athletes Differ on Olympic Boycott," *NYT*, May 9, 1980, 382; 387.

29 Sarantakes, "White House Games," 335–51.

30 Mary G. McDonald, "'Miraculous' Masculinity Meets Militarization: Narrating the 1980 USSR-US Men's Olympic Ice Hockey Match and Cold War Politics," in Wagg and Andrews eds., *East Plays West*, 231.

31 Oliver North quoted in ibid., 23.

32 Herb Brooks quoted in "Do You Believe in Miracles?" prod. Brian Hyland, 2001; HBO.

33 Mark Johnson quoted in ibid.

34 Al Michaels quoted in ibid.

35 Mike Eruzione quoted in ibid.

36 "Los Angeles 1984 Medal Table," https://olympics.com/en/olympic-games/los-angeles-1984/medals [accessed 8.1.2021].

37 Herring, *From Colony to Superpower*, 860.

38 Andrew Johns, "Competing in the Global Arena: Sport and Foreign Relations since 1945," in Dichter and Johns eds., *Diplomatic Games*, 5.

39 Ibid., 6.

40 Jaime Schultz, *Women's Sports: What Everyone Needs to Know* (New York: Oxford University Press, 2018), 30–1.

41 Susan Ware, *Title IX: A Brief History with Documents* (New York: Bedford/St. Martin's, 2007), 13.

42 Arthur Ashe quoted in Eric Morgan, "Black and White at Center Court," *Diplomatic History 36*, no. 5 (2012): 817.

43 Eric Allen Hall, *Arthur Ashe: Tennis and Justice in the Civil Rights Era* (Baltimore, MD: Johns Hopkins University Press, 2014), 149.

44 Ashe quoted in Moore, *We Will Win the Day*, 137.

45 Ashe quoted in "Arthur Ashe: More Than a Champion," 2015, BBC One.

46 Moore, *We Will Win the Day*, 136.

47 Edwards quoted in "Arthur Ashe: More Than a Champion."

48   Moore, *We Will Win the Day*, 137.

49   Ashe quoted in ibid., 138.

50   John Nauright, "Embodied Identities: Sport and Race in South Africa," in John Nauright, et al, eds, *Beyond C.L.R. James: Shifting Boundaries of Race and Ethnicity in Sports* (Fayetteville: University of Arkansas Press, 2014), 41.

51   Ryan M. Irwin, *Gordian Knot: Apartheid and the Unmaking of the Liberal World Order* (New York: Oxford University Press, 2012), 46; 174.

52   Ibid., 42.

53   Morgan, "Black and White at Center Court," 825.

54   Nauright, "Embodied Identities," 45–6.

55   Morgan, "Black and White at Center Court," 832.

56   Ibid., 834.

57   John Burns, "Won't Play in S. Africa, Ashe Declares after Visit," *NYT*, April 10, 1977, 291.

58   "Arthur Ashe Legacy Resources," *The Arthur Ashe Legacy*, URL: https://arthurashe.ucla.edu/legacy-resources/ [accessed 6.14.21].

59   Hall, *Arthur Ashe*, 151.

60   Ibid., 148–9.

61   Ibid., 150.

62   Ibid.

63   "Arthur Ashe," https://www.atptour.com/en/players/arthur-ashe/a063/fedex-atp-win-loss [accessed 6.14.21].

64   "The Arthur Ashe Legacy," UCLA, URL: https://arthurashe.ucla.edu/life-story/ [accessed 6.14.21].

65   Ashe quoted in Moore, *We Will Win the Day*, 139.

66   Billie Jean King quoted in "Arthur Ashe: More Than a Champion."

67   Susan Ware, *Game, Set, Match: Billie Jean King and the Revolution in Women's Sports* (Chapel Hill: University of North Carolina Press, 2015), 16.

68   Ibid.

69   King quoted in "Billie Jean King: Portrait of a Pioneer," produced by Ross Greenburg, Rick Bernstein, and Brian Hyland. 2006, *HBO Films*.

70   Ware, *Game, Set, Match*, 20.

71   King Quoted in "Billie Jean King: Portrait of a Pioneer."

72   Ware, *Game, Set, Match*, 26; 28.

73   Schultz, *Women's Sports*, 61.

74   Robert Lindsey, "Billie Jean King Is Sued for Assets over Alleged Lesbian Affair," *NYT*, April 30, 1981, 18.

75   Schultz, *Women's Sports*, 61.

76   King quoted in Ware, *Game, Set, Match*, 30.

77   Ibid., 31.

78   Ibid., 33.

79 King quoted in ibid., 35; 36.

80 Ibid., 38.

81 Billie Jean King with Cynthia Starr, *We Have Come a Long Way: The Story of Women's Tennis* (New York: McGraw-Hill, 1988), 142.

82 Ibid., 144.

83 Ibid., 145–6.

84 Ware, *Game, Set, Match*, 2.

85 King, *We Have Come a Long Way*, 46.

86 King quoted in ibid.

87 Josza Jr., *American Sports Empire*, 2.

88 Ibid., 124.

89 Letter from Curt Flood to Bowie Kuhn, December 24, 1969, reprinted in Marc Craig, "Curt Flood's Letter to Bowie Kuhn," *The Athletic*, December 24, 2019, URL: https://theathletic.com/1475428/2019/12/24/curt-floods-letter-to-bowie-kuhn-50-years-later-a-close-look-at-the-founding-document-of-free-agency/?redirected=1 [accessed 6.29.21].

90 For more on the racial animus Flood faced, see Charles P. Korr, *The End of Baseball as We Knew It: The Players Union, 1960–1981* (Urbana: University of Illinois Press, 2002), 95–7.

91 Korr, *The End of Baseball as We Knew It*, 85; 96. See also Terry Sloope, "Curt Flood," Society for American Baseball Research, URL: https://sabr.org/bioproj/person/curt-flood/ [accessed 7.1.2021].

92 Jackie Robinson quoted in Zirin, *A People's History of Sport*, 207.

93 Korr, *The End of Baseball as We Knew It*, 2.

94 Ibid., 3.

95 Ibid., 4.

96 Miller quoted in Zirin, *A People's History of Sport*, 206.

97 *Flood v. Kuhn* 407 US 258 (1972), June 19, 1972, JUSTIA, URL: https://supreme.justia.com/cases/federal/us/407/258/ [accessed 7.1.2021].

98 Korr, *The End of Baseball as We Knew It*, 101.

99 Roger Abrams, "Arbitrator Seitz Sets the Players Free," *Baseball Research Journal*, Society for American Baseball Research, 2009, URL: https://sabr.org/journal/article/arbitrator-seitz-sets-the-players-free/ [accessed 7.1.2021].

100 Korr, *The End of Baseball as We Knew It*, 3.

101 Abrams, "Arbitrator Seitz Sets the Players Free."

102 "Minimum Salary," *Baseball-Reference.com*, URL: https://www.baseball-reference.com/bullpen/Minimum_salary [accessed 7.6.2021].

103 Korr, *The End of Baseball as We Knew It*, 100; 85.

104 Elias, *The Empire Strikes Out*, 214.

105 Armou and Levitt, "Baseball Demographics, 1947–2016."

106 Ibid., 213; 229.

107   Ibid., 215.

108   Alan Klein, *Growing the Game: The Globalization of Major League Baseball* (New Haven: Yale University Press, 2006), 70.

109   "Valenzuela Granted $1 Million," *NYT*, February 20, 1983, 370.

110   Elias, *The Empire Strikes Out*, 215. Lasorda was alluding to the Mexican Cession that netted the United States most of Texas, Arizona, New Mexico, Nevada, California, and small portions of Colorado and Utah after the Mexican-American War (1844–8).

111   Gordon Edes, "Valenzuela Signs for 3 Years, $5.5 Million: Arbitration Avoided; He's Game's Richest Starting Pitcher," *Los Angeles Times*, February 16, 1986.

112   Joseph A. Reaves, "Korea: Straw Sandals and Strong Arms," in George Gmelch and Daniel Nathan, eds., *Baseball beyond Our Borders: An International Pastime* (Lincoln: University of Nebraska Press, 2017), 214.

113   Elias, *The Empire Strikes Out*, 218–19.

114   Ibid., 220.

115   Klein, *Growing the Game*, 128.

116   Andrew D. Morris, "Taiwan: Baseball, Colonialism, Nationalism, and Other Inconceivable Things," in Gmelch and Nathan eds, *Baseball Beyond Our Borders*, 249–81.

117   Ibid., 260–4.

118   Josh Chetwynd describes baseball's history in Great Britain as a "cycle of optimism and despair." He writes that "Britons have steadfastly protected their traditional sports. A popular antibaseball chant among detractors is that baseball is 'glorified rounders' …. Regrettably, this comparison hasn't changed much in more than a century." See Josh Chetwynd, "Great Britain: Baseball's Battle for Respect in the Land of Cricket, Rugby, and Soccer," in Gmelch and Nathan eds, *Baseball Beyond Our Borders*, 393–409. As Michael Clair reports, as of 2019, there has never been a British-born player on any MLB roster. See Michael Clair, "Here's How Baseball Has Grown in England, from Factory Towns to London Stadium," *MLB.com*, June 28, 2019, URL: https://www.mlb.com/cut4/baseball-in-england-has-a-fascinating-history [accessed 7.4.2021].

119   Klein, *Globalizing the Game*, 165.

120   Elias, *The Empire Strikes Out*, 230.

121   David Adler, "Every Back to Back World Series Champ in MLB History," *MLB.com*, November 6, 2020, URL: https://www.mlb.com/news/back-to-back-world-series-champions-c297636124 [accessed 7.3.2021].

122   For a good primer on this history, see Farid Rusdi, "How Jeffrey Loria Destroyed the Montreal Expos/Washington National," *Bleacher Report*, February 2, 2009, URL: https://bleacherreport.com/articles/118868-how-jeffrey-loria-destroyed-the-montreal-exposnationals [accessed 7.3.2021].

123   Colin Howell, "Canada: Internationalizing America's National Pastime," in Gmelch and Nathan eds, *Baseball beyond Our Borders*, 73.

124   Klein, *Globalizing the Game*, 165.

125   McGuire quoted in Elias, *The Empire Strikes Out*, 220.

126   Klein, *Globalizing the Game*, 104.

127 Elias, *The Empire Strikes Out*, 231.

128 Jozsa, Jr., *American Sports Empire*, 2.

129 Jerry West interview with Ernie Johnson, *NBA on TNT*, URL: https://twitter.com/
NBAonTNT/status/1255859453972238337?ref_src=twsrc%5Etfw%7Ctwcamp%5Etw
eetembed%7Ctwterm%5E1255859453972238337%7Ctwgr%5E%7Ctwcon%5Es1_&r
ef_url=https%3A%2F%2Fwww.talkbasket.net%2F83764-jerry-west-on-what-it-was-
like-to-play-in-the-60s-and-70s-in-the-nba [accessed 7.11.2021].

130 Leonard Koppet, "N.B.A. Players Threaten Strike in Dispute over Pension Plan,"
NYT, January 15, 1964, 34.

131 Dick Tinkham quoted in Terry Pluto, *Loose Balls: The Short, Wild Life of the
American Basketball Association* (New York: Simon and Schuster, 1990), 192–3.

132 Adam McKay, *Death at the Wing*, Episode 1: The Invisible Revolution, transcript,
URL: https://cdn.smehost.net/threeuncannyfourcom-neonhummediaprod/wp-
content/uploads/2021/04/Death-at-the-Wing-Episode-1_-The-Invisible-Revolution-
TRANSCRIPT.pdf [accessed 7.11.2021].

133 Ibid.

134 John Matthew Smith, "It's Not Really My Country," *Journal of Sport History* 36, no. 2
(2009): 232–3.

135 Al Bianchi quoted in ibid., 227.

136 Johnny Kerr quoted in ibid., 229.

137 Julius Erving, *Basketball Reference*, URL: https://www.basketball-reference.com/
players/e/ervinju01.html [accessed 7.10.2021].

138 Dana Hunsinger Benbow, "Bear Wrestling, Halter-Top Night and Wild Parties: ABA
Reunion in Indianapolis," *Indianapolis Star*. https://www.indystar.com/story/sports/
nba/pacers/2018/03/21/aba-reunion-indianapolis-trend-setting-league-julius-
erving-bob-costas-rick-barry-george-gervin/419479002/ [accessed 7.21.22].

139 Mike Goldberg quoted in Pluto, *Loose Balls*, 428.

140 "Julius Erving," *Basketball Reference*, URL: https://www.basketball-reference.com/
players/e/ervinju01.html [accessed 7.10.2021].

141 "NBA History—Points Leaders," *ESPN*, URL: http://www.espn.com/nba/history/
leaders [accessed 7.10.2021].

142 Michael Jordan, *For the Love of the Game: My Story* (New York: Crown, 1998), 15.

143 Bob Sakamoto, "Michael Jordan's Playoff Record 63 Points Isn't Enough for the
Chicago Bulls in a Loss to the Boston Celtics," *The Chicago Tribune*, April 21, 1986,
URL: https://www.chicagotribune.com/sports/bulls/ct-michael-jordan-playoff-
record-celtics-20160419-story.html [accessed 7.11.2021].

144 Jousza Jr., *American Sports Empire*, 2; 152; 122–34.

145 Ibid., 60–4.

146 David Stern quoted in ibid., 64.

147 Walter LaFeber, *Michael Jordan and the New Global Capitalism* (New York: W. W.
Norton & Company, 2002), 48.

148 Douglas Kelner, "The Sports, Spectacle, Michael Jordan, and Nike's 'Unholy Alliance'?"
in David L. Andrews, ed., *Michael Jordan Inc: Corporate Sport, Media Culture, and
Late Modern American* (New York: State University of New York Press, 2001), 42.

149 Ibid., 80.

150 Dir. Jason Hehir, *The Last Dance*, episode 5. 2020, ESPN. Also see *Sole Man* 30 for 30 ESPN Documentary.

151 Steve Rushin, "World Domination," *SI*, October 27, 1997, 82.

152 Kelner, "The Sport Spectacle, Michael Jordan, and Nike's 'Unholy Alliance'?," 56. See also LaFeber, *Michael Jordan and the New Global Capitalism*, 124–6.

153 LaFeber, *Michael Jordan and the New Global Capitalism*, 126.

154 William Rhoden, "Hodges Criticized Jordan for His Silence on Issues," *NYT*, June 4, 1992, 42.

155 "Death at the Wing," Episode 7.

156 "Men's Olympics—United States at Croatia, August 8, 1992," *Basketball Reference*, URL: https://www.basketball-reference.com/international/boxscores/1992-08-08-croatia.html [accessed 7.12.2022].

157 Kelner, "The Sports Spectacle, Michael Jordan and Nike's 'Unholy Alliance'?" 38.

Athlete Spotlight #4:
Carl Lewis

FIGURE 4.4 *The enigmatic Carl Lewis raises his arms in celebration after winning the 100-meter sprint at the 1984 Summer Olympics in Los Angeles, California. Lewis went on to match Jesse Owens's 1936 performance by winning four gold medals at those Games. (Bettmann/Contributor via Getty Images).*

In 1999, the IOC crowned Carl Lewis the Sportsman of the Century. Quite an honor considering all the Olympic legends worthy of consideration. But Lewis was a unique athlete. His nine gold medals, at the time, tied for the all-time Olympic record. He was flashy, cocky, and ambitious beyond just track and field. Lewis was a businessman, starred in movies, recorded albums, and delivered one of the most infamous renditions of the "Star-Spangled Banner" in television history. A journalist once compared Carl Lewis to "a child who has climbed a tree and lost himself in the self-absorption of seeing how far out on a limb he can go."[1]

Lewis was born in 1961 in Birmingham, Alabama, to a family of elite athletes, including two parents who stressed individualism and relentless competition. Carl was smaller than other kids his age but a gifted athlete, nonetheless. He excelled at soccer but bristled at authority. His talents, it turned out, flashed brightest when he was challenging other kids to race him. He met Jesse Owens when he was eleven, a moment Lewis later said changed his life. In high school, Lewis grew into a track and field phenom, adding the long jump to his game, and soon was beating world-class athletes at major competitions.

For all his success, however, Lewis seemed most obsessed with his image and marketability. His goal, he once noted, was to "[t]ranscend track and field and gain access to a diversity of Americans through stories in magazines such as *Esquire, Newsweek, GQ* and *Ebony*." Perhaps because it came so scripted, or because he was Black, eccentric, and dominant, but for much of his career Lewis struggled to capture the public's adoration like he wanted.[2]

Lewis's ascendance into Olympic lore came in Los Angeles in 1984, where he trained his sights on tying his idol Owens by winning four golds. He cruised in the 100 meters, and then with his first leap landed a long jump so far he skipped his final four attempts and still won gold—a move that provoked a chorus of boos from fans in the LA Coliseum. He proceeded to set an Olympic record in the 200 meters to win his third gold, and finished by anchoring the US 4x100 to another record-setting time and his fourth gold medal—matching Owens's 1936 performance.[3] "Without the inspiration of Jesse Owens," Lewis said afterward, "I wouldn't be here today …. It can't be topped. It's been the time of my life."[4]

Four years later, at the Seoul Olympics in South Korea, Lewis was part of history again. In what became known as "The Dirtiest Race in History," the Canadian sprinter Ben Johnson supplanted Lewis as the world's fastest man by winning the 100 meters in a record 9.79 seconds. Lewis finished second with an exasperated look on his face. Indeed, Lewis had been intimating other sprinters were using PEDs prior to the Games, and shortly after Johnson's victory, news broke that the Canadian had tested positive for a banned substance.

Johnson later admitted to doping; however, the details surrounding his positive test—including circumstantial evidence that an associate of Lewis might have drugged him—remain hotly contested. Lewis himself admitted in 2003 that he had tested positive for stimulants in 1988, although the IOC never made the results public and later removed the drugs Lewis had used from its banned substance list. Lewis was awarded Johnson's gold— his sixth overall at that point—and he added two more golds at the 1992 Barcelona Olympics and one in 1996 in Atlanta to make nine and tie the Olympic record. "People said I was arrogant and antisocial," Lewis later said about his iconoclastic career. "But I was like 'A track meet is work. I'm here to kick your ass, and then I'll go home and play with my friends'."[5] His focus on individual glory and commercial appeal also firmly linked Lewis to the broader athlete economic empowerment movement of his era.

Notes

1   "I Do What I Want to Do," *SI*, July 18, 1984, URL: https://vault.si.com/vault/1984/07/18/i-do-what-i-want-do [accessed 12.23.21].

2   Ibid.

3   Kenny Moore, "Triumph and Tragedy in Los Angeles," *SI*, August 20, 1984, URL: https://vault.si.com/vault/1984/08/20/triumph-and-tragedy-in-los-angeles [accessed 12.24.21].

4   George Solomon, "Lewis Gets Record with His 4th Gold," *WP*, August 12, 1984: URL: https://www.washingtonpost.com/archive/politics/1984/08/12/lewis-gets-record-with-his-4th-gold/f1fa0cdd-db9d-47eb-833b-bc1bd5d38b91/ [accessed 12.24.21].

5   Stephen Cannella, "Q+A Carl Lewis," *SI*, August 2, 2004, URL: https://vault.si.com/vault/2004/08/02/qa-carl-lewis [accessed 12.26.21].

5

Into the Twenty-First Century

US Sport in the World since 2000

Introduction

A few weeks after the September 11 terrorist attacks, President George W. Bush, formerly an owner of the Texas Rangers, climbed the mound at Yankee Stadium to toss out the ceremonial first pitch for game three of the 2001 World Series. The ruins of the World Trade Center still smoldering nearby, the president rocked and fired a strike and the stadium roared. America was headed back to war, and once again sport was coming with it. Bush fell back on baseball to steady Americans as his administration laid plans for a retaliatory offensive in Afghanistan and, soon with it, Iraq. Reactionary militarism produced staggering instability throughout the international system as the United States ran headlong into what became two decades of military occupations, political experimentation, and insurgent warfare throughout the Middle East.

New wars costing trillions of dollars and countless lives, compounded by an economic meltdown in 2008 and a resurgent brand of white nationalist politics, hastened the ebb of US hegemony and the weakening of its own democratic institutions. In sport, scandal and corruption were central to the story, but in other ways, paradoxically, over the last twenty years US sport has never seemed more vibrant, popular, or reflective of the country's democratic traditions. The activism and empowerment movements first championed in the twentieth century have produced an era in sport history where athletes have gained enormous control over the direction, purpose, and value of their sports. This chapter outlines some of the major developments and outstanding features in the global history of US sport in the twenty-first century. It also elevates several foreign sports—including golf, cycling, soccer, and gymnastics—that were peripheral in the prior century but gained broader cultural importance more recently. Exploring their histories widens the narrative and proves how far athlete activism and player empowerment have advanced.

The Highs and Lows of Global Sport Stardom

Several professional US athletes became international icons in the early twenty-first century. Arguably the greatest among them is tennis legend Serena Williams. Williams has brilliantly navigated the peaks and perils of sport celebrity, oftentimes with sister Venus at her side. Cecil Harris, who writes on the history of Black tennis players, argues that the "Williams sisters have done more than anyone else to revolutionize their sport," bringing "a previously unseen level of power, speed, and athleticism to [tennis] while essentially telling their opponents to adapt or get out of the way."[1] They debuted in the WTA in the 1990s, won their first Grand Slam Doubles title together in 1999, and by 2002 each had been ranked number one in women's tennis. Serena's first Grand Slam Singles title was in 1999 followed up by twenty-two more over the next two decades, making her the winningest female tennis player in the Open era. Her career earnings top $88 million; she has banked over $100 million in endorsements; and her net worth approaches $250 million.[2]

Williams represents the new era of Black activist athletes and proudly acknowledges the history that led to her career. She pushes back against sexist tropes in her sport—including what women should wear and how they should behave—and backs it up with utter dominance. Best of all, she is authentic. "Her style of play may not be every tennis fan's four o'clock cup of tea," writes Harris, and her "occasional racket-smashing and verbal outbursts may be over the top for some, but Serena is undeniably and unabashedly human."[3] Or, as she puts it, "nothing about me right now is perfect, but I'm perfectly Serena."[4] Scandal has not been part of her career, although her assertiveness as a Black female often chaps a certain class of commentators who label her "bad for tennis."[5] Such criticisms are vestiges of the kind Bill Russell and Kareem Abdul-Jabbar endured—reactionary catcalls triggered as much by the messenger as the message.

Having previously explored these patterns in US sport history, this section examines another kind of athlete. Williams was one of the brightest stars of the early 2000s but was not the only American to make global headlines in a foreign sport. In golf, Tiger Woods rewrote record books and became about as big a global celebrity as Michael Jordan. In cycling, Lance Armstrong achieved the impossible: overcoming stage-four, metastatic cancer to win a record seven-straight Tour de France races. Both Woods and

Armstrong climbed the summit of their sports, inked lucrative endorsement deals, and trained Americans' gaze on otherwise peripheral leagues. Both men projected and profited from a public image as sterling as their trophies. And, in the end, both proved to be liars, as inauthentic as Serena is genuine, and they paid a huge price for their duplicity. Their transgressions were not the same—indeed, it is fair to wonder whether Woods deserved the backlash he got, while Armstrong's deceit is hard to overstate. Their stories, however, share key themes and point to what happens when athletes cannot meet the standards they set for themselves.

The Tiger Effect

In 1996, as he tromped around the Witch Hallow golf course in Oregon to watch Tiger Woods win an unprecedented third US amateur championship, Nike CEO Phil Knight promised that what "Michael Jordan did for basketball, [Woods] absolutely can do for golf. The world has not seen anything like what he's doing for the sport."[6] Few people understood the nexus of global celebrity and athlete sensation better than Knight, who had navigated Jordan's ascent as a Nike and basketball icon. Like he was about Jordan, Knight was right about Woods. Four days later, Woods turned pro and signed a $40 million, five-year endorsement deal with Nike, followed by a $20 million deal with the golf equipment company Titleist—together the largest endorsement deals in golf history.

So began one of the most dominant and lucrative professional careers of all time. In 2020, Woods's net worth approached $800 million, of which $120 million came from PGA tour earnings, well beyond any other golfer. Yet all professional golfers cashed in on Tiger's rise. Before Woods joined the PGA, only ten players had ever earned $7 million in their career. Twenty years later, 218 golfers had reached that mark. Phil Mickelson, often pitted as Woods's closest rival, is a prime example of the "Tiger Effect" on golf. In 1996, after four years on the PGA tour, Mickelson had won about $4 million. In 2016, Mickelson reached $81 million in tour winnings, and hundreds of millions more thanks to endorsements that were possible only because of the popularity Tiger brought to golf. It was the same story with television ratings, broadcast rights, sponsorship deals, ticket sales, and tournament purses. By any metric, what Woods did to golf was nothing short of revolutionary.[7]

Born Eldrick Woods in 1975, Tiger (as his parents called him) toddled into the world of golf at the age of two, when he appeared on the Mike Douglas Show to demonstrate his uncanny striking and putting skills before a national television audience. His parents, Earl and Kultida, carefully managed every aspect of their only son's life. When Tiger was just six, CBS network executives told Earl they intended to chronicle his child's career "all the way to the 18th green at Augusta Country Club."[8] At eight, Tiger won the ten-and-under Junior World Golf Championship, his first amateur tournament win on the way to twenty more. He enrolled at Stanford University in 1994, where, along with his three US amateur titles, he won the 1996 NCAA men's golf championship. He notched two tournament wins and earned PGA Rookie of the Year after he turned pro in 1996, setting up what became a legendary sophomore season on tour.

In April 1997, at his first Masters tournament in Augusta, Georgia, Tiger won by a record-setting twelve strokes—three better than Jack Nicklaus had done in 1965. *Sports Illustrated* crowned him "The New Master," and Nicklaus came away believing Tiger was "more dominant over the guys he's playing against than I ever was." Woods's historic performance was about more than a record-smashing margin of victory—for Nicklaus, it was about *how* he did it. "He's so long [off the tee], he reduces the course to nothing," Nicklaus remarked. "Absolutely nothing."[9] Fellow PGA golfer Ben Crenshaw understood that what Tiger accomplished extended well beyond Augusta. "Something's changing," he told reporters. "Something's about to pass."[10]

What passed was one of the greatest displays of individual dominance in any professional sport, ever. Particularly in golf, where winning means mastering muscle memory, mental toughness, and body fatigue over four rounds and seventy-two holes, it is especially hard for one person to dominate the professional tours for a protracted amount of time. The sport itself dates back around the fifteenth century in Scotland (although that history is contested), making it one of the oldest international sports that remains popular and relevant today.[11] American golfers Babe Didrikson Zaharias and Ben Hogan earned names for themselves in the 1930s and made the game more popular in the United States. In the 1960s, golf enjoyed the consumer boom like many other sports. Arnold Palmer and Sam Snead, both Americans, along with the South African Gary Player, turned the sport into a commercial success. Other icons like the Mexican American Lee Trevino and the "Golden Bear" Jack Nicklaus also came of age in that era. Nicklaus played until the 1980s, winning seventy-three PGA tour events (second all-time) and eighteen major championships which is still the PGA record.[12] "His record for peak performance over a long career separates [Nicklaus] from all previous legendary golfers," historian George Kirsch writes.[13] No surprise it was Nicklaus's legacy that Tiger eyed as his career took off. Asked once if he would rather retire with 100 career wins or nineteen majors (one more than Nicklaus), Woods said nineteen. What about 100 career wins or seventeen majors (one fewer than Nicklaus)? "Nineteen," he said again.[14]

After the 1997 Masters, Tiger's career became an assemblage of tournament trophies, endorsement deals, interviews, autographs, and public appearances. What pundits called "Tigermania" spread quickly around the world. "Don't for a moment think that Tiger Woods is merely an American phenomenon," a UK-based journalist told *Sports Illustrated*. "In Britain we're obsessed with him too."[15] His talent made it happen, but Woods also cultivated a squeaky-clean public image that made him an advertiser's dream. Woods often acknowledged he was uncomfortable with his status and the loss of privacy that it carried. As his legend grew, however, his immersion into popular culture and global celebrity deepened. His exploits on the golf course were simply too incredible to ignore, even for fringe sport fans. In his first four years on the tour (1996–9), he won fifteen tournaments and two majors. Between 2000 and 2001, he achieved what became known as the "Tiger Slam" by winning all four majors (the US Open, the Open Championship, the PGA Championship, and the Masters) consecutively. By the end of 2006, his tenth year on tour and at the prime age of thirty-one, Tiger had amassed fifty-four PGA wins (sixth all-time) and twelve majors (second behind Nicklaus). He set the record for the lowest scoring average for a season in 2000 and led the PGA in average scoring nine times over his career.[16]

FIGURE 5.1 *Surrounded by a crush of fans, Tiger Woods launches a long iron shot off the tee during the final day of the 2002 Masters in Augusta, Georgia. Woods finished the tournament twelve-under par to notch his third green jacket. (Photo by Timothy A. Clary/AFP via Getty Images).*

Like Nicklaus predicted, Tiger's way of winning shook up the golf world as much as the victories themselves. Woods never led the tour in average driving distance—that honor usually fell to John Daly—but he ranked second four times and third twice in his first decade on tour. What distinguished Woods from more traditional bombers like Daly was that, while "Big John" generated power from a body mass made by McDonalds, M&Ms, Diet Coke, cigarettes, a few cocktails, and zero water ("I don't drink water ... I hate water. I cannot stand to drink water," he once declared), Tiger fueled his ferocious swing through a training regimen that had Woods looking more like a boxer than a golfer.[17]

"When I first turned pro, I was the only one in the gym," Tiger explained later in his career. But that started to change after other golfers took note of his physique. He watched as competitors started "getting bigger, stronger, faster, more athletic. They are recovering better. They are hitting the ball prodigious distances, and a little bit of that's probably attributed to what I did."[18] To his point, between 1996 and 2016, average driving distance jumped from 266.5 yards to 291.1, longer than what Daly averaged in 1996 as the PGA leader (288.8). Major advancements in golf equipment contributed to this as well. But as *Golf Digest* explained, "improvements in equipment as well as the overall fitness of tour pros (something that Woods *did* inspire) best explain the massive increase in driving distance on the PGA tour."[19] Tournament officials consequently began "Tiger Proofing" their courses. Between 1996 and 2016, the average length of PGA courses grew by about 300 yards. Augusta National lengthened their course for the Masters nearly 500 yards. Whereas only about half of the courses on the PGA tour were longer than 7,000 yards before Tiger arrived, twenty years later over 80 percent of courses stretched that far.[20]

Tiger transformed golf's culture as well. Although he famously told Oprah that he considered his ethnicity to be "Cablinasian" (an amalgam of his multiethnic background) and asserted his desire to control his identity, he also consented to Nike's decision to lean heavily on his African American roots to market Woods to the public. Nike's first commercials introducing Woods explicitly called attention to his Blackness both by historicizing his arrival on tour and by framing his immediate cultural impact. One of them filmed Woods alongside African American golfers Lee Elder and Charlie Sifford who played on the PGA tour in the 1970s along with other excellent Black golfers like the brothers Jim and Chuck Thorpe, Bobby Stroble, and Charlie Owens. In another ad, Nike claimed there were still courses Woods could not play because of the color of his skin. The company was exaggerating the state of golf's inclusivity, but they were drawing from very recent history. It took Augusta National until 1975 before allowing Black golfers to play in the Masters and only in 1990 did they accept their first Black member. "Nike's presentation of Woods thus invoked overtly political advertisements," writes historian Lane Demas, "and a corporate campaign that branded his racial identity. The result was the systematic removal of Woods's Asian heritage (and his Thai-Chinese mother, Kultida) from his public image, the very thing the golfer himself said he feared."[21]

While he made gobs of money from Nike's race-conscious advertising, Woods remained circumspect about his politics. Tiger aimed "to follow Jordan's model of presenting a public image that was relatively conservative, apolitical, and silent on the issue of race," Demas argues. Nike executives saw that as well, noting how Woods mimicked "the way Michael so carefully stays in that gray area—that in-between area where everything is neutral."[22] Jordan and Woods had many things in common, both being global businessmen wedded to Nike and beloved by fans like few others in history. Tiger's career dovetailed Jordan's and despite a twelve-year age gap, they developed a friendship that shaped Woods's career in more ways than he was probably expecting.

Whatever advice Jordan bestowed on the younger Woods, their time together in Las Vegas proved formative to Woods's maturation as a global celebrity. When his father Earl died in 2006, Woods began to frequent Las Vegas more often. Although he was married and a father by 2007, he maintained a web of affairs with multiple women that stretched from Nevada to where he lived in Orlando and, eventually, to his world travels on the PGA tour. Woods thought he was safe from scandal but salacious magazines like the *National Enquirer* began digging into his secret rendezvous, and soon found what they were looking for. Tiger managed to bury the first story about an affair with a waitress, but he could not outrun his infidelities forever.[23]

At the 2008 US Open held at Torrey Pines in California, Woods pulled off the unthinkable. Shortly before the tournament he underwent arthroscopic surgery on his left knee, during which doctors found multiple fractures in his leg and an obliterated ACL. Woods, however, refused to pass up a chance at another major, and entered the tournament playing effectively on one leg. Hobbled and in obvious pain throughout, Woods recovered from a rough first round to win his fourteenth major. The feat was superhuman. But what came next brought Tiger crashing down to earth. The torment his body suffered due to his training and ferocity as a competitor was catching up with him, but what finally broke his grip on golf were the lies. In 2009, after more rumors surfaced about an affair he was having with a Las Vegas socialite, Woods' wife, Elin, discovered Tiger's secrets from a text message on his phone. Around 2:00 am on Thanksgiving morning, the Florida Highway Patrol arrived on the scene of a car crash. Woods was the driver, the car had struck a fire hydrant and then rammed a tree near his house, and the car's back windows were shattered.

What was originally reported an accident was later pronounced a domestic dispute between Tiger and Elin, who allegedly smashed the car windows with a golf club when she learned Woods had been unfaithful. The news was followed by an onslaught of stories told by other women from all over the country claiming to have had intimate relationships with Woods. Professional athletes having affairs is not necessarily front-page news, but because Woods was a megastar who had built a public persona around his wholesome dedication to golf and his family, he faced relentless scrutiny in the media.[24] He lost nearly all of his endorsements, though Nike stayed with him. In 2010, Woods voluntarily entered a rehabilitation facility in Mississippi for sex addiction where he stayed for forty-five days.[25] Woods returned to golf the same year and played fairly well until injuries to his back required more surgeries and extensive physical rehabilitation.

In 2018, Tiger Woods won the PGA Tour Championship, his first tournament victory since 2013. A year later, he won his fifth green jacket and fifteenth major at Augusta. Afterwards, Woods reflected how he "had serious doubts" he could win again "after what transpired a couple years ago." Although "the body is not the same as it was," he said he was hopeful he could remain competitive on the tour.[26] But another car crash on February 23, 2021, nearly derailed his career for good. That morning, Woods lost control of his car driving at a high speed on a tight turn and flipped his SUV several times. Injuries to his legs required immediate surgery and there was even talk of amputation. A few months later, Woods told *Golf Digest* that his only goal now was "walking on my own."[27]

Incredibly, just before Christmas in 2021, Tiger was back on the links, competing in the PNC Championship scramble tournament with his son Charlie at his side. "The fact that I'm able to have this opportunity this year" was surprising, he said, admitting "even a couple weeks ago we didn't really know whether or not I would be doing this, but here we are." Over two days and thirty-six holes, father and son put on a show. Charlie's swing is a facsimile of Tiger's, as is his competitive nature. The duo shot twenty-five-under par over two rounds, including eleven birdies in a row, and finished two shots off the lead. Although he showed flashes of his former self, Tiger used a golf cart instead of walking the fairways and was in obvious pain throughout.[28]

Tiger Woods can make the case he is not only one of the greatest, but one of the absolute toughest and most resilient athletes of all time. He has weathered success, celebrity, scandal, and tragedy; endured several major injuries and multiple comebacks; and still he remains the commanding figure in the world of golf. After he and his son, John II, celebrated winning the 2021 PNC over Tiger and Charlie, Big John Daly was asked what he thought of Woods's performance and what was left for his career. Daly said that Woods "still looked great. He'll be back ... I could see it in his eyes. He's probably going to beat Jack Nicklaus' record and be the greatest of all time." It would take a herculean effort for Tiger to reach nineteen majors at this point. But it is never a good idea to argue with John Daly, or to count out Tiger Woods.[29]

"I'm Sorry You Don't Believe in Miracles"

From a tough childhood in Texas to the heights of international cycling, Lance Armstrong's fall from grace was even steeper than Tiger's. Woods lied about cheating on his wife; Armstrong lied about cheating at his sport. Armstrong's career raises additional questions about the gray areas of sport: the pressures to win at all costs; the use of PEDs; and the conflict between noble aims and wicked deeds. Despite his private scandals, Tiger Woods will likely always be remembered as a golf legend. Armstrong, on the other hand, must live with being a sport villain. Recently, Armstrong admitted that as his career took off, he "didn't understand that this story was going into the hearts and minds of Americans and embedding itself into American sports history." To sustain his unexpected stardom, he not only cheated but became a manipulative, spiteful person who wielded his enormous influence to punish critics and humiliate opponents. "I needed a fucking meltdown," he says, "and I got it."[30]

Armstrong was raised by his mother, Linda Gunderson, and stepfather, Terry Armstrong, whom Lance claims abused him when he was growing up. Armstrong sardonically credits his stepfather for fueling his passion to compete and win from an early age, when he feared Terry's belt as punishment for lackluster athletic performances. Armstrong was never suited for the more popular sports in Texas—football, basketball, and baseball—but soon discovered he was very fast as a swimmer, bike racer, and runner. He made an early name for himself as a triathlete and then at twenty-one joined Motorola's professional cycling team.[31]

In his first season in 1993, Armstrong began using PEDs through injections and blood transfusions but claims at that point he avoided the drug that was sweeping through the world of cycling known as synthetic erythropoietin, or EPO. Developed to help cancer patients and anemics, EPO triggers a rapid growth in red blood cells. For cyclists, stimulating red blood cell production boosts muscle performance and stamina. "In the sport of cycling, [EPO] turned out to be a miracle potion," writes Juliet Macur, one of Armstrong's biographers.[32] Armstrong's former teammate Jonathan Vaughters began taking EPO in 1996 and explained that:

> the performance enhancing benefit can be ten percent. Now consider that the difference between the last place rider and the first place rider of the Tour de France is two hours, and that's for a 100 hour race. So, from first to last is two percent and the difference of EPO is ten percent .... That gives you a lens into how much of a difference this particular drug made.[33]

Before he claims to have started taking EPO, Armstrong managed to win professional cycling's world championship in 1993 as the youngest cyclist ever and only the second American. But when he vied for the sport's crown jewel, the Tour de France, Armstrong was no match against his European rivals, many who were using the new drug. The Motorola team got crushed in 1994 and lost again in 1995. It was at that point, according to Armstrong, that he and his teammates joined the *peloton* and began taking EPO.

Throughout its history, dating back to 1868, professional cycling has been predominantly a European sport. Cycling cultures are an important part of many European histories and often reflect aspects of a country's national identity, particularly of its working classes. In 1900, the Union Cycliste Internationale (UCI) formed to govern the world of competitive cycling, and even though the United States was a founding member, the sport remained firmly under European control. Cycling was part of the inaugural 1896 Olympics and the Tour de France itself began in 1903. It winds thousands of miles around the country and lasts twenty-one days (though its distance and duration have varied over time). For eighty-three straight years, a European won the tour.[34] Only until Greg LeMond completed the final stage in 1986 did an American take home the trophy. LeMond won two more times, making him the most famous American cyclist ever. Yet between LeMond's era and Armstrong's, cycling became overrun by PEDs. Some argue the inherent dangers in cycling—the extreme physical exertion required to complete a race like the Tour de France, combined with the looming threat of injury or even death—made doping an easy decision for professional cyclists, figuring they were already putting their lives at risk doing what they loved. When EPO hit the cycling world, riders were enticed by its performance benefits and near undetectability, even as reports of life-threatening side effects became known.[35]

Armstrong says he started taking EPO in 1996, the same year he joined the US Postal Service cycling team, and the same year he was diagnosed with advanced testicular cancer. He had ignored a pain in his testicles for months and by the time of the diagnosis the cancer had spread to his brain, lymph nodes, and lungs. Doctors gave Armstrong little chance of survival. After several surgeries and chemotherapy, however, his cancer was gone. As he fought, Armstrong noticed that an emphasis on survival was missing in Americans' attitudes toward cancer treatment, both culturally and clinically. So, he set out to fix that.

Armstrong's personal recovery was a compelling story in its own right. But what he did for the societal-wide fight against cancer was legitimately transformative. Armstrong launched a modest cancer fundraising event in 1997 that quickly mushroomed into a much broader initiative called Livestrong. In its first eight years, the Livestrong Foundation pulled in more than $89 million directed to cancer treatment and research. As he kept winning, Armstrong found he could leverage his influence with sponsors like Nike to support his Livestrong foundation. Nike made annual donations of $7.5 million, and it was Nike who came up with the idea of selling yellow bracelets for $1 to promote the Livestrong cause. Soon, Livestrong bracelets became a cultural phenomenon. Nike reported $53 million in sales from the bracelets alone.

They could be seen on the wrists of prominent athletes, celebrities, and politicians—including then-presidential candidate John Kerry. "For many people, the money raised was the least of Armstrong's impact on the cancer community," Macur writes. "He made it fashionable ... [to identify] as part of a club of cancer survivors or those affected by a loved one's battle."[36]

Armstrong returned to cycling in 1999 on the heels of an intense doping investigation into the previous year's Tour de France that the legendary Italian cyclist Marco Pantani won. Allegations against scores of riders still hung over the cycling world, and top UCI officials promised that the sport was finally going to clean itself up. Instead, the next year Armstrong set a new Tour de France time record on his way to his first of seven yellow jerseys. The French press, dubious that a recent cancer patient could perform as he did without PEDs, printed a story claiming to have proof one of Armstrong's drug tests contained traces of cortisone, a steroid and banned substance. According to individuals involved with the situation, Armstrong worked quietly with UCI officials and his team members to discredit the story. They engineered an alibi, relying on complicit racing officials and doctors, claiming that prior to the race he had used a cortisone skin cream for saddle sores. The UCI declared the excuse credible and closed the case. Afterward, Armstrong accused the French government and media of trying to pin the sport's troubles on an American agitator. "It's a scary time right now for cycling in France," he said in an interview. "They're hungry for a story, both the press and the minister of sport, they want to start trouble .... You hope that people are good and true and fair and correct, but you never know."[37]

The taste of victory drove Armstrong to push the pace of cycling and the intensity of his team's doping regimen to new extremes. He grew unabashed in his drug use and demanded the same from his teammates. He and a team of doctors constructed an elaborate doping program centered on EPO but that also involved, in some instances, dozens of injections of various PEDs in a day and, in others, blood transfusions administered on the side of the road in between stages of a race. "To put it concisely," Armstrong's teammate Vande Verde said, "the biggest thing was that we were going to train harder than everybody else, we were going to have a better diet than everyone else, and we were going to dope better than everybody else."[38]

In 2005, Armstrong won the Tour de France a record seventh time. Standing on the winner's platform he told his audience, "the last thing I'll say to the ... cynics and the skeptics, I'm sorry for you, I'm sorry that you can't dream big. I'm sorry you don't believe in miracles."[39] It was the pinnacle of his career. He had earned millions from tour winnings and tens of millions more in endorsements. And had he not tried a comeback in 2008, Armstrong might have kept his money, and secrets, in hand. But he had burned too many bridges, humiliated and alienated too many friends and teammates, and when he returned in 2008, his enemies and the European press were ready to pounce. The testimony of his former teammate Floyd Landis plus a public fallout between Armstrong and Greg LeMond set the wheels in motion.

The Food and Drug Administration (FDA) and the US Anti-Doping Agency (USADA) filed suit against him and secured the testimony of Armstrong's closest teammates who admitted that they, and he, had doped as part of the US Postal Service team. After shielding Armstrong for years, enabling his doping, and riding his coattails, in 2012 the UCI announced it was banning him from the sport and stripping him of his titles.[40]

Within forty-eight hours of the USADA's report becoming public, Armstrong lost all of his endorsements. He finally told the truth to Oprah on national television in 2013, at which point lawsuits were stacking up, including a $100 million suit with the US federal government for defrauding the Postal Service that Armstrong settled for $5 million. No longer a miracle, or the embodiment of hard work and perseverance, Armstrong was even pushed out of Livestrong, which by that point had raised more than $500 million towards cancer research.[41]

After he came clean, Armstrong still refused to concede that what he had done was beyond the pale, at least in the modern era of cycling. The world, like his legacy, was shades of gray, not black and white. "No good guys and bad guys," he reasoned. "We've all done something wrong. I handled myself in the wrong way and I'm paying for it."[42] Many others do not see it that way. Even his teammates have a hard time reconciling Armstrong's legacy. "Thirty years knowing someone, you either love them or hate them," teammate Bobby Julich once said. When it comes to Armstrong, "I still haven't decided where I stand after all that."[43]

US Professional Sport after the American Age

The prominence of American athletes in international sports like tennis, golf, and cycling underscored the extent to which US sporting culture had been globalized by the twenty-first century. The same was true in other foreign sports, including hockey. American stars like Patrick Kane, Jonathan Quick, and John Carlson have led dynasties to Stanley Cups and pushed for gold medals at the 2002 and 2010 Olympics. The league's top talent still tilts toward Canada and Europe. Between 2000 and 2021, only one American (Kane) has won the award given to the NHL's best player in the regular season, whereas thirteen times the award went to a Canadian. Yet at the franchise level, the United States dominates the world of professional hockey. The last Canadian-based team to win a championship was the Montreal Canadiens in 1993. Since then, teams like the Chicago Blackhawks, Pittsburg Penguins, Los Angeles Kings, and Tampa Bay Lightning have helped keep the cup an American possession.[44]

This section considers how globalization continues to shape the "Big Three" American sports—baseball, basketball, and American football—before taking up the curious case of soccer in America. US sport history between 2000 and 2020 proves that globalization cuts two ways, by invigorating professional leagues and, depending on who you ask, threatening the "heritage" of American sports. MLB is currently hostage to a mounting tension between its reliance on foreign markets and a domestic fanbase easily affronted by change and difference. The NBA, by comparison, has come to embrace multiculturalism and built a modern identity that is nothing if not cosmopolitan. Somewhere in the middle are football and *fútbol*—arguably the two most popular sports in the world—and yet both struggle to make inroads where the other thrives.

Wither Baseball?

Steroids took on an outsized role across many sports as PED research advanced in the new century. In baseball, PED use intensified in the late twentieth century and affected the game in obvious and profound ways. Cheating and players looking for a competitive edge are not new in baseball. Over the years, measures taken to enhance performance range from pitchers spitting on the ball to players ingesting amphetamines. Baseball's steroid scandal, however, was on a different level, revealing a seedy web of users and enablers—players, doctors, and league officials alike—who worked together to produce an era of ballooning biceps and record-breaking power numbers.

Anabolic steroids became a problem in MLB in the late 1980s. Sluggers Jose Conseco and Mark McGwire, then teammates on the Oakland Athletics, were known as the "Bash Brothers," but what truly bonded them was their mutual steroid habit. "I was the godfather of the steroid revolution in baseball," Canseco later admitted, "but McGwire was right there with me as a living, thriving example of what steroids could do to make you a better ball player."[45] With baseball's addiction to PEDs deepening, the 1994 players' strike threatened to bury the sport completely. Players returned in 1995 to find league-wide attendance down about 20 percent while MLB's operating revenue fell $500 million and stayed at those levels for years.[46]

Steroids unequivocally helped re-popularize baseball in the late 1990s—a development MLB officials understood full well under the commissionership of Bud Selig. Selig was the game's biggest cheerleader when McGwire and the Cubs' Sammy Sosa raced to see who could eclipse Roger Maris's single-season record of sixty-one homeruns in 1998. The race became a major national story and vaulted baseball back in the spotlight. In the end, both surpassed Maris, with Sosa hitting sixty-six and McGwire setting the new record with seventy homers. All throughout MLB homeruns were the story. In the 1990 season, there were 3,317 homeruns across both leagues. By 1995 it was over 4,000. In 1998, the year McGwire hit seventy, batters slugged over 5,000 homeruns. In 2000, the apex of the steroid era, 5,693 balls left the park.[47]

Steroid-induced power hitting generated huge interest in the game, more attention for the big hitters, and enormous contracts to match—inevitably making other stars envious. Barry Bonds was a prolific power hitter and in his early professional years, playing for the Pittsburg Pirates, his all-around baseball talent drew comparisons to Willie Mays. Before Bonds ever took PEDs, he was a Hall-of-Fame-caliber player. But steroids helped Bonds overtake McGwire's record with seventy-three longballs in 2003, and then take aim at baseball's holiest grail: Hank Aaron's career homerun record of 755.

With Bonds marching closer to Aaron, baseball's steroid problem became public knowledge. In 2005 Conseco published *Juiced*, a book detailing an incessant doping culture in MLB. Congress called hearings that put ten players—including McGwire and Sosa—in front of cameras and under oath. McGwire deflected questions about his PED usage (he later admitted to doping in 2010) while Sosa outright lied, swearing to Congress, "I have never taken illegal performance-enhancing drugs." A couple of years later, reports surfaced that Sosa had, in fact, tested positive for PEDs in 2003, shortly after signing a four-year extension with the Chicago Cubs worth $72 million.[48]

Rumors, confessions, and investigations surrounding MLB's steroid problem reached critical mass as Bonds neared Aaron's record. Bonds came under scrutiny for his relationship with a company named BALCO that had been supplying PEDs to athletes. In 2006, two San Francisco-based journalists published *Game of Shadows*, which carefully documented their years of research into Bonds's relationship to BALCO, his PED regimen, and efforts to cover the trail. After a decade of acceding to steroid use in baseball, and then dragging his feet to stem the tide, Commissioner Selig announced an internal investigation that published its findings in December 2007, just four months after Bonds had hit career homer 756. The report named Bonds along other MLB stars like Rafael Palmeiro, Gary Sheffield, and Roger Clemens. More investigations followed accusing other stars, including Alex Rodriguez—one of the most vociferous deniers—of taking PEDs. In 2009, Rodriguez finally admitted to using PEDs early in his career and swore he would never dope again. In fact, he never stopped doping and got caught a second time in 2013, leading to a full season suspension.[49]

Two decades of speculation and investigations into which ballplayers were doping, which records were legitimate, and who, if anyone, in the league was clean left a black eye on the game. Baseball's declension had other causes, however. The infusion of new statistical analyses—what baseball insiders call Sabermetrics, named after the Society of American Baseball Research (SABR)—played a part as well.[50] Pioneered by baseball researcher Bill James and eventually adopted by MLB front offices, Sabermetrics fundamentally altered what was valued in a baseball player. Isolated slugging percentage (ISO), weighted runs created (wRC), and fielding independent pitching (FIP), for example, overtook traditional metrics like batting average (BA), runs batted in (RBI), and earned-run average (ERA) when it came to evaluating players. Hitters who take lots of walks and hit lots of homeruns—even if they strikeout often—better improve a team's chances of winning than low-power, steady hitters who put the ball in play. Pitching likewise evolved around these new principles. Sabermetrics also popularized defensive shifting strategies that take defenders out of their normal positions and into areas on the field individual hitters are statistically more likely to hit the ball. Shifts turn batted balls that once were safe base hits into easy outs.[51]

Those changes, plus an infusion of hard-throwing, situational bullpen pitchers led to a surge in what baseball statisticians call the "three true outcomes": strikeouts, walks, and home runs. The effect has been a marked decline in the number of balls put in play, leading to less action and excitement on the field, but more walks, strikeouts, pitching changes, and home runs. The percentage of at-bats ending in a strikeout, walk, or homerun has gone up from 26 percent in 1970 to over 36 percent in 2020. That year, more than a quarter of all at-bats ended in a strikeout. The average strikeout rate for hitters has nearly doubled in the last forty years; batting averages have declined about twenty points; and average game length stretched almost forty extra minutes.[52] Meanwhile overall scoring is down, attendance is slumping, and so are television ratings. According to the *Denver Post*, the "average viewership for the World Series has declined dramatically since the 1970s, from 44.2 million in 1978 to a record low 9.8 million viewers in 2020." Even worse, the average age of baseball fans grows higher every year. In 2010, MLB's average television viewer was fifty-two years old. In 2016, it was fifty-seven and only 7 percent of MLB viewers were under the age of eighteen.[53] In short, the game is slower, there is less action, younger people are tuning out, and MLB's most loyal fans are turning gray.

In contrast to its slide at home, at the international level baseball looks as robust as ever. The infusion of Latin players in the game, constituting almost one-third of MLB players today, has kept baseball popular in the western hemisphere. MLB academies in the Caribbean continue to bring in high-quality players. Over the last few decades, Latin players have become predominant among baseball's brightest stars. Although still relatively small, the number of Asian players on MLB rosters has also grown steadily since 2000, culminating in the arrival of the Babe Ruth-like hitter and pitcher Shohei Ohtani.

Baseball's global enterprise, erected over two centuries, added a new edifice in 2006 when MLB and the International Baseball Federation organized the World Baseball Classic (WBC). League officials hoped the WBC would showcase MLB's best talent and showoff its international reach. But the inaugural event was ripe with nationalism and geopolitical signaling. Teams protested the ongoing US occupation of Iraq, while the United States tried and failed to block Cuba from competing. South Korea knocked out America on the way to finishing third in the tournament. The Japanese team, led by the great Ichiro Suzuki, defeated Cuba in the championship game, the first of two consecutive WBC titles for Japan. The Dominican Republic won in 2013, and in 2017 the United States finally prevailed. As Robert Elias writes:

> Despite the tensions, the World Baseball Classic gave MLB what it wanted. Its objective wasn't to reproduce the Olympic message of peace and friendship .... Instead, MLB's media campaign focused entirely on individual stars .... John Kelly called this the "Jackie Robinsonization of international baseball".... The impression was that the pioneers have colonized the major leagues and not vice versa. Individual players can break down boundaries.

For some baseball diehards, however, even as their ship sinks, they complain about who has come to bail them out. The influence of Latin players in particular has created a new culture war in baseball. Today's MLB stars, like Fernando Tatis Jr. and Javier "El Mago" Baez, play with a flair and passion that many observers see as the bridge between baseball's past and its youthful future. But baseball nativists, who have forever misunderstood the international heritage of the game, remain indignant that MLB's fate might hang with foreigners. When Latin players began flipping their bats and erupting in celebration after a home run, "purists" (often a pseudonym for nativist) decried what they said was the desecration of the game and an affront to the "unwritten rules" of baseball. "If you're going to come into our country and make our American dollars," groused Bud Norris of the San Diego Padres, "you need to respect a game that has been here for over a hundred years."[54] Others disdain the players for not speaking English. Hall of Fame third baseman Mike Schmidt has insisted teams cannot build around talented Latin players because guys who speak Spanish simply "can't be ... that kind of player."[55] Yet if baseball is to remain relevant as both a national and an international sport, its dependence on foreign influence must continue to grow. To what extent today's new cast of MLB superstars can win over its aging white male audience and reach the younger generations who have lost interest has become an existential question for the game of baseball.

From Yao to the Eurostep

When Jordan retired in 2003, some wondered if the NBA would struggle to stay relevant. The early 2000s were not like the golden decades that preceded them, but soon enough electrifying young superstars took over the league and further popularized the NBA at home and abroad. Kobe Bryant, LeBron James, Kevin Durant, and Steph Curry became cornerstones of great dynasties, won Olympic gold medals, and now sit atop the record books alongside Jordan, Abdul-Jabbar, and Russell. There has also been a surge in the number international players serving as franchise-changing stars since 2000. Several foreign players, including Vlade Divac from Serbia and Patrick Ewing from Nigeria, had Hall-of-Fame careers in the 1990s.[56] In the new century a wave of elite international talent turned the league into a microcosm of the greater basketball universe.

China's basketball infatuation grew steadily over the twentieth century. In 1995, the Chinese Basketball Association (CBA) formed as part of FIBA and quickly became the epicenter of professional-level basketball in Asia. When NBA commissioner Stern was asked his thoughts on the future of basketball in China, he exclaimed, "you have 1.2 billion people, 1.2 billion! With that many people, you should become the world's largest basketball market, bigger than the US."[57] In 2001, Wang Zhizhi debuted with the Dallas Mavericks, becoming the first Chinese-born player in NBA history. Although Wang's career was less decorated than some hoped, in any case it was overshadowed by the arrival of the 7'6" center Yao Ming.

Yao played for the Shanghai Sharks as a teenager and quickly became a folk legend in international basketball circles. Brook Larmer, author of *Operation Yao Ming*, explains how challenging it was for NBA representatives to pry Yao from the CBA, which included official negotiations between the leagues and even bizarre offers to help Yao defect.[58] After the Houston Rockets made him the first pick in the 2002 draft, the Chinese government consented to letting him go only after Yao and the league agreed he would play for the PRC national team whenever he was asked, even at the expense of his NBA career.

Over an abbreviated career, Yao was a powerful force on the court and plugged the NBA into the fabled China Market. He was an NBA All-Star eight times, even during seasons he was injured, thanks in part to the millions of Chinese fans who voted for him. When he and another Chinese player, Yi Jianlian, squared off for a regular season game in November 2007, an estimated 100–200 million people in China tuned in to see the game—comparable to the total global viewership for recent Super Bowls.[59] Yao also appeared on multiple All-NBA teams, and had his jersey number 11 retired by the Rockets after multiple foot and leg injuries made it impossible to keep playing.[60] In 2017 Yao became chairman of the CBA and remains the face of Chinese basketball around the world. When a confrontation erupted in 2019 after then-Rockets general manager Daryl Morey criticized an ongoing PRC crackdown against pro-democracy activists in Hong Kong, the PRC and Yao's CBA threatened to cut off all ties between the NBA and the mainland. "I'm hoping that Yao and I can find accommodation," NBA commissioner Adam Silver said at the time. "But he is extremely hot at the moment, and I understand it." Only after the league and other Rockets officials apologized for Morey's criticism did basketball relations between the United States and PRC normalize.[61]

Yao never won an NBA title but came close a couple of times. One of his best chances was in 2005, when his Houston Rockets lost to their Texas rival Dallas Mavericks, led by their own legendary international star Dirk Nowitzki. Nowitzki, who is German, exemplified the surge in European players that began in the 1990s. When he joined the league there were thirty-eight international players representing twenty-seven countries; when he left, there were more than 100 players from over forty countries, comprising about a quarter of NBA rosters. In the 2017 NBA draft alone, about half of the players selected were foreign-born.[62] Nowitzki developed his skills through FIBA and became the ninth pick in the 1998 NBA draft. He played twenty-two years for the Mavericks and led them to a championship in 2011. A fourteen-time All-Star and the regular season and Finals MVP in 2011, most contemporaries still consider Nowitzki the greatest international player ever—at least for now.

Nowitzki's impact on the game extends beyond the stat sheet. For one, unlike Yao Ming, he was not a prototypical seven-footer who played the game close to the basket for short-range shots and to defend the rim. Nowitzki, instead, came over as a seven-footer who could dribble, pass, and, above all, shoot from distance. He was a lethal three-point shooter, steady from the stripe, and possessed a unique jump shot that was virtually unblockable. His shooting form—often off one foot and twisting away from the defense—was unorthodox but he made it iconic. Nowitzki's rise represented more broadly what was happening to basketball outside of the United States, and how those changes were coming back to America to inflect the game in new ways. Throughout much of the NBA's history, big men rarely handled or shot the ball beyond a few feet from the basket. In European leagues, however, all players, regardless of size, train seriously in ball-handling skills and long-distance shooting. Nowitzki's arrival in 1998 introduced the NBA to what fans like to call the "basketball unicorn": a seven-footer who can shoot, pass, and dribble the ball up the court. And that was Dirk. Legendary NBA coach Greg Popovich called him "arguably the best pure shooter we've seen. He worked himself into a position where he was impossible to defend."[63]

In today's NBA, unicorns are everywhere. The 2021 NBA MVP was Nikola Jokić, the lumbering, six-eleven, point-guard/center from Serbia. He is a deadeye from deep and one of the deftest passers and ballhandlers in the NBA. Like Nowitzki, Jokić has a shooting style and pace of play that defy conventional NBA wisdom. The Slovenian phenom Luka Dončić is another. At six-seven, Dončić is smaller than Nowitzki and Jokić, but nonetheless flashes a distinctly European skillset that makes him difficult to stop on the court. Dončić's all-around style embodies what sport journalist Jonathan Abrams calls "the difference between the way players develop in the United States, where the emphasis has traditionally been on athleticism, and the way they develop in Europe, where young players tend to spend hours on skill development."[64]

Another detectable European influence on the NBA is the proliferation of a move dubbed the "Eurostep," which involves a ballhandler taking

FIGURE 5.2 *German-born Dirk Nowitzki of the Dallas Mavericks attempts his patented fall-away jump shot over the tough defense of Chicago's Jimmy Butler during the 2016 season. Arguably the greatest foreign player in NBA history through his era, Nowitzki won an MVP award in 2007 and an NBA championship in 2011. (Photo by Jonathan Daniel/Getty Images).*

two lateral steps to avoid the defense for a layup. Šarūnas Marčiulionis, a Lithuanian guard who bounced around the NBA in the 1990s, gets credit for inventing the move and soon other Europeans, including Dražen Petrović, used it with success. It took American players decades to adopt the move but now the Eurostep is an important weapon in many players' arsenals. NBA coaches also have incorporated plays and systems from the European game, particularly the focus on ball movement, pace, and spacing in the half court. International basketball relies heavily on swift passing and wide spacing on offense, while in the NBA offenses traditionally encouraged isolating individual players so they can create action off the dribble. Recently, however, NBA teams have adopted elements of the European approach. Former coach Jay Triano confessed that he "stole a bunch of plays." His imperative was "to incorporate the same athleticism of our players into the ability to run continuity and movement sets the way that the European teams do."[65]

The NBA's assimilation of these basketball immigrants and their cultures coincides with the league's most concerted effort yet to bring its product to the world. In 2017 the league opened NBA Academies in Mexico, Senegal, India, and China and a Global NBA Academy in Australia. The academies operate as feeder schools that rely on regional talent evaluators and local coaches to identify young players and recommend them for academy admission. From there, they get a residential athletic and academic training experience. Australia serves as the final hub for the best players from the regional academies. They study English, prepare for the SAT, and compete against some of the best international talent in world-class facilities. Greg Colluchi helps run the academies and explains that, before anything else, "the first idea is to get ... as many kids dribbling a basketball with their hands versus their feet. That's the first goal." In places like India, where basketball is only starting to grow, the evaluation process is more basic, with scouts simply "looking for attributes of basketball players: big feet, long arms, move well." In Africa, however, where the "potential there is still exploding" according to Colluchi, player development is far more advanced.[66]

The NBA's first African-born player arrived in 1984, when Hakeem "The Dream" Olajuwon from Nigeria began his Hall-of-Fame career. In 2021, fifteen African-born players were on NBA rosters, including superstars Joel Embiid from Cameroon and Giannis Antetokounmpo who was born in Nigeria and grew up in Greece. In addition to the NBA Academy in Senegal, another initiative called NBA Africa established the Basketball Africa League in 2021 with teams from twelve countries. Several African-born former NBA players drive the NBA Africa initiative, including Dikembe Mutombo and Loul Deng, and recently the organization brought aboard former US president Barack Obama as a strategic partner. "The NBA has always been a great ambassador for the United States," Obama said after signing on, "using the game to create deeper connections around the world, and in Africa, basketball has the power to promote opportunity, wellness, equality, and empowerment across the continent."[67] His sentiments not only reinforce how sport can function as a form of soft power. They also capture the essence of the NBA's modern history, which is nothing if not global. The NBA is now the best-positioned professional US sport league to capitalize on the globalization happening in the twenty-first century. Baseball sits at a crossroad, while with the NFL the question remains: Can American football ever become internationally popular?

Global Football or American Fútbol?

The NFL's modest global footprint is not for a lack of trying. In 1991, NFL Europe launched with the goal of selling American football across the Atlantic. It shut down in 2007 after major financial losses. In its place, the NFL began playing regular season games in London in 2007, two years after the NFL hosted its first-ever regular season game outside the continental United States in Mexico. The Canadian Football League (CFL) has existed since 1958 and has a moderately strong fanbase. The International Federation of American Football formed in 1998 and governs competitive football around the world with more than a hundred participating clubs. And within the US empire itself, football has shown evidence it can be popular in other parts of the world, such as American Samoa.[68]

Despite its oversized role in America, however, football as a consumer and participatory sport has not managed to build the kind of international ecosystem as have basketball and baseball. Even as it tries to duplicate the NBA's blueprint for global growth with its NFL International initiative, league rosters are bereft of foreign players. In 2019, out of 1,696 players, only twenty-three were foreign-born (1.3 percent).[69] Mark Waller, who works for NFL International, admits that the game's provinciality makes it "a lonely job being a fan of a sport that isn't played" in most parts of the world. Although the Super Bowl itself can draw tens of millions of global viewers, a sustained interest in the league and the growth of the game as a participatory sport in most countries still lag.[70] Why is that? What about football makes it so appealing to Americans but so foreign to everyone else?

Some like Waller believe it has to do with football's intricate rules and scoring system that can make even baseball seem streamlined. "Watch a basketball game or a soccer game, you have a pretty good idea, pretty quickly, what the goal is," he explains. "It's less obvious in football."[71] Any football game is naturally herky-jerky. Pile on commercial timeouts and injury stoppage, and NFL games feel especially stuttering. But what Waller describes is also a function of football's early roots in American culture. Walter Camp's vision of a sport that ran like a factory floor, based on highly individualized tasks all serving a common goal, can overwhelm the uninitiated by the amount of movement and physical contact taking place.

One also wonders about the abiding militarism long present in US society, to what extent it has conditioned Americans' lust for combat, and whether football fills a certain void. In a 1977 essay for *The New Republic* titled "The Moral Equivalent to Football," historian Wilcomb Washburn brilliantly elucidated this dynamic, as have other historians since.[72] "The game of football is a better barometer of American character than any other aspect of our culture because it reflects the true—and not the ideal—nature of our people," Washburn wrote. "The brutality and insensitivity (along with the courage and intelligence) that characterize the game are integral parts of our national character." His essay explores similarities in how wars are waged, and football is played, and notes to the "extent that American national character is male and chauvinistic, football reflects that." Washburn concluded:

> As an observer of my society—as a historian—I see a general acceptance of the values of controlled physical violence in our society, expressed most clearly in the approbation and support of football at all levels. It may not be the moral equivalent of war, but it is an equivalent that satisfies the majority of the American people.[73]

Or could it be the name? Can a sport, where foot rarely touches ball, hope to challenge a more popular, older, and more suitably named game that shares the same handle? For billions of people, of course, football, or *fútbol*, is the official name of the "beautiful game"—what Americans still call soccer. Asking global audiences to abandon one for the American other is a daunting proposition. Even more so when comparing the styles of play. Soccer is the antithesis to American football in many ways. The immediate skillset and rules system are straightforward, logical, and apply to everyone but the goalie—use mostly feet, no hands—equipment costs are modest, physical contact is limited, scoring is low, and the pace is fluid and fast. Incidentally, basketball enjoys similar characteristics with soccer—except for the low scoring and use of hands—and no doubt that helps its burgeoning popularity around the world. In the current global sport landscape, no matter how much the NFL tries to export its game, it is hard to imagine football matching baseball or basketball's rate of adoption, to say nothing of the behemoth that is the beautiful game.

Indeed, the differences between American football and soccer extend to their perfectly inverse relationship within the world of sport. Whereas football dominates in America and struggles abroad, soccer is just the opposite: king of the world but a pauper in the States. Certainly, in the case of women's soccer, which the next section explores at length, this has not been true since the 1990s. But for professional men's soccer, and for the US Men's National Team (USMNT), major success has been elusive. Once again, the question is: Why? How can soccer control so much space in the world of sport but in America, one of the sport-thirstiest countries on Earth, flounder at the men's level?

There have been several attempts to make soccer a major US national sport. Historians Andrei Markovits and Steven Hellerman call soccer's early history in the United States a "motley patchwork of respectable marginality" dating back to its introduction in the nineteenth century.[74] Early iterations resembling today's game of soccer reach back to China before the common era (BCE), and historian Mary Miller has shown that a sport resembling team soccer was wildly popular in Mesoamerica almost 3,000 years ago.[75] Its modern form, however, usually dates to the 1860s in England, although the time and place of its invention remain hotly contested.[76] In the United States, immigrants from Europe brought "soccer" (itself a British term used to distinguish between the new sport and "rugby football") with them.[77] Organized groups called football clubs formed soon after. According to Markovitz and Hellerman, "cities and towns that retained strong first-generation cultural identification with particular nationalities became 'soccer islands,' mostly throughout the eastern United States."[78]

Until the 1990s, however, there were very few successful American soccer players and "the world's most popular team sport never reached beyond mediocrity, at best, on American soil."[79] Scholars point to the early institutionalization of the Big Three American sports, plus the crowding in by hockey, as impediments to soccer's growth over the century. Professional leagues formed in the 1890s, 1930s, and 1970s, but each one petered out due to funding problems, constrained talent pools, and the balkanization of Americans' sport interests.[80] The United States sent teams to the World Cup—the premier global soccer tournament first held in 1930—but hardly ever advanced out of the group stage. In many instances the USMNT failed to qualify for the event, including as recently as 2018. The Olympic record is much the same. The USMNT came close to medaling at the Sydney Games in 2000, finishing fourth, but then failed to qualify for four out of the next five Olympics.

Things improved somewhat when the United States hosted the 1994 World Cup and made it to the round of sixteen for only the second time in history. America's foray into World Cup relevance coincided, and likely helped spur along, a major surge in recreational soccer happening at the youth level in the United States. Historians estimate that in 1980, fewer than 200,000 US high school athletes played soccer. Three years after the United States hosted the World Cup, that number had spiked to over 500,000. Estimates put the total number of Americans of all ages playing soccer in 1997 at over 18 million—almost a 20 percent increase in just a decade.[81] But according to Markovitz and Hellerman, although "soccer's proliferation at the recreational level ... has been quite prolific," the structural headwinds it faces due to its secondary sport status in America "prevent its full utilization for complete entry into American hegemonic sports culture."[82]

Nowhere is the precarious future of men's soccer in America more evident than with Major League Soccer (MLS). The origins of MLS are bound up with the 1994 World Cup, which FIFA agreed to give to the United States partly out of its "desire to help a professional league get off the ground as soon as possible" in America.[83] The league was announced in 1994 and immediately distinguished itself from other professional leagues by operating as a "single-entity" sport league, meaning players, teams, and the league functioned as a vertically integrated operation. Other leagues, like the NFL, NBA, and MLB, behave as confederations: the league approves of and regulates team franchises, facilitates the draft, and schedules their seasons, but private individuals or groups own the teams and teams hold player contracts. In MLS, the process is much more centralized.

MLS league play launched in 1996 and opened with ten teams split between its Eastern and Western conference divisions. Over the next twenty-five years, seventeen more franchises were added, and plans are in place to grow the league further over the next decade. Franchise expansion only happened as attendance figures at MLS games grew, which they did over the decades and remain one of the league's few signs of strength. But in the case of television ratings, MLS continues to struggle mightily, and its broadcast deals tell the story. Under its current deal, MLS brings in about $90 million a year to put its games on television. By comparison, the NHL's television deal is worth $225 million a year; the NBA's is over $2.6 billion annually (and expected to grow substantially); while the NFL's new deal signed in 2021 is worth $10 billion a year. To put a finer point on MLS's marginality: in 2022 NBC will pay five times the amount ($450 million) to broadcast the English Premier League (EPL) than what other companies pay MLS for its product. And for good reason. More Americans watch the EPL and Liga MX (the professional Mexican league) than MLS games.[84]

It is certainly plausible that US men's soccer could become a more compelling product and play a bigger role in US sport culture. American history is replete with examples of the nation's capacity to produce world-class athletes in any sport. Developing major, US-born soccer superstars could do for MLS what Dr. J. and Michael Jordan did for the NBA. In 2021, there were three Americans playing in the EPL, which boasts the best competition in the world. That is a strikingly small number, to be fair, but still a sign it can be done. MLS needs the number of elite US men to multiply, and then convince them not to play in Europe, for its fortunes to grow like the other major professional sports. In any case, soccer *is* alive and well on the women's side of things. One could even argue that, globally speaking, US women's soccer is the most dominant form of American sport today.

US National Sport in the Twenty-First Century

The US Olympic movement regained some of its lost momentum once the Cold War was over. At the 1996 Atlanta Games, golden-soled Michael Johnson streaked into Olympic lore when he became the first man to win the 200-meter and 400-meter races at the same Olympics, setting new world time records in both. Four years later in Sydney, Johnson defended his 400-meter title—another Olympic first in men's track and field.[85] The Sydney Olympics also saw the debut of the greatest Olympian ever, the US swimmer Michael Phelps, who splashed onto the scene at the age of fifteen. At the 2004 Olympics in Athens, Phelps won six gold medals, and four years later in Beijing he won eight golds, one for every event he competed in, surpassing the American Mark Spitz's former record of seven golds won at the 1972 Munich Games. From there, Phelps just kept on winning: in 2012 in London, he captured four golds and two silvers, and then came out of retirement for the 2016 Rio Games at the age of thirty-one to take another five golds and one more silver. Phelps's twenty-three gold medals is the record for any individual Olympian. The next closest are Spitz, Carl Lewis, and two others with nine total gold medals each.[86]

Johnson, Phelps, and other Americans like Jenny Thompson and Lindsey Vonn headlined one of the most decorated eras in US national sport history. Between 1996 and 2018, covering six Summer and six Winter Games, the United States won the most gold medals five times and the most overall medals seven times. Across all six Summer Olympics, America won the most golds in all but one (2008), and the total medal count every time. At the 2010 Winter Olympics in Vancouver, the United States finished with the most total medals—the first Winter Games where it had done so since 1932 in Lake Placid.[87]

The accomplishments of American women in soccer and gymnastics exemplify this new golden era of US national sport. Their histories also reflect the trajectory women's sport has taken over the last thirty years, combining standout individual performances with masterful teamwork and group chemistry. Unfortunately, and in different ways, women's soccer and gymnastics have endured some of the most toxic elements that exist in competitive athletics. From misogyny and political persecution, to staggering levels of sexual abuse, their histories portray what is best and what remains debased about American sport culture today.

The USWNT

Women's soccer did not figure prominently in US national sport until recently because women's soccer as a major, global sport did not really exist until the 1990s. In 1971, there were fewer than ten women's national teams in the world. Twenty years later there were thirty-two, and by 2020 there were 120. The sudden growth in women's soccer unquestionably corresponds to the success of the US Women's National Team (USWNT), which won the first-ever Women's World Cup in 1991. Women's soccer became a medal event at the Olympics only in 1996—and the USWNT won that tournament, too. Yet even in the 1990s, the fate of women's soccer was far from certain, and much of the (male-dominated) sport world continued to dismiss the USWNT as a quaint, but ultimately insignificant, story. The doubters were quite wrong. "A team that had been used to flying under the radar was about to be the talk of a nation," writes Caitlin Murray, author of *The National Team*. "They were going to set records, inspire a new generation, and change the landscape of sports in America."[88]

Winning the first-ever Women's World Cup was as much a reality check for the USWNT as it was a time to celebrate. FIFA awarded tens of millions of dollars to the top men's teams at the conclusion of their World Cup. The USWNT received thank-you cards in the mail and $500. Making women's soccer legitimate was one thing; making it lucrative was something else entirely. Fortunately, the USWNT got what any aspiring sport or professional league needs if it wants to flourish: a marketable star. A handful of terrific players led the USWNT to its first World Cup, but Mia Hamm stole the show.[89]

Hamm enrolled at the University of North Carolina before becoming a key member of the 1991 team. Hamm's brilliance on the pitch, her calm and comfortable demeanor, plus a natural beauty that fans and marketers adored turned her into the first true soccer star—male or female—in American history. Nike recognized her appeal instantly and became her first sponsor after she graduated from UNC in 1994. The deal's financials were modest, but it was a watershed moment. "For the first time ever," writes Murray, "a female soccer player wasn't going to need to think about getting a 'real' job after college." Instead, Hamm would make her living playing the game she loved.[90]

There are striking parallels between women's soccer in the 1990s and women's tennis in the 1970s. Struggling for respectability, demanding fair treatment and equitable pay, and fighting off endemic sexism are hallmarks in the history of both sports. To succeed, players needed sharp elbows, endless patience, and an unflinching determination to prove the world wrong. Luckily, the USWNT had the ultimate coach to guide them on their way. Shortly before the 1996 Olympics, Billie Jean King met with Hamm and her teammates. The USWNT detailed the major discrepancies between men's and women's soccer—including tournament bonuses, per diem on the road, travel and lodging accommodations, and uniform and equipment quality—and asked King what they should do. "You just don't play. That's the only leverage you have," she advised.[91] The team agreed. Just weeks before the Atlanta Games kicked off, the USWNT told the US Soccer Federation they were boycotting training camp until they had a new contract that offered fairer treatment and compensation. The gambit worked. Although the terms of the deal were still unequal to the men's team, the USWNT secured a better payout structure for the upcoming Olympics. The team reassembled and proceeded to win the first gold medal in women's Olympic soccer history.

More than 75,000 people attended the gold medal match between the United States and China—yet the networks chose not to air the game live, so most Americans were unaware of the history that was made. Turning success into broader commercial gain became one of the biggest challenges for the USWNT. Evidence of the sport's soaring popularity was visible at the ground level. Attendance at USWNT camps and clinics, and especially at their matches, often stunned organizers. Just before the 1999 World Cup, the USWNT played an exhibition in Washington, DC, and again nearly

75,000 fans showed up to watch. When the match was over, only about 15,000 stayed for a second game that featured MLS teams and members of the USMNT.[92]

The 1999 World Cup proved a formative moment in the USWNT's history. The team advanced to the championship where once again they faced China. Heightened geopolitical tensions hung over the game due to a misbegotten US missile strike in Yugoslavia the month prior that hit the Chinese embassy and killed three Chinese. The match itself, played in the Rose Bowl Stadium in Pasadena, California, was loaded with consternation. Regulation ended in a 0–0 tie and the game went to a penalty kick shootout. The Chinese team missed just one of their kicks, but the USWNT was perfect. The image of Brandi Chastain celebrating her game-winning goal appeared on front pages and homepages everywhere. The *New York Times*, which ran a headline calling the moment "Soccer's Move: From Grassroots to the Grand Stage," reported that the television ratings for the game—upward of forty million viewers—doubled network expectations. April Heinrichs, captain of the 1991 USWNT team that won first Women's World Cup, told the *Times*: "[w]hen we look back in twenty years, I really think that the Billie Jean King-Bobby Riggs tennis match, Title IX, and the 1999 Women's World Cup are the three largest pillars supporting women's sports in this country." The USWNT proved that "if you put enough money into women's sports, people will come to watch it."[93]

The 1999 World Cup team made women's soccer commercially relevant in America. But like they did for Wilma Rudolph, Billie Jean King, and other major US female athletes, the press and the public insisted on making the story about sex. "Talented and Sexy—US Team Has It All," boasted the *Orlando Sentinel*, while another outlet called it "The Babe Factor in Soccer Team's Success."[94] However the players felt about it personally—and some were definitely uncomfortable with their sudden status as sex symbols—both they and US Soccer understood that the public's infatuation with the team was elevating the sport's status in America. But as Murray shows, sex appeal only went so far. Most fans, male or female, were drawn to the USWNT because of the players' skill and the team's incandescent success. By the 2000s, the audience for the sport had reached new highs.[95]

From the players' perspective, whatever the reason, their newfound popularity presented the perfect time to try a professional league. Their first attempt came in 2001 and was called the Women's United Soccer Association (WUSA). Although the league included USWNT stars like Hamm and Brandi Chastain, the WUSA was doomed from the start. The economic shock brought on by the September 11 attacks compounded the financial issues the league faced from its beginning, and it never got on solid ground. The WUSA folded after three seasons. The next attempt came in 2008 when a league called Women's Professional Soccer (WPS) launched shortly after the USWNT won gold at the 2008 Olympics in Beijing. Without the star power of Hamm and other 1990s-era USWNT players, the WPS instead brought in some of the best foreign talent to complement the US-born players on league rosters, including the legendary Brazilian soccer star Marta Vieira da Silva. Nonetheless, financial hardship once again dogged women's professional soccer. After downsizing to just six teams in 2011, in 2012 the WPS suspended its operations permanently.[96]

The arrival of a new generation of USWNT luminaries like Alex Morgan, Hope Solo, and Megan Rapinoe carried on the USWNT's winning traditions and helped solidify the third, and current, effort at women's professional soccer. After another gold medal at the 2012 London Games, members of the USWNT helped organize the National Women's Soccer League (NWSL), and games opened in 2013. An important element to the NWSL's construction was that anyone who played for the USWNT also had to play in the NWSL. Murray explains that, while the players could have made more money playing abroad, they agreed to that arrangement because they "wanted to grow the game at home in the United States and committed themselves to the NWSL."[97] In 2017, the NWSL landed a television deal with A&E Networks, who purchased a 25 percent stake in the league. Three years later, CBS and the streaming service Twitch bought the rights to air NWSL games for around $5 million. The NWSL stands on sturdier financial footing than its predecessors, but familiar problems persist. Maximum contracts for the 2021 season were capped at $52,500, and many of the players made much less than that. Stories that sound like the early days of the NBA abound, with players picking up odd jobs in the off-season or living with their parents to make ends meet.[98]

Although challenges remain, and its future is far from certain, the NWSL is the most advanced and credible effort yet at professional women's soccer in America. However, the USWNT remains the key measurement for the sport's overall health. No team is perfect, and the USWNT has had poor showings and heartbreaking losses to fierce rivals. But since 1991, no women's soccer program in the world has accomplished more than the USWNT. The United States has won four of the first eight Women's World Cup tournaments and four of the first six Olympic gold medals for women's soccer. And almost as important, the United States has done so with waves of talented players who have become sport celebrities and cultural lightning rods. Hope Solo, the legendary goalkeeper who led the USWNT from 2000 to 2016, wore her emotions on her sleeves and ignited several media firestorms for the team. She was an audacious goalie who backstopped the USWNT's road to glory in the early twenty-first century. She also disparaged opponents, criticized her teammates, and questioned her coaches in front of the media. Solo's soundbites became fodder for outlets like ESPN and *Sports Illustrated*, and eventually led to her dismissal from the team in 2016.

Another USWNT star with enough bravado to fill a stadium is Megan Rapinoe. She is not only an all-time great women's soccer player—in 2019 alone, she won awards for Best FIFA Women's Player, FIFA Women's World Cup Golden Ball, FIFA World Cup Golden Boot, and FIFA World Cup

FIGURE 5.3 *USWNT star Megan Rapinoe scores a goal against the Netherlands during the championship match of the 2019 FIFA Women's World Cup. It was Rapinoe's sixth of the tournament. The USWNT won the match 2–0, and Rapinoe earned the Golden Ball (best player) and Golden Boot (top goal-scorer) of the tournament. (Photo by Maja Hitij/ Getty Images).*

Final Player of the Match—but also a fearless disciple in the tradition of the activist athlete. She has been an outspoken advocate of LGBTQ+ rights ever since she came out in an interview in 2012. "I feel like sports in general is homophobic," she told the magazine *Out*. "People want—they *need*—to see that there are people like me playing soccer for the good ol' US of A."[99]

Rapinoe's activism also extends to the problem of unequal pay in women's sports and, most contentiously, as a powerful advocate of the Black Lives Matter movement. When the NFL's Colin Kaepernick chose to kneel during the national anthem before a game in 2016 as a way to call attention to police brutality in America, the sport world became engulfed in questions about the politicization of sport, free speech, and peaceful protest, and whether athletes deserved to have their voices heard. Some Americans, ignorant of their own country's history, insisted that social justice movements were out of bounds for professional athletes. President Donald Trump demanded Kaepernick lose his job for using his First Amendment right to free speech and then suggested Kaepernick and other players who were protesting should be kicked out of the country. "Get that son-of-a-bitch off the field right now. Out! Out! He's fired!" seethed Trump to his adoring hordes at a campaign rally in Huntsville, Alabama.[100] When NBA superstar LeBron James weighed in on race relations and the role of Black athletes in contemporary society, Fox News host Laura Ingraham told her audience James should "shut up and dribble."[101]

Into the lion's den jumped Rapinoe. She began kneeling in solidarity with Kaepernick in 2016 and soon after published an article titled "Why I'm Kneeling" for the *Player's Tribune*, a publication by and for professional athletes that New York Yankees legend Derrek Jeter founded in 2014. "I am kneeling because I have to do *something*. Anything. We all do," she began. Athletes in her position must use their "platform to elevate the millions of voices being silenced and support them in the tremendous work already being done." Rapinoe acknowledged that she, and Kaepernick, and the other athletes who took a knee, would be viewed the same way that Tommie Smith and John Carlos were in 1968 when they protested the anthem at the Mexico City Olympics. But like Carlos and Smith, the anthem protests that began in 2016 were about striving for the ideals America claimed to represent—not disgracing them. "I can understand if you think that I'm disrespecting the flag by kneeling, but it is because of my utmost respect for the flag and the promise it represents that I have chosen to demonstrate this way," Rapinoe explained. "When I take a knee, I am ... staring straight into the heart of our country's ultimate symbol of freedom—because I believe it is my responsibility, just as it is yours, to ensure that freedom is afforded to *everyone* in this country."[102]

Rapinoe represents a generation of sport stars who have picked up the activist athlete mantle first raised in the early twentieth century and carry it forward in the new millennium. And their efforts are still needed. Much has improved since the time of Jack Johnson and Babe Didrikson Zaharias. But if anything, the last twenty years have shown that the darkest corners in sport—where deceit, corruption, and abuse lurk—still fester. The recent history of US women's gymnastics, in particular, involves iniquities and misdeeds that are difficult to fathom.

The Devil and the Goat

On January 16, 2018, midway through her victim impact statement, Jeanette Antolin, who competed for USA Gymnastics (USAG) from 1995 to 2000, told the courtroom: "I will never fully understand the evil that motivates an adult to abuse an innocent child, but I do understand the evil that motivates organizations like USA Gymnastics and Michigan State to turn a blind eye to this abuse." Antolin was fourteen when she joined the US national team and helped earn a silver medal for her country at the 1999 Pan American Games. "It is the evil that puts money and medals above the welfare of children," she stated. Antolin then turned and addressed her abuser directly. "Larry," she said, "you made me believe that you were my friend. You deceived me, you manipulated me, and you abused me. I truly believe that you are the spawn of Satan."[103]

The 2016 sexual abuse scandal that centered on the actions of the doctor and athletic trainer Larry Nassar implicated not only USAG, where for eighteen years Nassar was the women's team doctor, but also the USOC, which did nothing to protect the child athletes, and Michigan State University (MSU), where Nassar worked as a physician and professor for over ten years. The constellation of bad actors and conspirators who enabled Nassar's abuse is astonishing. Among his hundreds of victims are US Olympians, NCAA athletes, high school students, and the six-year-old daughter of a family friend. The decades during which he preyed on helpless, trusting children from his positions of considerable power span the most successful era in US gymnastics history. "To me, it was like a cult," explains Jamie Dantzscher, who starred for the 2000 US Olympic team. "Leaders of the cult were all about money and medals. If there are sacrifices in a cult, the sacrifice was the gymnasts ... [and] their physical, mental, and emotional well-being."[104]

The story starts back in the Cold War, when Eastern European gymnasts dominated the Olympics like so many other athletes from the communist bloc. The Romanian national team was a powerhouse, and its program was unique. Under the direction of Béla and Mártha Károlyi, Romanian gymnasts were incredibly young—often prepubescent—and their training was beyond intense. The children were hit, starved, and degraded, broken emotionally and mentally, and repurposed into Olympic medal-winning machines. Greatest among them was Nadia Comăneci, who in 1976, at the age of fourteen, completed an Olympic-first by scoring a perfect ten in an event—then repeated her feat six more times—and won three gold medals. Four years later, the Károlyis defected to the United States, where the USOC hired them to remake USAG as they saw fit. The couple instituted the program they designed in Romania, and before long, the USOC had its own army of child gymnasts conditioned to sacrifice everything on behalf of their coaches, country, team, and sport.

The breakout year was 1996, when the "Magnificent Seven" won America's first gold medal in the all-around team competition. The gymnasts who shined on the US included Dominque Dawes, Shannon Miller, and Dominique Moceanu—young women who performed brilliantly on the greatest stage and then became marketing icons to the benefit of USAG and the USOC. Another legendary member of the 1996 team was Kerri Strug, whose individual heroics to clinch the gold medal personified the culture USAG and the Károlyis cultivated. In her first attempt at her final event, the vault, Strug landed awkwardly and fell, tearing ligaments in her ankle. Strug was in obvious agony, but Béla ordered her to try again. "We need you one more time for the gold," he shouted. She limped back to the starting line, dashed down the runway, and somehow landed her second try, securing her team's gold on one foot. The image of Béla carrying Strug around the arena afterward, while she waved and clutched a bouquet of flowers, became an enduring portrait of the American win-at-all-costs spirit that had stamped

US Olympic history since turn of the twentieth century. Yet another image, captured on television before Károlyi paraded Strug in his arms, proved equally revealing. As Strug writhed in pain on the mat following her second vault, Mártha Károlyi picked her up and guided Strug into the outstretched hands of Larry Nassar, who took her to a stretcher and then whisked her away to a training room for evaluation.

Nassar came to USAG in 1986, and by the 1996 Atlanta Games he had become its national medical coordinator. The next year, MSU hired Nassar as a team physician and assistant professor in the College of Osteopathic Medicine. During his first year at MSU, Nassar sexually assaulted a sixteen-year-old during physical therapy by performing a "treatment" he called an "intravaginal adjustment." She went to MSU athletic officials, and her story was corroborated by another MSU gymnast, but university administrators intimidated the victims into staying quiet, and the report went nowhere. Nassar continued performing his treatment on MSU and USAG gymnasts, as well as high school athletes. According to court documents, it was around this time when Nassar began molesting a six-year-old whose parents Larry and his wife befriended.[105]

Besides MSU's administrative malfeasance, another reason Nassar's assaults persisted for so long is that he learned to take advantage of the culture of fear, abuse, and indoctrination that the Károlyis instilled within USAG. A focal point in this history is the Károlyi Ranch: a USAG training facility tucked deep in the woods in Huntsville, Texas. USAG gymnasts visited the ranch several times a year and stayed for week-long training sessions. No parents were allowed, phone service was spotty, and the coaches brutalized the girls physically and emotionally. Madison Kocian, who competed on the 2016 US Olympic team, described the tenor at the camps as one where "you can never be good enough ... everything would be criticized." The gymnasts were told it was all "part of the normal procedures of the national team camp," but it became "like a trap you can't really escape."[106] Nassar positioned himself as the girls' ally, someone whom Dantzscher said "seemed like he was on our side."[107] Nassar offered encouragement, not criticism, snuck food to the hungry girls, and inquired about their personal lives, all the while grooming them and gaining their trust. Moceanu, one of the stars on the 1996 team, explained:

> Mártha really loved Nassar. He would do what she would say. Give clearance to the athletes ... and then he got to go on the trips, go to the Olympics, got to be the team doctor, he got to be celebrated. It fed his ego: "I'm untouchable now. I have all access to these kids." All people cared about was ... medals. They were just hungry for medals and success. The coverage was catapulting these people that harmed so many gymnasts because of how the broadcasts were glorifying the Károlyis. No one had the confidence and courage to speak up because they were scared of the backlash.[108]

The US national team's success insulated the Károlyis from outside criticism about how they trained the gymnasts. After winning gold in 1996, USAG won silvers in the all-around team event at the 2004 and 2008 Olympics, then golds consecutively in 2012 and 2016. Gymnasts like Simone Biles, Gabby Douglas, and Aly Raisman secured dozens of individual medals at the Olympics and other international competitions. The winning kept the Károlyis in power, and they made sure Nassar remained the team doctor, despite growing numbers of accusations by USAG gymnasts and other female athletes. Between 1997 and 2015, at least seven young women reported to authorities that Nassar had assaulted them. Not only were those accusations ignored or dismissed, but Nassar was allowed to continue his work with MSU and USAG athletes largely unsupervised. In 2015, USAG gymnast Maggie Nichols informed her coach and parents about Nassar's intravaginal procedure, which he had performed on her at the Károlyi Ranch. Nichols's coach reported Nassar to the head of USAG, Steve Penny. Penny waited five weeks to inform the FBI. The FBI branch in Indianapolis, where USAG is based, passed the report on to another branch, where again nothing happened. As Nichols and her family waited for resolution, she continued training for the Olympics, and Nassar continued abusing gymnasts.

Three weeks after the US women won the team gold at the 2016 Rio Olympics, and nearly thirty years after Nassar started working for the team, the rot that had become USAG was laid bare. Following an *Indianapolis Star* investigation into the USAG's broader culture of abuse, Rachel Denhollander, a former gymnast and Nassar victim, contacted the paper and told them her story. On September 12, 2016, the paper published Rachel's account and named Nassar as her abuser.[109] USAG tried distancing itself from Nassar, claiming they had relieved him of his duties as team doctor in 2015 (Nassar and his attorney disputed USAG's framing, and insisted Nassar had retired in 2015 on his own accord). Eight days later, the FBI executed a search warrant at Nassar's home, and discovered computer hard drives containing over 37,000 images of child pornography. MSU fired Nassar the same day; several administrators and MSU's president later resigned; and eventually the university agreed to a $500 million settlement with his victims. Over the next three months, lawsuits and criminal charges against Nassar and his enablers mounted. By June 2017, more than 100 women had come forward alleging sexual abuse. Nassar pleaded guilty to child pornography charges in July and multiple counts of criminal sexual misconduct in November. In December he was sentenced to sixty years in prison for possession of child pornography. During his trial for criminal sexual misconduct in January 2018, 156 women read victim impact statements over the course of eight days in front of Nassar and the court. When they finished, the judge sentenced Nassar to an additional 40–175 years in federal prison.[110]

The day before the victim impact statements began, Simone Biles, the winningest American gymnast ever, posted her survivor story on Instagram. "For too long I've asked myself, 'Was I too naïve? Was it my fault?'" she wrote. "I will not and should not carry the guilt that belongs to Larry Nassar, USAG, and others." Reckoning with the reality of what had happened was going to be "a process, and one that I need more time to work through." But with one post, Biles had leveraged her superstar power and forced USAG to permanently close the Károlyi Ranch and take stock of the cancer it had spawned. Major figures within USAG resigned, were fired, and some criminally charged for their complicity. But America's gymnasts, who had endured impossible torment in the name of winning, continued their march of greatness, while the rest of the country grappled with a sport culture that could produce such evil.[111]

In 2018 and 2019, Biles led the United States to team golds at the gymnastics world championships. Biles won seven individual gold medals, including the all-around gold at both tournaments. Her brilliance is indescribable. The tally of her accomplishments surpasses anything else in gymnastics history, and to the human eye she defies reality. She has twenty-five world-record titles—two more than any other male or female gymnast—and four gymnastic skills named after her because she was the first woman to perform them at major global competitions. One of her skills—the Biles on the balance beam—is so difficult that gymnastics officials have tried to legislate the move out of the women's sport. "That's how good Simone Biles is," writes journalist Jane Coaston. "The international body that determines the scoring for the sport thinks that her moves are so difficult other gymnasts shouldn't risk trying them." When Biles learned how her balance beam skill would be scored—that she was being penalized for being *too* great—she replied simply, "hahaha … bullshit."[112]

Biles's official nickname, according to the USAG website, is "$imoney"—so sure to win you can take it to the bank. But to her fans, she is the "GOAT": Greatest of All-Time. Not only because she has achieved more than any US gymnast, or because watching her can leave one breathless. She is the GOAT because she is an exemplary leader, a beloved teammate, and the moral conscience of a sport gone terribly wrong. In 2019, in an interview during a tune-up competition before the 2020 Tokyo Olympics, Biles was asked about how she was processing the fallout from the Nassar scandal and how she viewed her role as an advocate for change. Her response beautifully captured her humanity as well as the mentality of the activist athlete and the heart of a champion:

> I think it's important because we have a platform … and when we [speak] it obviously goes a long way. So we're blessed to be given a platform, so people will hear and listen. But it's not easy coming back to the sport, coming back to the organization that has failed you …. I feel like every day is a reminder of what I went through and what I've been through and what I'm going through and how I've come out of it. I try to just not think about it but it is hard.

It's like did you guys really not like us *that* much that you couldn't just do your job? … I don't mean to cry but it's hard coming here for an organization and having had them failed us so many times. And we had one goal and we've done everything that they asked us for, even when we didn't want to and they couldn't do one damn job. You had one job, you literally had *one job* and you couldn't protect us ….

I'm strong, I'll get through it, but it's hard.[113]

No one has accomplished more in their sport than Simone Biles, and no American athlete has carried the dual burdens of greatness and activist under circumstances like hers. As a gymnast, she deserves to be called the GOAT. In the annals of American history, she stands with a handful of other consequential athletes whose greatness in the arena mirrored their enormous impact on society.

Notes

1   Cecil Harris, *Different Strokes: Serena, Venus, and the Unfinished Black Tennis Revolution* (Lincoln: University of Nebraska Press, 2020), 2.

2   Ibid., 5.

3   Ibid., 20.

4   Serena Williams quoted in ibid.

5   Darren Rovell, "Are Venus and Serena Bad for Tennis?" *ESPN*, February 3, 2003, URL: https://www.espn.com/sportsbusiness/s/2003/0202/1503084.html [accessed 8.10.21].

6   Phil Knight quoted in Tim Rosaforte, *Raising the Bar: The Championship Year* (New York: MacMillan, 2000), 51.

7   Ryan Herrington, "What Golf Looked Like before Tiger Woods Turned Pro and Changed the Game Forever," *Golf Digest*, August 28, 2016.

8   Quoted in Lane Demas, *Game of Privilege: An African American History of Golf* (Chapel Hill: University of North Carolina, 2017), 242.

9   Jack Nicklaus quoted in Rick Reilly, "Strokes of Genius," *SI*, April 21, 1997, 45.

10   Ben Crenshaw quoted in Michael Bamberger, "All Is Changed," in ibid., 48.

11   Kirsch, *Golf*, 3.

12   "Jack Nicklaus," *PGATour.com*, 2021, URL: https://www.pgatour.com/players/player.01869.jack-nicklaus.html [accessed 8.8.22].

13   Kirsch, *Golf*, 184.

14   *Tiger*, HBO Documentary directed by Matthew Hamacheck and Matthew Heineman, 2021.

15   Derek Lawrenson, "Tiger Goes Global," May 5, 1997.

16   "By the Numbers: Woods' 82 Wins," *PGATour.com*, October 27, 2019, URL: https://www.pgatour.com/statsreport/2019/10/27/golf-numbers-tiger-woods-record-tying-82-pga-tour-wins.html [accessed 8.8.22].

17   Garry Lu, "John Daly's Diet Would Have Killed a Lesser Man," *Boss Hunting*,
      April 9, 2021, URL: https://www.bosshunting.com.au/sport/golf/john-daly-diet/
      [accessed 8.8.22].

18   "How Tiger Woods Changed the Game of Golf," *Today's Golfer*, April 17, 2019, URL:
      https://www.todaysgolfer.co.uk/news-and-events/tour-news/2019/april/how-tiger-
      woods-changed-the-game/ [accessed 8.8.22].

19   Herrington, "What Golf Looked Like" [emphasis in original].

20   Ibid.

21   Lane Demas, *Game of Privilege* (Chapel Hill: University of North Carolina, 2017), 267.

22   Ibid., 265.

23   *Tiger,* HBO Documentary, Part II.

24   Jim Peltz, "Tiger Woods Hurt in Car Accident in Front of His Florida Home," *LA
      Times*, November 28, 2009, URL: https://www.latimes.com/archives/la-xpm-2009-
      nov-28-la-sp-tiger-woods28-2009nov28-story.html [accessed 8.8.22].

25   Andrew Stern, "Tiger Woods Case Puts Spotlight on 'Sex Addiction,'" *Reuters*, February
      19, 2010, URL: https://www.reuters.com/article/us-woods-addiction/tiger-woods-case-
      puts-spotlight-on-sex-addiction-idUSTRE61I61S20100219 [accessed 7.25.2021].

26   "Tiger Woods 2019 Masters Press Conference," *CBS Sports*, URL: https://www.
      youtube.com/watch?v=BvEFexY6lQc [accessed 8.10.21].

27   Daniel Rapaport, "Tiger Woods Discusses His Rehab," *Golf Digest*, May 27, 2021,
      URL: https://www.golfdigest.com/story/tiger-woods-speaks-about-recovery [accessed
      7.25.2021].

28   Bob Harig, "What Comes Next for Tiger Woods," *ESPN*, December 19, 2021, URL:
      https://www.espn.com/golf/story/_/id/32905231/what-comes-next-tiger-woods-
      knows-even-caddie [accessed 12.28.21].

29   Dan Lyons, "John Daly," *SI*, December 21, 2021, URL: https://www.si.com/golf-
      archives/2021/12/21/tiger-woods-probably-beat-jack-nicklaus-major-championships-
      record-john-daly-pnc [accessed 12.28.21].

30   Armstrong interviewed in ESPN 30 for 30 Documentary *Lance*, Part I, directed by
      Marina Zenovich (ESPN Films, 2020), URL: https://www.espn.com/watch/catalog/
      d58966fd-bc67-46d8-b5f3-2b0465102489/lance/_/bucketId/3989 [accessed 8.8.22].

31   See Reed Albergotti and Vanessa O'Connell, *Wheelmen: Lance Armstrong, the Tour de
      France, and the Greatest Sports Conspiracy Ever* (New York: Avery, 2013).

32   Juliet Macur, *Cycle of Lies: The Fall of Lance Armstrong* (New York: Harper, 2014), 54.

33   Jonathan Vaughters quoted in *Lance*, Part I.

34   Tim Bonville-Ginn, "Tour De France Winners," *cyclingweekly.com* (Cycling Weekly,
      August 27, 2020), https://www.cyclingweekly.com/news/racing/tour-de-france/tour-
      de-france-list-winners-128885 [accessed 8.8.22].

35   *Lance* pt. I, dir. Zenovich; "Blood Doping and EPO: An Anti-Doping FAQ: USADA,"
      US Anti-Doping Agency (USADA), January 3, 2020, URL: https://www.usada.org/
      spirit-of-sport/education/blood-doping-epo-faq/ [accessed 8.8.22].

36   Macur, *Cycle of Lies*, 258.

37   "Lance Armstrong Early Doping Denial," *Trans World Sport*, URL: https://www.
      youtube.com/watch?v=PCfYUf3qLfk [accessed 8.10.21].

38   Vande Verde quoted in *Cycle of Lies*, 141–2.

39   Armstrong quoted in ibid., 260.

40   Ibid., chapter 24.

41   Ibid.

42   Armstrong quoted in ibid., 403.

43   Julich quoted in *Lance*, HBO Documentary.

44   See Stu Cowen, "A Lament For the Stanley Cup Drought That Has Left Canada Dry," *WP*, July 9, 2021, URL: https://www.washingtonpost.com/opinions/2021/07/09/montreal-canadiens-stanley-cup-canada-drought/ [accessed 11.2.21].

45   Jose Canseco, *Juiced: Wild Times, Rampant 'Roids, Smash Hits, and How Baseball Got Big* (New York: Harper Collins, 2005), 75.

46   "The 1994 Strike Was a Low Point for Baseball," *ESPN*, August 10, 2004, URL: https://www.espn.com/mlb/news/story?id=1856626 [accessed 8.8.22].

47   "League by League Totals for Home Runs," *Baseball Almanac*, URL: https://www.baseball-almanac.com/hitting/hihr6.shtml [accessed 8.15.21].

48   Michael Schmidt, "Congress to Review Sosa's Testimony," *NYT*, June 17, 2009.

49   The 2018 documentary *Screwball* chronicles Rodriguez's extensive relationship with the Miami-based company Biogen, whose records MLB used to prove Rodriguez's continual and extensive PED usage.

50   For a good summation of this argument, see the Theo Epstein interview on the R2C2 podcast, hosted by C.C. Sabathia and Ryan Ruocco, URL: https://open.spotify.com/episode/3wg1m6E0mL5RvvySJNCDYn?si=KlzgtqSWSQuoTlOb5WCrJg&dl_branch=1&nd=1 [accessed 8.15.21].

51   For an excellent primer on Sabermetrics, including the metrics mentioned above, see *FanGraphs*, "Getting Started," URL: https://library.fangraphs.com/getting-started/#1 [accessed 8.15.21].

52   See "League Batting Encyclopedia" and "Miscellaneous Encyclopedia," *Baseball Reference*, URL: https://www.baseball-reference.com/leagues/majors/bat.shtml [accessed 8.15.21].

53   Patrick Saunders, "The State of Baseball," *The Denver Post*, March 28, 2021, URL: https://www.denverpost.com/2021/03/28/the-state-of-baseball-game-needs-fresh-ideas [accessed 8.15.21].

54   Chris Lamb, "When Latino Players Flip Their Bats It's Called Disrespectful," *WP*, October 20, 2015, URL: https://www.washingtonpost.com/posteverything/wp/2015/10/20/when-it-comes-to-baseballs-ethnic-tensions-problems-run-deeper-than-bat-flips/ [accessed 8.15.21].

55   Evan Grossman, "Here's Why Mike Schmidt Says You Can't Build Around Players like Odubel Herrera of the Phillies," *New York Daily News*, June 6, 2017, URL: https://www.nydailynews.com/sports/baseball/schmidt-build-latin-players-due-language-barrier-article-1.3226063 [accessed 8.15.21].

56   For more on their story, see the ESPN 30 for 30 documentary *Once Brothers*.

57   Stern quoted in Brook Larmer, *Operation Yao Ming: The Chinese Sports Empire, American Big Business, and the Making of an NBA Star* (New York: Gotham Books, 2005), 113.

58 Ibid., 207–8.

59 "Hundreds of Millions in China Watch Yao vs Yi," *Associated Press*, November 10, 2007, URL: https://www.ctvnews.ca/hundreds-of-millions-in-china-watch-yao-vs-yi-1.263650 [accessed 8.16.21].

60 "Yao Ming," *Basketball Reference*, URL: https://www.basketball-reference.com/players/m/mingya01.html [accessed 8.16.21].

61 Stephen Wade, "Could Mao Mend the Fences between the NBA and China?" *AP*, October 8, 2019, URL: https://apnews.com/article/aba5856440624249962f060660 2e5098 [accessed 8.21.21].

62 Jeff Zillgitt, "Dirk Nowitzki Changed the NBA's Perception of International Talent," *USA Today*.

63 Eddie Sefko, "Spurs Coach Greg Popovich on 'Impossible to Defend' Nowitzki," *Dallas Morning News*, February 11, 2016, URL: https://www.dallasnews.com/sports/mavericks/2016/02/12/spurs-coach-gregg-popovich-on-impossible-to-defend-dirk-nowitzki-arguably-the-best-pure-shooter-we-ve-seen/ [accessed 8.16.21].

64 Jonathan Abrams, "An N.B.A. Move that Crossed an Ocean," *NYT*, November 17, 2010.

65 Triano quoted in ibid.

66 Greg Colluchi interview on the "World of Basketball with Fran Fraschilla" podcast, URL: https://open.spotify.com/show/64tLWxvsjYEQSN3oNNYo2t [accessed 8.8.22].

67 "Former President Barack Obama Joins NBA Africa as a Strategic Partner," *NBA.com*, July 27, 2021, URL: https://www.nba.com/news/former-president-barack-obama-joins-nba-africa-as-strategic-partner?%24web_only=true&_branch_match_id=948385142986509388 [accessed 8.19.21].

68 See Joel S. Franks, "Pacific Islanders and American Football: Hula Hula Honesy, Throwin' Samoans and the Rock," *IJHS* 26 no. 16 (2009): 2397–2411.

69 Jabari Young, "The NFL Plans to Expand Its International Players Program," *CNBC*, March 9, 2020, URL: https://www.cnbc.com/2020/03/09/the-nfl-plans-to-expand-its-international-players-program.html [accessed 8.20.21].

70 Jason Margolis, "Many International Fans of American Football Are 'Born' on Super Bowl Sunday," *The World*, February 1, 2019, URL: https://www.pri.org/stories/2019-02-01/many-international-fans-american-football-are-born-super-bowl-sunday [accessed 8.20.21].

71 Ibid.

72 Chris Serb, *War Football: World War I and the Birth of the NFL* (New York: Roman & Littlefield Publishers, 2019).

73 Wilcomb E. Washburn, "The Moral Equivalent to Football," *The New Republic*, July 23, 1977, URL: https://newrepublic.com/article/71260/the-moral-equivalent-football [accessed 8.20.21].

74 Andrei Markovits and Steven Hellerman, *Offside: Soccer and American Exceptionalism* (New Jersey: Princeton University Press, 2001), 99.

75 Erin Blakemore, "Where Did Soccer Start?" *National Geographic*, June 15, 2018, URL: https://www.nationalgeographic.com/science/article/soccer-world-cup-origins-mesoamerica-ball-games-archaeology-science [accessed 8.21.21].

76 For a primer see: Ben Johnson, "Association Football or Soccer," *History Magazine*, nd., URL: https://www.historic-uk.com/CultureUK/Association-Football-or-Soccer/ [accessed 8.21.21].

77 Uri Friedman, "Why Americans Call Soccer 'Soccer,'" *The Atlantic*, June 13, 2014, URL: https://www.theatlantic.com/international/archive/2014/06/why-we-call-soccer-soccer/372771/ [accessed 8.23.21].

78 Markovits and Hellerman, *Offside*, 100.

79 Ibid., 104.

80 Ibid., 104–19.

81 Ibid., 171–3.

82 Ibid., 174.

83 Ibid., 182.

84 Graham Ruthven, "MLS Is Pulling Fans into Stadiums, but TV Audiences Remains Underwhelming," *The Guardian*, August 25, 2000, URL: https://www.theguardian.com/football/2020/aug/25/mls-tv-audiences-viewing-figures; Jayna Bardahl, "FC Cincinnati Doubled Average MLS Viewership," May 20, 2021, *Cincinnati Enquirer*, URL: https://www.cincinnati.com/story/sports/soccer/fc-cincinnati/2021/05/20/mls-tv-ratings-fc-cincinnati-tql-stadium-opener-drew-720-000-viewers/5185912001/; Jabari Young, "NBA Is Next Up for a Big Rights Increase," *CNBC*, March 22, 2021, URL: https://www.cnbc.com/2021/03/22/nba-is-next-up-for-a-big-rights-increase-and-75-billion-is-the-price.html [accessed 8.30.21].

85 "Michael Johnson's Astonishing Olympic Success," *Olympics.com*, URL: https://olympics.com/en/video/michael-johnson-s-astonishing-olympic-success [accessed 9.2.21].

86 "Michael Phelps," *Olympics.com*, URL: https://olympics.com/en/athletes/michael-phelps-ii [accessed 9.2.21].

87 "Olympic Games," *Olympics.com*, URL: https://olympics.com/en/olympic-games [accessed 9.3.21].

88 Caitlin Murray, *The National Team: The Inside Story of the Women Who Changed Soccer* (New York: Abrams Press, 2019), vii.

89 Ibid., 12.

90 Ibid., 15.

91 Ibid., 21.

92 Ibid., 38.

93 Jere Longman, "Soccer's Move: Grass Roots to Grand Stage," *NYT*, July 10, 1999, 43.

94 Quoted in Murray, *The National Team*, 51.

95 Ibid.

96 Ibid., 80–158.

97 Ibid., 199.

98 Candace Buckner, "Sick of Side Hustles," *WP*, August 10, 2021, URL: https://www.washingtonpost.com/sports/2021/08/10/nwsl-side-hustles-salaries/ [accessed 11.18.21].

99   Jerry Portwood, "Fever Pitch," *Out*, July 2, 2012, URL: https://www.out.com/travel-nightlife/london/2012/07/02/fever-pitch [accessed 11.15.21].

100   Bryan Graham, "Donald Trump Blasts NFL Anthem Protesters," *The Guardian*, September 23, 2017, URL: https://www.theguardian.com/sport/2017/sep/22/donald-trump-nfl-national-anthem-protests [accessed 8.8.22].

101   Emily Sullivan, "Laura Ingraham Told LeBron James to Shut Up and Dribble," *NPR*, February 19, 2018, URL: https://www.npr.org/sections/thetwo-way/2018/02/19/587097707/laura-ingraham-told-lebron-james-to-shutup-and-dribble-he-went-to-the-hoop [accessed 11.15.21].

102   Megan Rapinoe, "Why I am Kneeling," *The Players' Tribune*, October 6, 2016, URL: https://www.theplayerstribune.com/articles/megan-rapinoe-why-i-am-kneeling [accessed 8.8.22].

103   "Nassar Victim: Jeanette Antolin Statement," *NBC News* Detroit, Local 4, WDIV, URL: https://www.youtube.com/watch?v=fT6JGR0z6pM [accessed 11.23.21].

104   Dantzscher interviewed in "Defying Gravity" Documentary, directed by Bess Kargman and Lucy Walker (2020).

105   "Larry Nassar: A Trail of Sexual Abuse," *The Detroit News*, January 17, 2018, URL: https://www.detroitnews.com/story/news/local/michigan/2018/01/17/larry-nassar-career-abuse-timeline/109560512/ [accessed 11.24.21].

106   Madison Kocain interview, "Defying Gravity."

107   Dantzscher quoted in ibid.

108   Dominique Moceanu quoted in ibid.

109   Tim Evans, et al., "Former USA Gymnastics Coach Accused of Abuse," *Indianapolis Star*, September 12, 2016, URL: https://www.indystar.com/story/news/2016/09/12/former-usa-gymnastics-doctor-accused-abuse/89995734/ [accessed 11.24.21].

110   "Larry Nassar: A Trail of Sexual Abuse."

111   Simone Biles, "Feelings …" Instagram Post, shared January 15, 2018, URL: https://www.instagram.com/p/Bd_C55cHWUQ/?hl=en [accessed 11.24.21].

112   Jane Coaston, "Simone Biles Is the Greatest Female Gymnast Ever," *Vox*, October 13, 2019, URL: https://www.vox.com/culture/2019/10/10/20908435/simone-biles-gymnastics-best-ever [accessed 11.25.21].

113   Liz Clarke, "Simone Biles Blasts USA Gymnastics," *WP*, August 7, 2019, URL: https://www.washingtonpost.com/sports/olympics/simone-biles-lashes-out-at-usa-gymnastics-in-tearful-statement/2019/08/07/20037d80-b93a-11e9-b3b4-2bb69e8c4e39_story.html [accessed 5.23.22].

Athlete Spotlight #5:
Michelle Kwan

FIGURE 5.4 *Michelle Kwan, the daughter of first-generation Chinese immigrants, glides to victory at the 1996 US Figure Skating Championships. Kwan is one of the winningest US figure skaters in history and after retirement became a diplomat for the US government. (Photo by David Madison/Getty Images).*

Michelle Kwan embodies the global identity of modern American athletes. Born in 1980 to Chinese immigrants who left Hong Kong for California a decade prior, Kwan grew up obsessed with the sport of ice skating and the dream of Olympic glory. Her parents could not afford the coaching most ice-skating prodigies enjoy; nonetheless, Kwan and her sister Karen dutifully trained together, and, when she was twelve, she competed in the US senior nationals. By then, Kwan's talent caught the eye of the premier skating instructor Frank Carroll, who coached her for a decade.[1]

When she was thirteen, Kwan took second at the infamous 1994 US Championships in Detroit, Michigan. Nancy Kerrigan was a favorite heading into the event until a man attacked her in a hallway by the rink, hitting her across the knees with a baton. Although Kwan finished second behind another skater, Tonya Harding, US officials awarded Kerrigan the second Olympic spot, and named Kwan an alternate. She traveled with the US team to Norway and watched Kerrigan earn a silver medal. Harding came in eighth, but a bad Olympic showing was the least of her problems. Prior to the Games, investigators discovered that it was Harding's bodyguard who attacked Kerrigan, and that her ex-husband was involved in the plot as well. Harding eventually pleaded guilty to obstructing the investigation and was sentenced to three years' probation and a $100,000 fine. The United States Figure Skating Association stripped Harding of her 1994 US Championships title and banned her for life.[2]

Kwan emerged from the scandalous 1994 Games well positioned to compete for a spot at the next Winter Olympics set for Nagano, Japan. She won the 1996 World Championships but in 1997, after placing second at the US Championships, she fractured her left foot and was in a cast until a few weeks before the 1998 US Championships. Even still, Kwan delivered a performance the *LA Times* called the "gold standard for future generations of figure skaters." She earned perfect scores from six judges and cemented her spot as the US favorite heading into the Nagano Games.[3]

In Japan, Kwan's tightest competition came from her teammate, Tara Lipinski. Kwan won the short program and then executed a flawless long routine, but admitted afterward she felt like she held something back. Lipinski followed with a dazzling performance full of explosive jumps and inspired skating—and she won the gold. Kwan took home silver and almost immediately her attention turned to the 2002 Salt Lake City Olympics. She also dismissed Carroll, her longtime coach, and decided to train solo. She came into Salt Lake the clear favorite but uncharacteristically faltered twice and settled for the bronze. Although an Olympic gold eluded Kwan, her two Olympic medals, to go along with five world championships and nine US championships, represent one of the greatest careers in the history of skating.

After Salt Lake, Kwan's attention turned to other worldly matters. She earned a BA in international studies from the University of Denver and then an MA from Tuft's University in law and diplomacy. Kwan was an invited guest at a 2006 White House luncheon with China's president Hu Jintao, and afterward signaled her interest to take a more active role supporting US diplomacy. Kwan became involved in the State Department's sport diplomacy initiative that dates back to the Cold War, working for both the Bush and Obama administrations as a public envoy in the Bureau of Educational and Cultural Affairs as well as the Office of Global Women's Issues. In December 2021, President Biden nominated Kwan to be the US ambassador to Belize. "If confirmed, I will be very proud to serve my country," Kwan told the press. She added her priorities would be "working with the Belizean government on economic issues, to put an end to [the Covid-19] pandemic, and to address the root causes of migration."[4]

Notes

1   E. M. Swift, "Into the Light," *SI*, February 9, 1998, 157–65.

2   Taffy Brodesser-Akner, "Tonya Harding Would Like Her Apology Now," *NYT*, January 10, 2018, 1.

3   Mike Penner, "Victorious Kwan Close to Perfection," *LA Times*, January 11, 1998, URL: https://www.latimes.com/archives/la-xpm-1998-jan-11-sp-7342-story.html [accessed 12.27.21].

4   Jim Tankersley, "Olympian and a Kennedy Picked as Envoys by Biden," *NYT*, December 16, 2021, 14.

Conclusion

Tokyo ~~2020~~ 2021

Seven-foot Frenchman Rudy Gobert, star center for the Utah Jazz, finished his post-game press conference on March 9, 2020, by touching every microphone and recording device his long arms could reach, in a strained attempt at humor. The NBA was encouraging social distancing in the wake of the news that a pandemic had arrived in America—and Gobert thought the whole thing was silly. Two days later, Gobert became one of the first reported cases in the United States of Covid-19, the SARS-based virus (quickly dubbed the coronavirus) that broke out in China in 2019 and spread rapidly throughout the world. Gobert, like others at the time, dismissed the magnitude of the pandemic encircling the globe. But just hours after he tested positive, the NBA announced it was suspending the remainder of its season.[1]

Other leagues, including the EPL and MLB, followed suit, canceling or postponing their seasons as public health officials and national leaders scrambled for information about the coronavirus. The NBA eventually resumed its season five months later in what was dubbed "The Bubble": a tightly controlled compound in Disney World where players lived under strict medical supervision and played before empty arenas. The WNBA built its own bubble nearby in Bradenton, Florida. MLB's postponement lasted until August and predictably included a contentious labor dispute that stalled the season's start and cost the league a golden opportunity to pageant its dwindling product before an entire world deprived of other sports. Instead, baseball settled on an abbreviated sixty-game schedule that started after the NBA and European soccer had already resumed. Within weeks, teams like the St. Louis Cardinals and Miami Marlins suffered major Covid-19 outbreaks. The NFL managed a full season—and some teams even allowed fans to attend games—but they too struggled with contagion on their rosters.[2]

The pandemic also coincided with some of the most tumultuous racial strife in the United States since the 1960s, following the horrific police killing of George Floyd, an African American, in Minnesota, in May of 2020. In the basketball bubbles, the hardwood courts were stamped with the Black Lives Matter slogan and stitched on the backs of players' jerseys, where their last names normally appear, were phrases like "Equality," "Anti-Racist," "I Can't Breathe," and "Vote." As evidence of the transnational bonds that define the contemporary world of sport, soccer players in Europe took a knee before their national anthems and displayed Black Lives Matter on their video boards as an act of solidarity. Even MLB, which had been resistant to athlete activism for virtually all of its history, stenciled "BLM" behind the pitcher's mounds. It was a striking change in the tenor of professional sport in America, underscored by NFL commissioner Roger Goodell's mea culpa over how the league scapegoated Colin Kaepernick for protesting police brutality almost a decade earlier.[3]

Meanwhile, the 2020 Summer Olympics set for Japan were postponed until 2021, although at the time no one knew if those Games would ever take place. Tensions were already high among the Japanese people, who had been agitating against their country hosting the Olympics since well before the Covid-19 pandemic began. Their dissent was multifaceted: some

FIGURE 6.1 *Inside the WNBA's "bubble" during the 2020 finals between the Las Vegas Aces and Seattle Storm were signs of the times, with Black Lives Matter embossed on the hardwood and game officials sitting courtside wearing protective medical masks as preventive measures against the novel coronavirus sweeping the globe. (Photo by Julio Aguilar/ Getty Images).*

protested the ballooning costs to build the requisite Olympic infrastructure (jumping from an initial estimate around $7 billion to a final sum three to four times that amount); others fretted that the government's desire to showcase Japan's recovery since the devastating 2011 nuclear meltdown in Fukushima was misguided, premature, and could risk the health of Japanese citizens and Olympic athletes. When the pandemic erupted, new fears emerged that the Olympics would become a super-spreader event—another cost the Japanese people would incur so their government could look competent and powerful on the world stage.[4]

Still, the Games went on. Thanks to the stunning achievement by the world scientific community, coronavirus vaccines became available in the United States under emergency FDA approval in November 2020 just days after President Donald Trump, who had downplayed the severity of the virus and spread misinformation about its origins, effects, and treatments, only to become severely sick from the disease himself, was voted out of office. By early 2021, America and much of Western Europe were inoculating large percentages of their population, yet global vaccine distribution was slower and uneven. The IOC made vaccines available for all Olympians, and upward of 85 percent of all those who competed in the Games were estimated to have been vaccinated beforehand. Others, however, were unmoved by scientific explanations about the need to protect themselves and the broader public and refused the vaccine. The chief medical officer for the USOC, Jonathan Finnoff, told the *New York Times* that while most athletes understood the public health imperative for mass vaccination, "there are other people who don't believe the virus exists and that it's a global conspiracy and that the vaccine is a tracking device."[5]

After a hellacious year of public health, economic, and political crises, the United States could look forward to the Tokyo Olympics with reasonable optimism. The USOC fielded some of its greatest teams and athletes ever to compete at an Olympics, including the 2019 World Cup-winning USWNT; a US basketball team led by the surefire Hall-of-Famer Kevin Durant; swimming sensation Katie Ledecky; and, of course, the GOAT: Simone Biles. The stoutness of America's competition was also in question. The IOC banned Russia from official participation in Tokyo after they were caught again for systematic doping; however, many individual Russian athletes were allowed to compete as members of the Russian Olympic Committee. But most observers expected America's toughest challenger would be China.

In the words of PRC Olympic Committee chairman, Gou Zhongwen, China had settled on an Olympics strategy with a singular focus: "We must resolutely ensure we are first in gold medals." Their plan was a familiar one. "Rooted in the Soviet model," the journalist Hannah Beech writes, "the Chinese system relies on the state to scout tens of thousands of children for full-time training at more than 2,000 government-run sports school." They emphasize "less prominent sports that are underfunded in the West or sports that offer multiple Olympic gold medals." No surprise, Beech adds, "that nearly seventy-five percent of the Olympic golds China has won since 1984 are in just six sports: table tennis, shooting, diving, badminton, gymnastics and weightlifting."[6]

Heading into the last day of the Games, China's plan looked to be working. Chinese athletes won golds in air rifle and pistol shooting, weightlifting, fencing, synchronized diving, and rowing all in the first week of events. Over the second week, Chinese added more golds in table tennis, badminton, sailing, shot put, and cycling. Much like the Soviets during the Cold War, women won a major portion of China's gold medals in events like air rifle shooting, weightlifting, fencing, sailing, and badminton. By August 4, China had thirty-two gold medals—five more than the United States who otherwise led in the overall medal count. And in one of the biggest spotlights of all, the Chinese were winning golds in women's gymnastics over a USAG squad beset by more trouble.

Consternation set in early, when during her first event, the floor exercise, Biles received a huge point deduction for stepping out of bounds. As the journalist Meredith Cash wrote, "while Biles has been known to teeter out of bounds from time to time due to the immense power on some of her passes, Sunday's error was more jarring than usual." She did not just land out of bounds: "Biles flew clean off the mat."[7] Biles tried to shake it off, but the falter proved a harbinger of a bigger problem. America's GOAT was in the midst of a mental health crisis, and almost no one knew it at the time. Biles later explained to her fans and media that she had a case of the "twisties": an occurrence gymnasts can experience whereby, in the middle of a jump, they lose their orientation and have no idea when or where they will land. The twisties are very dangerous, especially for someone like Biles who elevates so high in the air and performs so many aggressive flips and turns. "She is doing some of the most difficult skills in the entire world," explained former US gymnast Jordyn Wieber, "and if you're not mentally in a great place, or have the twisties, then it can be a matter of life or death."[8]

Two days after the faulty floor exercise, Biles performed an erratic looking vault and promptly withdrew from the remaining events of the team competition. She explained to her fans and the media that it had "been a really stressful Olympics as a whole … It's been a long week, a long Olympic process, and a long year." She had previously disclosed that the pandemic and the delay it caused to the Olympic calendar had exasperated her mental struggles from the Larry Nassar scandal and USAG's failures to protect the athletes. "I don't think the extra year helped," she told *Time* magazine right before the Olympics began. It meant twelve more months full of daily reminders of her abuse and public accounting of her life as a survivor. "How much more can I take before I had enough?"[9]

Remarkably, and true to form, Biles steeled herself in time to compete in one individual event—the balance beam—and earned a bronze. Her USAG teammates filled in for her during the team competition, and, despite losing their ace, fought hard and won silver. Most everyone celebrated the bravery

FIGURE 6.2 *The embodiment of her era of American sport, Simone Biles briefly levitates in front of empty seats, the result of the covid-19 pandemic, during the women's gymnastics qualification round at the Tokyo Olympics. After withdrawing from team competition because of mental health concerns, Biles returned to win bronze on the balance beam during individual events. (Photo by Ulrik Pedersen/ NurPhoto via Getty Images).*

Biles exhibited by prioritizing her mental health, stepping aside for the good of the team, and becoming USAG's biggest cheerleader as they came up just short to Russia for the gold. Yet certain reactionaries attacked Biles for being a "quitter." Right-wing pundits and politicians were especially vitriolic. The Republican Deputy Attorney General in Texas, Aaron Reitz, took to Twitter to call out "our selfish, childish national embarrassment, Simone Biles." Others, including Donald Trump acolyte and far-right activist Charlie Kirk, told audiences that America was "raising a generation of weak people like Simone Biles," and called her a "shame to the country."[10]

Biles, of course, rose above what charlatans in the press and politicians waging culture wars were trying to do to her. She patiently explained the mental struggles she was enduring and articulated how dangerous the twisties can be for gymnasts. After the Olympics, Biles was already looking back on her decision as one of the formative moments of her life. Having "the courage to take care [and] put myself first" was a turning point, she said, and one she only made because of her maturity and prior struggles. "Sixteen-year old [Simone] would never" have done that, she admitted.[11]

The invective Biles endured was not the only case in which prominent Americans back home ridiculed US Olympians for subpar performances in Tokyo. The USWNT, stalwart of so many US Olympic achievements and positioned to become the first women's team ever to win a World Cup and

Olympic gold consecutively, struggled mightily. During the group stage of play, Sweden drubbed the United States 3–0, and in the quarter finals the team barely won a ragged game against the Netherlands. Then, in the seventy-fourth minute of their semi-final match against Canada, the United States was flagged for a penalty that set up Canadian striker Jessie Fleming for a free kick which she promptly buried in the back of the net. The game ended 1–0 and Canada advanced to the gold medal game. Even though the USWNT won their bronze medal game against Australia, their detractors back home let the women know what they thought of them. "If our soccer team, headed by a radical group of Leftist Maniacs, wasn't woke," former president Donald Trump said in a statement, "they would have won the Gold Medal." He added that the "woman with the purple hair [Megan Rapinoe] played terribly and spends too much time thinking about Radical Left politics and not doing her job!"[12]

The disconnect between US athletes using their constitutionally protected right to free speech and certain flag-waving Americans trying to silence them remains one of the most disorienting features of US sport today. To see powerful Americans with massive public platforms openly root against and disparage US athletes for using the very freedoms, their critics accuse them of dishonoring underscores how fraught sport's evolution in America has been over the last 150 years. The USWNT, where its athletes are not only activists, but women, and some of them LGBTQ+, helps simplify the matter. Reactionaries hate them not just because of their message, but because of who they are. Sport provides a unique route to power and success for people who do not conform to the dominant—often repressive—social norms that govern most other parts of life. Those who are threatened by difference and change have a hard time reconciling the success and power of those they think are beneath them, and so they contort themselves into knots insisting that only *they* are the true Americans, while the ones achieving greatness for their country and acting out what free speech looks like are infidels.

Behind to China in the gold medal count, and with two of its winningest national programs caught in a media maelstrom, the Americans would need a strong final week to turn the narrative around. For a minute, it appeared the US men's basketball team, another pre-Olympic favorite to win gold, might also falter in 2021. In their first exhibition game against Nigeria, the US team lacked the cohesion and chemistry that the Nigerians exhibited and lost 90–87. It was a shocking defeat and left many observers wondering if basketball's global growth had finally caught up to the NBA's American stars. Those questions persisted after the US lost their next exhibition game against Australia, and then lost their first tournament game against France. "The gap in talent shrinks every year as there are more and more great players all over the world," US coach Greg Popovich told the media after the game. Chris Mannix with *Sport Illustrated* declared the US was no longer the Olympic favorite in basketball and pointed out that after losing "three of its last five [games]," America's "work is clearly cut out for them. And time is running out."[13]

Through the brilliant play of the team's leader, Kevin Durant, the US men steadied the ship and finished the preliminary round with two straight victories, and then comfortably handled Spain and Australia in the first two games of the knockout round, setting up a rematch with France for the gold. The championship game was competitive throughout. France, led by the face of the NBA's coronavirus troubles, Rudy Gobert, along with other NBA players including Evan Fournier and Nicholas Batum, jumped out to an early lead but with two minutes left in the first quarter, Durant drilled a three-pointer to tie the game, and the United States never trailed again. The game got close in the fourth quarter, but Durant was irrepressible, and the United States prevailed 87–82.

Durant, who earlier in the tournament became Team USA's all-time scoring leader, finished with twenty-nine points, six rebounds, three assists, and a block, and was named the tournament's Most Valuable Player. "He's the most skilled basketball player ever," insisted US assistant coach (and Golden State Warriors head coach) Steve Kerr, who had played alongside Michael Jordan for the Chicago Bulls in the 1990s. "There's nobody who's his size—6' 11"—who combines shooting and ballhandling skills and athleticism. We've never seen it before." By helping add a gold medal to America's rising tally, Durant told the press he treasured the opportunity "to build the camaraderie with the most talented guys in the world, to play for your country, to represent my little section of the United States, my family— it's special to come together for a common cause."[14]

Great as Durant was for America, the nation's brightest star in 2021 was Katie Ledecky, who earned four medals, including two golds, in women's swimming. Ledecky became an Olympic sensation as a fifteen-year-old in London in 2012, where she won her first gold, and solidified her place atop the world of women's swimming in 2016 in Rio, where she secured four gold medals. Her two golds in Tokyo—including a third-consecutive gold in the 800-meter freestyle—gave her six total in her career. Like Phelps did in his day, Ledecky is eyeing more. "That was not my last swim—I'm at least going to [2024]," she said after winning the 800-meter. "Maybe [2028], we'll see."[15]

Team USA's victory over France and Ledecky's brilliance in the water helped move the United States closer to China in the gold medal count. Heading into the last day, the United States was well ahead in the overall medal count but still trailed the PRC by two golds, thirty-six to thirty-eight. But in the final hours of play, America's women came through again, winning golds in women's basketball, volleyball, and track cycling. The United States finished the Olympics with thirty-nine golds and 113 overall medals. China's gold-or-bust strategy nearly panned out, and they could have added more on the final day. But they came up short in rhythmic gymnastics and women's middleweight boxing, and left Tokyo two golds shy of their goal.

The US women's basketball team, who blasted their competition on way to a rout of Japan in the gold medal game, was a fitting courier for their country's 2021 Olympic glory. Composed of WNBA stars like Brittney Griner and Sue Bird (fiancée to USWNT star Megan Rapinoe), many of its players had endured harsh criticism over the prior year for speaking out on racial and social justice issues, akin to other athletes including their NBA brethren. The actions of some members of the women's Olympic team invited the scorn of then-US senator Kelly Loeffler, who was also part-owner of the WNBA franchise the Atlanta Dream. She accused the players of "radically changing America" for protesting the national anthem and supporting organizations like Black Lives Matter. "I don't think they have a place in sports," Loeffler said. "Sports need to be about unity and bringing people together."[16]

By winning the gold medal for their country (the seventh in a row for US women's basketball!) and helping move America ahead of China on the last day, the greatest female basketball players on the planet showed what greatness and patriotism were all about. "It's twenty years of sacrifice, putting everything aside and just wanting to win," said WNBA star and five-time gold medalist Diana Taurasi.[17] Bird seemed to appreciate the broader significance of her particular group of athletes coming through in the clutch for the United States on the greatest stage in world sports. "Hopefully we've left a legacy with the younger players," she said, "where they now can carry that torch."[18]

It seems appropriate that the competition between the United States and China overwhelmed the Tokyo Olympics. Sport, as it has for the last 150 years, once again reflects key forces shaping world events as the twenty-first century reaches the quarter mark. China and the United States have been uneasy cohabitants of the international community for better than a century. Despite salient economic and cultural linkages that bind the countries together, tensions between the two steadily rise. With some observers calling it the "new Cold War" and others breathlessly insisting that a military confrontation is just around the corner, it is hard to know exactly in what direction US-Chinese relations are headed. The eagerness with which some pundits describe a looming crisis between the two superpowers is often hyperbolic, if not wholly irrational. There is no doubt, however, that the United States and China view each other, at the very least, as rival competitors. How this new superpower contest plays out is unpredictable. Yet, it is clear sport will, again, serve a role.[19]

Beijing hosts the next Olympics, in the winter of 2022. American athletes will be on hand, but the United States elected to diplomatically boycott the Games, citing the ongoing humanitarian catastrophe in China's Xinjiang province, where millions of ethnic Muslims known as Uyghurs have been forced into "reeducation camps." Global outcry over what the Chinese government at first denied and now downplays is sharpening, but what action can be taken to force the PRC's hand and open the camps remains unclear. Additionally, one of China's top female tennis stars, Peng Shuai, recently went missing after she accused a top PRC official of sexual assault.

Her disappearance has only added to international pressure against the PRC's inhumane treatment of its people.[20]

Paraphrasing from Jimmy Carter's playbook, President Biden decided to signal his opposition to China's crimes against humanity by diplomatically boycotting the 2022 Winter Games. He did not, however, require Americans to boycott or compete in an alternative set of games, like Carter did in 1980. Jen Psaki, press secretary for the Biden administration, said the president did not feel "it was the right step to penalize athletes who have been training, preparing for this moment," but added the US government felt it was imperative to send a message to leaders in Beijing. The PRC, in turn, ordered the United States to "stop politicizing sports" and threatened "resolute countermeasures" as retribution for the diplomatic slight. Most observers agreed that Biden's boycott accomplished little more than to further highlight the PRC's oppressive regime. But it was also another step in the direction of an adversarial relationship between the two countries. If history is any guide, sport will likely remain a helpful barometer for measuring the intensity of that rivalry. Not a substitute for war, but an approximation of the state of play between great powers and their competing visions for world order.[21]

✳ ✳ ✳

The Tokyo Olympics captured much about how sport, America, and the world have evolved over the last 150 years. Alongside superpower competition, political signaling, international crises, and enormous economic investment were individual acts of grace, sacrifice, and glory. The world looks much different than it did during the Cold War, or the era of empire preceding it, yet many of the tensions that shaped the prior century remain. The fallout from the collapse of the Soviet Union and the Eastern bloc, like the aftershocks of decolonization, continues to drive international relations. The maturation of the global sporting community combined with the persistence of international rivalry suggests that sport will stay a vital form of soft power for the United States and other countries for the foreseeable future.

The international history of American sport points to several lessons that can help guide present observers of the contemporary world of sport. Foremost, the United States is still a nation of immigrants. The country's relationship with its "golden door" grows more complicated by the year, but nothing changes the fact that diversity is still one of America's most obvious and vital national characteristics. Sport will continue to be an essential vehicle of assimilation for the various ethnicities and cultures that comprise US society. Teams and leagues will likewise continue to draw heavily from a diverse cast of athletes to make up their rosters, win games, and capture medals. Imperfect as it may be, American democracy and the pluralistic society it holds together still bolster the country's image on the world stage. Time has shown that sport is uniquely suited to reflect and advance the state of its democratic system.

The multiculturalism of American sport also means that athlete activism is not likely to fade anytime soon. American athletes have been using their platforms and privilege to call out injustice for over a century—and their ferocity only grows. Thanks to social media and an audience of younger sport fans that overwhelmingly supports social activism, incidents of athlete civil protest, united messaging, and agitation for political causes will surely remain prominent features of American sport. Athlete activism will continue to define and redefine athletes' relationship with fans, as well as their influence on the ever-growing business end of sport.

Indeed, the commercialization of sport shows no signs of stopping. Like the radio and television, new media technologies and new forms of corporate sponsorship will continue to grow professional leagues into multibillion (trillion?) dollar entities and plunge American sporting culture further into the world of consumer entertainment. Sport gambling has gone mainstream in the last few years, and its immersion within the fan and game experience now seems ubiquitous. Naming rights, corporate logos, streaming services, and hefty sponsorships enrich owners, management, and players like never before.

Sport's position as one of the most lucrative and culturally resonant features of the United States today is indisputable. Those who want to diminish sport's importance confess to a profound misreading of modern society. Rather, given how broadly sport shapes the United States and many other countries today—culturally, economically, politically, and diplomatically—we would do well, as fans, citizens, and students of history, to take sport even more seriously. Sport is deeply meaningful. It has become one of the fullest expressions of the human condition. Between the lines of American history, its story also signals the possibilities of a truly democratic society.

Notes

1   "Visual Timeline of the Day That Changed Everything," *ESPN*, March 11, 2021, URL: https://www.espn.com/espn/story/_/id/30546338/visual-line-day-changed-everything-march-11 [accessed 12.4.21].

2   Joseph Zucker, "Timeline of Coronavirus' Impact on Sport," *Bleacher Report*, n.d., URL: https://bleacherreport.com/articles/2880569-timeline-of-coronavirus-impact-on-sports; Gabe Lacques, "Why MLB May Be Sports' Biggest Loser during Covid-19 Pandemic," *USA Today*, June 5, 2020, URL: https://www.usatoday.com/story/sports/mlb/2020/06/05/mlb-biggest-sports-loser-during-covid-19-pandemic/3154841001/ [accessed 12.4.21].

3   "In Photos: The Sports World Has Been Taking a Stand," *CNN*, October 1, 2020, URL: https://www.cnn.com/2020/08/27/world/gallery/sports-protests/index.html [accessed 12.4.21].

4   David Zirin, "Covid's Devastating Toll on the Tokyo Olympics," *MSNBC*, August 9, 2021, URL: https://www.msnbc.com/opinion/covid-s-devastating-toll-tokyo-olympics-n1276307 [accessed 12.4.21].

5   Victor Mather and Andrew Keh, "IOC Offers Vaccine to All Tokyo Game Participants," *NYT*, May 6, 2021, URL: https://www.nytimes.com/2021/05/06/sports/olympics/tokyo-olympics-vaccine.html [accessed 12.4.21].

6   Hannah Beech, "The Chinese Sports Machine's Single Goal," *NYT*, July 29, 2021, URL: https://www.nytimes.com/2021/07/29/world/asia/china-olympics.html [accessed 12.4.21].

7   Meredith Cash, "Simone Biles Faltered in Her First Event in Tokyo," *Insider*, July 25, 2021, URL: https://www.insider.com/simone-biles-floor-error-finishes-second-gymnastics-qualifying-2021-7 [accessed 12.5.21].

8   Weiber quoted in Alice Park, "Simone Biles Has the Twisties," *TIME*, July 30, 2021, URL: https://time.com/6085776/simone-biles-twisties-gymnastics/ [accessed 12.5.21].

9   Alice Park, "Simone Biles Is Already the Best Gymnast Ever," *TIME*, June 24, 2021, URL: https://time.com/6075185/simone-biles-tokyo-olympics/ [accessed 12.5.21].

10   Brady Langmann, "If You're Criticizing Simone Biles, This Is the Company You Keep," *Esquire*, July 28, 2021, URL: https://www.esquire.com/sports/a37154782/simone-biles-olympics-mental-health-criticism/ [accessed 12.5.21].

11   Aimee Lutkin, "Simone Biles Says She Would Never Have Withdrawn from Olympics as a Teen," *Elle*, October 16, 2021, URL: https://www.elle.com/culture/celebrities/a37980051/simone-biles-reflects-on-tokyo-withdrawal/ [accessed 12.5.21].

12   Tom Lutz, "'Woke Means You Lose,'" *The Guardian*, August 5, 2021, URL: https://www.theguardian.com/football/2021/aug/05/donald-trump-uswnt-usa-soccer-olympics-bronze-megan-rapinoe-tokyo-2020 [accessed 12.8.21].

13   Chris Mannix, "US Men's Basketball's Loss to France Is a Reminder That They're Not the Gold Medal Favorite," *SI*, July 25, 2021, URL: https://www.si.com/olympics/2021/07/25/team-usa-loss-france-tough-road-ahead-olympics [accessed 12.8.21].

14   Barry Svrluga, "USA Basketball Faced a Lot of Questions at These Olympics," *Washington Post*, August 7, 2021, URL: https://www.washingtonpost.com/sports/olympics/2021/08/07/kevin-durant-usa-basketball-tokyo-olympics/ [accessed 12.8.21].

15   Matt Norlander, "Katie Ledecky Makes History with 6th Individual Gold," *CBS Sports*, August 8, 2021, URL: https://www.cbssports.com/olympics/news/katie-ledecky-makes-history-with-6th-individual-gold-cements-olympic-icon-status-and-shell-be-back-in-2024/ [accessed 12.8.21].

16   Adam Well, "Atlanta Dream Co-Owner Kelly Loeffler Criticizes Players, BLM after WNBA Protest," *Bleacher Report*, August 28, 2020, URL: https://bleacherreport.com/articles/2906682-atlanta-dream-co-owner-kelly-loeffler-criticizes-players-blm-after-wnba-protest [accessed 12.8.21].

17 "2021 Olympics," *The Athletic*, August 8, 2021, URL: https://theathletic.com/news/2021-olympics-us-womens-basketball-wins-seventh-consecutive-gold-medal/bklgd7MgunM6/ [accessed 12.8.21].

18 Brian Windhorst, "Team USA Women's Hoops Wins Seventh Straight Gold Medal at Tokyo Olympics," *ESPN*, URL: https://www.espn.com/olympics/story/_/id/31984277/team-usa-women-hoops-wins-seventh-straight-gold-medal-tokyo-olympics [accessed 12.8.21].

19 See for example Alan Dupont, "The US China Cold War Has Already Started," *The Diplomat*, July 8, 2020, URL: https://thediplomat.com/2020/07/the-us-china-cold-war-has-already-started/ [accessed 12.11.21]; Stephen Walt, "Everyone Misunderstands the Reason for the US-China Cold War," *Foreign Policy*, June 30, 2020, URL: https://foreignpolicy.com/2020/06/30/china-united-states-new-cold-war-foreign-policy/ [accessed 12.11.21]. For a more nuanced and historically grounded assessment of contemporary US-China tensions, see Hal Brands and John Lewis Gaddis, "The New Cold War: America, China, and the Echoes of History," *Foreign Affairs* 100, no. 6 (November/December 2021), URL: https://www.foreignaffairs.com/articles/united-states/2021-10-19/new-cold-war [accessed 8.22.22].

20 Emma Graham-Harrison, "China Has Built 380 Internment Camps in Xinjiang, Study Finds," *The Guardian*, September 23, 2020, URL: https://www.theguardian.com/world/2020/sep/24/china-has-built-380-internment-camps-in-xinjiang-study-finds [accessed 12.11.21].

21 Zolan Kanno-Youngs, "US Will Not Send Government Officials to Beijing Olympics," *NYT*, December 6, 2021, URL: https://www.nytimes.com/2021/12/06/us/politics/olympics-boycott-us.html [accessed 12.11.21].

SELECTED BIBLIOGRAPHY

Ariail, Cat. *Passing the Baton: Black Women Track Stars and American Identity*. Champaign: University of Illinois Press. 2020.

Borish, Linda, et al., eds. *The Routledge History of American Sport*. New York: Routledge. 2016.

Buford, Kate. *Native American Son: The Life and Sporting Legend of Jim Thorpe*. Lincoln: University of Nebraska Press. 2010.

Burgos Jr., Adrian. *Playing America's Game: Baseball, Latinos, and the Color Line*. Berkeley, CA: University of California Press. 2007.

Cayleff, Susan. *Babe: The Life and Legend of Babe Didrikson Zaharias*. Champagne: University of Illinois Press. 1996.

Crawford, Bill. *All American: The Rise and Fall of Jim Thorpe*. Hoboken, NJ: Wiley & Sons, Inc. 2004.

Cunningham, Carson. *American Hoops: U.S. Men's Olympic Basketball from Berlin to Beijing*. Lincoln: University of Nebraska Press. 2010.

Davies, Richard. *Sports in American Life: A History*, Third Edition. Malden, MA: Wiley Blackwell. 2017.

Dichter, Heather L., ed. *Soccer Diplomacy: International Relations and Football Since 1914*. Lexington: University Press of Kentucky. 2020.

Dichter, Heather L. and Andrew L. Johns, eds. *Diplomatic Games: Sport, Statecraft, and International Relations since 1945*. Lexington: University Press of Kentucky. 2014.

Dyreson, Mark. *Crafting Patriotism for Global Domination: America at the Olympic Games*. London: Routledge. 2009.

Dyreson, Mark. *Making the American Team: Sport, Culture, and the Olympic Experience*. Urbana: University of Illinois Press. 1998.

Edwards, Harry. *The Revolt of the Black Athlete: 50th Anniversary Edition*. Urbana: University of Illinois Press. 2017.

Elfers, James. *The Tour to End All Tours: The Story of Major League Baseball's 1913–1914 World Tour*. Lincoln: University of Nebraska. 2003.

Elias, Robert. *The Empire Strikes Out: How Baseball Sold U.S. Foreign Policy and Promoted the American Way Abroad*. New York: New Press. 2010.

Gems, Gerald R. *Boxing: A Concise History of the Sweet Science*. New York: Roman & Littlefield. 2014.

Gems, Gerald R. *Sport and the Shaping of Italian American Identity*. New York: Syracuse University Press. 2013.

Gmelch, George and Daniel Nathan, eds. *Baseball Beyond Our Borders: An International Pastime*. Lincoln: University of Nebraska Press. 2017.

Gorn, Elliot. *A Brief History of American Sports*. Second Edition. Champagne: University of Illinois Press. 2013.

Gray, Frances Clayton and Yanick Rice Lamb. *Born to Win the Authorized Biography of Althea Gibson*. Hoboken: John Wiley & Sons. 2004.

Guthrie-Shimizu, Sayuri. *Transpacific Field of Dreams: How Baseball Linked the United States and Japan in Peace and War*. Chapel Hill: University of North Carolina Press. 2012.

Hall, Eric Allen. *Arthur Ashe: Tennis and Justice in the Civil Rights Era*. Baltimore, MD: Johns Hopkins University Press. 2014.

Hardy, Stephen and Andrew Holman. *Hockey: A Global History*. Champaign: University of Illinois Press. 2018.

Heaphy, Leslie. *The Negro Leagues, 1869–1960*. Jefferson, NC: McFarland & Company. 2003.

Josza, Frank Jr. *American Sports Empire*. Westport: Praeger Publishers. 2003.

Keys, Barbara. *Globalizing Sport: National Rivalry and International Community in the 1930s*. Cambridge, MA: Harvard University Press. 2006.

Kirsch, George. *Baseball in the Blue and Gray: The National Pastime during the Civil War*. Princeton: Princeton University Press. 2013.

Klein, Alan. *Globalizing the Game: The Globalization of Major League Baseball*. New Haven: Yale University Press. 2006.

Korr, Charles P. *The End of Baseball as We Knew It: The Players Union, 1960–1981*. Urbana: University of Illinois Press. 2002.

Kuska, Bob. *Hot Potato: How Washington and New York Gave Birth to Black Basketball and Changed America's Game Forever*. Charlottesville: University of Virginia Press. 2004.

LaFeber, Walter. *Michael Jordan and the New Global Capitalism*. New York: W. W. Norton & Company. 2002.

Lamb, Chris. *Conspiracy of Silence: Sportswriters and the Long Campaign to Desegregate Baseball*. Lincoln: University of Nebraska Press. 2012.

Lamb, Chris, ed. *From Jack Johnson to Lebron James: Sports, Media, and the Color Line*. Lincoln: University of Nebraska Press. 2016.

Larmer, Brook. *Operation Yao Ming: The Chinese Sports Empire, American Big Business, and the Making of an NBA Star*. New York: Gotham Books. 2005.

Levine, Peter. *Ellis Island to Ebbets Field: Sport and the American Jewish Experience*. New York: Oxford University Press. 1993.

Markovits, Andrei and Steven Hellerman. *Offside: Soccer and American Exceptionalism*. New Jersey: Princeton University Press. 2001.

Moore, Louis. *I Fight for a Living: Boxing and the Battle for Black Manhood, 1880–1915*. Urbana: University of Illinois Press. 2017.

Moore, Louis. *We Will Win the Day: The Civil Rights Movement, the Black Athletes, and the Quest for Equality*. Denver, CO: Praeger. 2017.

Murray, Caitlin. *The National Team: The Inside Story of the Women Who Changed Soccer*. New York: Abrams Press. 2019.

Oriard, Michael. *Brand NFL: Making and Selling America's Favorite Sport*. Chapel Hill: University of North Carolina Press. 2010.

Peavy, Linda and Ursula Smith. *Full Court-Quest: The Girls from Fort Shaw Indian School, Basketball Champions of the World*. Norman: University of Oklahoma Press. 2008.

Peterson, Robert. *From Cages to Jump Shots: Pro Basketball's Early Years*. New York: Oxford University Press. 1990.

Peterson, Robert. *Only the Ball Was White: A History of Legendary Black Players and All-Black Professional Teams*. New York: Oxford University Press. 1970.

Pluto, Terry. *Loose Balls: The Short, Wild Life of the American Basketball Association*. New York: Simon and Schuster. 2007.

Pope, S.W. *Patriotic Games: Sporting Traditions in the American Imagination, 1876–1926*. New York: Oxford University Press. 1997.

Pope, S.W. and John Naught, eds. *Routledge Companion to Sports History*. New York: Routledge. 2011.

Rider, Toby C. *Cold War Games: Propaganda, the Olympics, and U.S. Foreign Policy*. Champagne: University of Illinois. 2016.

Rider, Toby C. and Kevin B. Witherspoon, eds. *Defending the American Way of Life: Sport, Culture, and the Cold War*. Fayetteville: University of Arkansas Press. 2018.

Riess, Steven, ed. *A Companion to American Sport History*. Malden, MA: Wiley Blackwell. 2014.

Riess, Steven. *City Games: The Evolution of American Urban Society and the Rise of Sports*. Urbana: University of Illinois Press. 1991.

Roberts, Randy. *Papa Jack: Jack Johnson and the Era of White Hopes*. New York: The Free Press. 1985.

Rofe, Simon, ed. *Sport and Diplomacy: Games within Games*. Manchester: Manchester University Press. 2018.

Rosen, Charley. *The First Tip-Off: The Incredible Story of the Birth of the NBA*. New York: McGraw-Hill Education. 2008.

Sarantakes, Nicholas. *Dropping the Torch: Jimmy Carter, the Olympic Boycott, and the Cold War*. New York: Cambridge University Press. 2011.

Schultz, Jaime. *Women's Sports: What Everyone Needs to Know*. New York: Oxford University Press. 2018.

Serb, Chris. *War Football: World War I and the Birth of the NFL*. New York: Roman & Littlefield Publishers. 2019.

Silver, Mike. *Stars in the Ring: Jewish Champions in the Golden Age of Boxing*. New York: Roman & Littlefield. 2016.

Stark, Douglas Andrew. *Wartime Basketball: The Emergence of a National Sport during World War II*. Lincoln: University of Nebraska Press. 2016.

Thomas, Damion. *Globetrotting: African American Athletes and the Cold War*. Champaign: University of Illinois Press. 2012.

Tygiel, Jules. *Past Time: Baseball as History*. New York: Oxford University Press. 2000.

Wagg, Stephen and David Andrews, eds. *East Plays West: Sport and the Cold War*. Oxfordshire: Routledge. 2007.

Ware, Susan. *Game, Set, Match: Billie Jean King and the Revolution in Women's Sports*. Chapel Hill: University of North Carolina Press. 2015.

Ware, Susan. *Title IX: A Brief History with Documents*. New York: Bedford/St. Martin's. 2007.

Zeiler, Thomas W. *Ambassadors in Pinstripes: The Spalding World Baseball Tour and the Birth of the American Empire*. Boulder, CO: Rowman & Littlefield Publishers. 2007.

Zeiler. Thomas W. *Jackie Robinson and Race in America: A Brief History with Documents*. New York: Bedford/St. Martin's. 2014.

Zirin, Dave. *A People's History of Sport: 250 Years of Politics, Protest, People, and Play*. New York: The New Press. 2008.

INDEX

9 781350 134706